The Assault on Childhood

The Assault on Childhood
The Hardboiled Dicks
Lineup Tough Guys
The Sword Swallower

The Assault on Childhood

by
Ron Goulart

SHERBOURNE PRESS, INC. LOS ANGELES

Manufactured in the United States of America
by Heritage Printers, Inc., Charlotte, N. C.
Library of Congress Catalog Card Number 69–20138
First Printing

This one is for Fran & Sean again.
And for Walt & Mauriça for future reference.

Acknowledgments

I am grateful to Hobart MacQuarrie, Terry Wollter, Don and Margaret Thompson, Alfred Bester, and William F. Nolan for providing assorted reference and background material. I appreciate, too, the cooperation of the various toymakers, psychiatrists, physicians, public relations men, animators, comic book artists, copywriters, and account executives I talked to in the course of writing this book. Many of them were not quite sure what I was up to. All interpretations of research and opinions are mine.

Contents

1. The Assault on Childhood

To understand either childhood or society, we must expand our scope to include the study of the way in which societies lighten the inescapable conflicts of childhood with a promise of some security, identity, and integrity. In thus reinforcing the values by which the ego exists, societies create the only condition under which human growth is possible.

ERIK H. ERIKSON
Childhood And Society

I have a friend who says, "Business is business, and anything you do in it is fair as long as you don't cheat children." But there's such a good profit in cheating children that businessmen can easily deceive themselves about what they're doing. They can even publicize themselves into honors and awards for it.

PAULINE KAEL
McCall's

Many of the children in America will never grow up. The odds are mounting, the obstacles and hazards increasing. Most of our kids are under attack, and the attack has both physical and psychological effects. Physically, of course, most of them will probably survive. They all stand, however, in danger of never growing up inside, of being trapped for the length of their lives in an endless childhood or a false adulthood." Childhood should be a journey, and one of its joys is being able to travel through it to the next stage. How hard and how fulfilling this journey is depends chiefly on the child and

1

the parent. Increasingly, though, outsiders are intruding and setting up blocks to progress.

These outsiders, the people to whom kids are big business, will be the subject of this book. Rather, they are one of the three main subjects. The other two are our kids and ourselves. As parents, we do not tell the child his destination and we should not deliver him to a predetermined adulthood. At best we guide and counsel. Therefore we have a legitimate right to be concerned with and angered by those who hinder and side-track our children, and those who exploit them: the television producers, the toymakers, the cereal manufacturers, the comic book publishers, and the army of others who make a living by selling things to youngsters.

The men in the kid business, while at first glance seemingly engaged in the manufacture of trivia, do create some of the major outside influences on children. One of our duties as parents is understanding—understanding not only our children and ourselves, but the objects and diversions of the child's world. A physician I talked to while doing this book referred to its overall subject as "the mass assault on children." This sums up the situation. There is an assault going on. While its main purpose is to sell products, the assault isn't a simple, single-faced one, nor is there an agreed-upon conspiracy. So that we may better understand the assault on childhood, and to avoid getting bogged down in mass condemnations and blanket prohibitions, most of our time together is going to be devoted to exploring—to examining the dimensions and implements of the assault, the people engaged in it, and their products and purposes. After that will come some conclusions of my own and of other people who are concerned with children and growing up.

There are physical hazards, plenty, potential in the products of the kid business: unsafe toys, harmful foods, false products. These are important and will be detailed. More important, since a physical injury often heals faster than a psychological one, are the injuries to the child's self that the pressures of the kid business contribute to. Being pressured and programmed into growing up falsely, or never growing up fully at all, is the worst thing that can happen to a child.

Many of the teenagers and young adults who feel most hopeless today are the ones who grew up, in Paul Goodman's phrase, "absurd." Kids who saw no reason to continue on to adulthood; kids who were persuaded, in good part by our mass media, that adult life is pointless and hollow, or who were seduced into believing that childhood is all. To drop out, to smash, to set fire, can be attempts to deny there is an adult world or an admission that you are not ready for it. More hopefully, they can be gestures toward realizing that the self was lost somewhere in childhood and must now be found.

For many of the manufacturers of mass products, the word *consumer* is synonymous with *childlike*. It is not an exaggeration, as I think will be abundantly clear by the end of this book, that many of these manufacturers would like the worst characteristics of children—selfishness, impulsiveness, delight in the simple-minded, uncontrolled aggressiveness, and prejudice —to survive into adult life. Much too much adult advertising presupposes a residue of childishness in the viewer. The advertising aimed at children begins what can turn into a lifelong assault. As psychologist Rollo May has pointed out, no child "moves on to responsible selfhood if it remains chiefly the reflection of the social context around it." And he also tells us that "the healthy child, who is loved and supported by his parents, will proceed in his development."

Not to grow up, not to realize the adult self, means an individual is never fulfilled. "To the extent that we do fulfill our potentialities," says May, "we experience the profoundest joy to which the human being is heir. When a little child is learning to walk up steps or lift a box, he will try again and again.

And finally, when he does succeed, he laughs with gratification, his expression of joy in the use of his powers. But this is nothing in comparison to the quiet joy when the adolescent can use his newly emerged power for the first time to gain a friend, or the adult's joy when he can love, plan and create." Childhood then must be open-ended, must be an expansion. The mass media men do not sufficiently acknowledge that the child is going someplace. The child is on his way to adolescence, and from there to adulthood and his transitions shouldn't be interfered with by the giants of the kid business. The meanings and pleasures of growing up should not be imposed from outside.

While the kid business is not the sole cause of not growing up, it is, in collaboration with the mass culture, an important contributor. The kid business helps create an increasingly evident type—a person who is not a kid any more, but who is not really an adolescent or an adult either. He is not fully recovered from childhood. He is Superkid.

One of the byproducts of the kid business, Superkid may well be the typical representative of the first generation to grow up under television or of the generation which is now following it. He comes in two forms: active and passive. Superkid in his passive form is less noticed. He doesn't excite or bother as many people, since his childishness manifests itself in quieter and less troublesome ways than that of the active Superkid. Basically he is a consumer. He graduates from kid consumer to affluent teenage consumer to young married consumer. He goes from having 2.6 billion dollars worth of toys bought for him each year to spending 20 billion dollars a year on lingerie, surfboards, motorcycles, deodorants, hamburgers, skis, mouthwash, eye makeup, phonograph records, used cars, movies, etc., to being 100 billion dollars in debt through installment buying. Though passive, Superkid moves around. He likes to drive, to move fast, and in his late teen phase he is responsible for one-third of all fatal auto accidents.

As a teenager, probably living in a suburban enclave of Superkids, he says, "Yes, I'd say I'm spoiled. I could get anything I wanted to. The majority of kids in school aren't exposed to people who are badly off," he adds. Superkid is only peripherally aware that half of the children in the world live where the average income is under $100 and that hundreds of millions of children and young people go hungry, a surprising number of them right here in America. Superkid is from ten to twenty pounds overweight. As he grows physically older, the absence of a real self becomes harder to hide. A suburban minister comments, "Because of the anonymity of the city you can hide emotional immaturity. But suburbia is living together. They feel they've got to put up this front. The front looks ritzy, but behind it, everything's a shambles. This confuses the kids."

Superkid in his active form gets most of the press. His methods, like those of a sort of gigantic Katzenjammer, involve noise, fireworks, and demolitions. Superkid has been able to adapt the tantrum to the political arena and can throw himself on the ground or yell until his demands are met. Active Superkid destroys and smashes and calls it passive resistance, because he is still a child inside and can understand only the labels and broader surface workings of this grownup concept. In the vocabulary of the active Superkid, words like "speed" and "trip" recur to label different objects and events, but they are always synonyms for the same thing—the getaway. The active Superkid is overly ready to accept any escape as valid, since he's been conditioned by mass media and mass values to believe that everything, even self-awareness and adulthood, is easy to get. He has a loud, but vague, conviction of his freedom. It isn't necessary at the moment to rehearse further the exploits and philosophies of the active Superkid. You know all about that; we see it in *Look* and live it in *Life*. One of the aims of this book is to slow down the production of Superkids.

During Prohibition, whenever gangster Frank Costello installed one of his slot machines in a candy store he always provided a little stool so that the smaller children would be able to reach up and play. Today kids are involved with a great many people whose only concern for them is of roughly the same kind. The only important and universally shared aim of the entire kid business is to turn children into consumers. Whatever is done for kids is done primarily to get them to hold out the hand with the money in it.

Any real concern for children, the kind we should feel as parents, has to include a critical examination of the methods being used to accomplish the goals of the kid business and some careful consideration of the possible physical and emotional results. Kids are spending more time with the kid business advertisers than they are with us, they get more education from them than they get from school. As one writer on children has said: "The best preparation for life is surely to live fully as a child." It requires an effort to keep our children from becoming merely consumers and to balance the effects of the kid business.

There are physical effects, centered around the selling of dangerous foods and harmful toys. It's still quite possible for a little girl to be burned by an inflammable doll, for a boy to be permanently deafened by an air-blast gun. In discussing the safety standards governing the testing of flammable materials in toys, the *Consumer Bulletin* reported: "There has been some criticism of the tests for fabrics as being insufficiently rigorous. Fabrics may comply with requirements, yet burn comparatively quickly. . . . Some fabrics resist flame propagation by melting and falling away. Hot, melted residues are a burn hazard, too." When, in 1966, *Consumer Reports* ran their independent tests on the compressed-air sonic blaster gun, they found sound levels of the blast could do "permanent damage to the hearing" and possible damage to the ear drum. This toy is no longer produced. When I asked the manufacturers why it was withdrawn they told me, "It didn't sell." What about the *Consumer Reports* findings? "We don't agree with them. We'd still be making the gun if it was selling sufficient units."

When the skateboard craze hit us in 1965, a number of safety councils and medical groups became concerned about the more serious accidents connected with the toy, not the scratches and abrasions but the fractures and concussions. Asked about proposed safety ordinances, one skateboard maker replied, "They don't mean nothing. The more they ban, the more they buy." At this writing there is no uniform code that covers all finished toys. Whatever testing done is undertaken by the manufacturer himself, not by any government agency or even an industry-sponsored testing center. As a parent you must simply take the word of the toymaker that the toy won't give your kid an electric shock or burn him and that its paint won't poison him.

Every now and then, usually at Halloween, a neighborhood eccentric hands out poisoned fruit or laxative candy to kids. He's usually arrested, or committed. You can't help thinking one of the reasons he got into trouble was for operating on such a small scale. If he'd called himself the Neighborhood Eccentric Candy Company and spent a million dollars on advertising, he'd probably still be on the good side of everyone. Right this minute in any supermarket your child can get a soft drink or gelatin mix or candy containing a synthetic sweetener which can cause stomach troubles and diarrhea. The sweetener is usually sodium cyclamate, a sugar substitute the Food and Drug Administration originally tried to restrict to adults. Your little girl can get the stuff in many of the home cooking toys she buys. Also available may be a chocolate bar that has been

contaminated with salmonella bacteria, which can produce
flu-like symptoms. Kids can still easily pick up a package of
hot dogs made in part from the carcass of a tubercular steer,
from meat originally intended for dog food, containing chemical additives, like sulfite, not permitted in human foods.

Besides containing artificial sweeteners and dubious preservatives, many of the foods kids buy are almost entirely synthetic. Not only is it difficult to tell what your children are
actually eating, it's sometimes impossible to tell what they're
missing. We'll take a full chapter later on to sort out some of
the false notions about nutrition the food wing of the kid
business beams at our kids (and us). A dietician told me, "Six
out of ten school girls are malnourished. The foods they eat
are full of calories and little else." While some nations are
plagued with starvation, the United States has an increasing
population of children who are overfed and undernourished.
There is even a serious obesity problem in American kids.
We're often told, especially on kid shows, that as long as vitamins are taken in nobody can go wrong. Many pharmaceutical
houses have found that their vitamin sales can be increased
incredibly by going into the candy-flavored chewable vitamin
field. The FDA has long been concerned with the way vitamins
are advertised and states that "Except for persons with special
medical needs, there is no scientific basis for recommending
routine use."

Though cigarettes are not supposed to be a children's product, a considerable amount of cigarette advertising is still aired
during the prime hours of child viewing. Complete with cowboys. A study by Dr. Ela J. Salber of the Harvard School of
Public Health shows that "before the age of 15, most youngsters have already decided whether or not they plan to smoke."
The president of the American Cancer Society has said that
while "an impressive and mounting number of American adults

have quit smoking, . . . youngsters in grade school and high school continue to court lung cancer, heart disease, and other cigarette-caused diseases to a discouraging degree." The tobacco industry reacts by contending there is no proof that cigarettes are harmful to anyone, by fighting and protesting any regulations on what can be said in a cigarette commercial and when it can be said. So far only one major tobacco company has made any effort to keep cigarette ads off kid-hour shows. The whole tobacco industry spent $194,079,300 on television advertising in 1966, and our kids saw most of it.

"There are pains of childhood that never come to light in any routine examination," says Dr. Benjamin Spock. "Wounds too deep to be seen by the human eye." Many of the results of the efforts to sell children are like this. There are millions of advertising dollars being spent to teach our children that their personality can be defined by the possession of things. The message of the medium is that all the pleasures of life are objects, objects which can be replaced. We allow kids to be told for several hours each and every day that violence and shooting are solutions to almost any problem, that anyone who is ugly or different should be wiped out. We let them be talked to by strangers who have all the oily harshness of used car dealers. When the advertisers are not openly lying, they are conning and shucking kids with misleading labels, false packaging, and phony offers. When psychiatrist Fredric Wertham talked about "the seduction of the innocent," some accused him of being melodramatic. Despite its popular sexual connotation, *seduction* means "to lead astray, to entice, to cajole and tempt." Kids are being seduced by television as much as six times per half hour. Their naiveté is being traded on, and any half-formed instinct is searched out and exploited.

Too much of the entertainment offered to children doesn't imply any standard of conduct or exercise any judgment. Ask

your 6-year-old why the hero of the cartoon show just blew
up twenty aliens, and he'll answer, "Because they were bad."
How does he know they were bad? "Because he killed them."
Talk to an executive producer of cartoon shows and ask why
he shifted from rabbits and cats to masked heroes burning
dozens of identical Martians and giant whales burying dozens
of identical natives. The producer shrugs and answers, "It's
what the kids want. Monsters and superheroes." But think
back to Karloff as the Frankenstein Monster or Charles Laugh-
ton as the Hunchback of Notre Dame, and you'll remember
that even horror and violence can be presented with compas-
sion. A killing can be used to make the point that life is valuable and its loss a tragedy. It was the ignorant peasants who
laughed at the hunchback for his ugliness.

A generation ago in a Western-like *Destry Rides Again*,
Jimmy Stewart didn't strap on his guns until the last reel. In
any recent TV Western, the hero has killed somebody while
the opening credits are rolling by and killed a few more and
stepped on somebody's face before the first commercial. The
mass media, as we'll examine in detail in a later chapter, aren't
providing children with enough alternatives to the false notion
that masculinity is built upon the ability to kill and hurt. Commenting on what he calls the code of blood shows, *San Francisco Chronicle* television columnist Terrence O'Flaherty reflected: "The most depressing thing about this . . . is there is no
turning back. It means violence and more violence until it
becomes meaningless to all but sadists and masochists. A lot
of otherwise good storytelling has been spoiled by resorting to
the fist and the gun for dominance, instead of intelligence, persuasion, or even cunning. . . . Take a look at the 11 P.M. news-
casts and you'll see a living continuation of the entertainment
programs which have preceded them since 7:30." Young
people have been taught the virtue of violence and the gun as
a solution for so long that they are even using it on themselves,

and the rate of suicide among children and young people rises each year.

Our kids must grow up, too, with the constant din of images being smashed and classics being ripped down. In the current children's world, Alice In Wonderland is a technicolor cartoon, Peter Pan is a peanut butter, Moby Dick is the sidekick of two Saturday morning cartoon kids, Huckleberry Finn and Tom Sawyer belong to the Hanna-Barbera Studios, Mowgli is a stuffed toy, and Abraham Lincoln is a robot who works at Disneyland. Contemplating the children's book of the future, Randall Jarrell had a vision of "a book that, pressed, says: *I'm your friend*; teaches the child Crime Does Not Pay; does not exceed thirty words; can be used as a heating pad . . . and has three-dimensional illustrations dyed with harmless vegetable matter and flavored with pure vanilla." Many children's entertainments have become such crazy quilts that any appreciation of individuality or even merit is almost impossible. When you put Lewis Carroll, J. M. Barrie, Rudyard Kipling, the Brothers Grimm and even, surprisingly, Upton Sinclair into the machine, and they all come out Walt Disney, you are doing kids a disservice. We'll consider the scope of the affable vandalism of Walt Disney further on.

Everyone has the right to be left alone, the right to occasional solitude. Everyone, that is, except children. "Every individual needs both to communicate with others and to keep his thoughts and beliefs from others," Justice William O. Douglas has said. "This dual aspect of privacy means that a person should have the freedom to select for himself when he will share his thoughts and attitudes with others." This sort of freedom simply doesn't exist for kids, and one of the most disturbing things about the mass media assault on children is the enormous invasion of their privacy that has accompanied it. "We must keep in mind that every step in personal growth needs isolation," writes psychiatrist Joost Meerloo in *The Rape Of The Mind*, "needs

inner conversation and deliberation and a reviewing with the
self. Television hampers this process and prepares the mind
more easily for collectivization and cliché thinking."

The intrusion doesn't stop with television, with the other
obvious media. To the advertising man, all the world is media
and he pursues our children accordingly. Advertising follows
kids to school, keeps hustling them even in the classroom. In a
given day at school, your child may see a documentary made
by an ad agency, see a film of an old television show with its
commercials still intact, use a workbook produced by a group
of companies in the kid business, take notes with a sloganed
pencil, study out of books whose protective covers have advertising messages on them. Book covers plugging the local sav-
ings and loan, and documentaries on the Congo with breakfast
food commercials in the middle, are only part of the intrusion.
Many schools are now testing labs for new products and allow
their pupils to be quizzed and probed by motivational research
people. The largest youth research company in the country
promises its clients "a field staff of over 8,000 high school and
college leaders and faculty instructors."

Dwight Macdonald has remarked that "the questionnaire is
to our civilization what art and philosophy were to the Greeks,
or law and sewers to the Romans—a natural form of self-
expression." Advertisers and researchers are making increasing
use of the questionnaire with children. Numerous requests for
information are now being mailed directly to kids. When
Golden Magazine, for instance, wanted to find out about its
young readers, a firm of marketing research consultants was
hired to design and send out "a special illustrated booklet
questionnaire." The addresses were selected from a list of children who'd entered a contest in the magazine early in 1965.
After a battery of questions about preferences and possessions,
the booklet asked, "Do your parents *own* or *rent* the home in
which you live?" Then, "If your parents own the house, about

how much would it sell for today?" The final query is, "The total family income of your mother and dad is approximately . . .?" followed by a list of salaries to pick from. This kind of information was once considered your private business. Even today a credit company or private investigator would have to make a few phone calls to find it out.

Every time your children answer a mail questionnaire or enter a contest or send for a premium or subscribe to a magazine, they immediately are thought of as a possession of the people who have their name and address. While a magazine will never flaunt its felt ownership of your child directly in his face (or yours), it will brag about it behind his back. The trade papers and business magazines have a locker room effect on advertisers and ad writers. They say things there they wouldn't say in public. The Boy Scout periodical *Boys' Life* in its pitch to the readership of *Advertising Age* says, "Look into *Boys' Life* now—especially if you're interested in moving mountains of your brand." Their boy readers are described as "an active, acquisitive market," and the magazine as the best way "to get to" them. *Boys' Life* is talking about the same Boy Scouts that Dan Beard helped found. The same Dan Beard who advised, "Money spent on fancy sporting apparatus, toys, etc., would be better spent upon tools." That was in another era.

Since there has been a United States, there has been a kid market here. The abusing and exploiting of children has a venerable history, though there has never before been anything like today's situation. The Second World War, something no member of the youth market remembers, was the basic cause. The war reshaped family patterns, allowing for a youth culture to grow and spread. It brought a new affluence.

The confrontation of kids and advertisers was also encouraged by the rise of television. Advertisers found the teenagers first, then children from 12 on down. In 1939 only $300,000 was spent on advertising to young people on network radio. In less than twenty years, the budget for youth advertising, on television, rose to over 100 million dollars.

Our kids today represent yearly gross sales that have been estimated as high as 50 billion dollars. There are several billion more to be made from adult sales influenced by child pressure. About two and a half billion of the annual take goes to the toy tycoons. There are 1500 companies making toys, games, and wheel goods, but 80 to 85 percent of the total dollar volume is done by the top 400, headed by Mattel, Hasbro, Milton Bradley, Aurora Plastics, Ideal, Remco, Kenner, Tonka, and Marx. Mattel, Inc., leads all the rest, selling 125 million dollars worth of toys a year. Based in Southern California, they are the creators of the Barbie doll. They spend 12 million dollars a year on advertising. Hasbro has risen to near the top in the '60's, chiefly because of their war doll, G.I. Joe. We'll get to know Mattel, Hasbro, and the rest in a later chapter.

Another big share of the youth market profits goes to the soft drink makers. They sell almost three and a half billion dollars' worth of flavored water a year, much of it to kids. Coca-Cola does 40 percent of all this business, trailed by Pepsi-Cola and Royal Crown. Candy costs us a billion and a half dollars. Children spend 25 million dollars just on bubble gum. Of children, a bubble gum vice president says, "That's who we're after every day, every month, all the time." The breakfast food industry persuades kids to consume 650 million dollars' worth of dry cereal annually. To do this, Kellogg, General Mills, Quaker Oats, General Foods, and Ralston spend 100 million dollars on advertising. "The cereal companies often spend more to promote," reports *Forbes*, the business magazine, "than to produce what they sell." Kellogg alone puts out something like 15 million dollars on network television advertising, putting them up in the top twenty of television advertisers and giving them considerable control over what kind of programs kids will see.

Our children read 35 million comic books a month, which is 4 million dollars' worth. The two major companies in the comics magazine field are pulp veteran Martin Goodman's Marvel Group and National Periodicals, Inc. National, which owns Superman, Batman, MAD, and the Independent News Distributing Company, grosses nearly 70 million dollars a year. Marvel owns The Fantastic Four and Captain America. Mickey Spillane used to write for them.

Both critics and defenders of the consumer conditioning of children seem to agree on its aims. David Riesman, as long ago as 1950, observed in *The Lonely Crowd* that the long-range object of the mass media assault on children was to build up in the child "habits of consumption he will employ as an adult." In the early 1960's, social anthropologist Jules Henry pointed out that all cultures train children "for the roles they will fill as adults." In our society, "the central aims of our culture are to sell goods, . . . create consumers, . . . educate children to buy." The leaders of the kid business and of advertising in general have been saying the same thing. A trade magazine called *Media/Scope* puts it plainly: "Youth is advertising's frontier market—young, wild, and sprouting everywhere, and just barely being exploited." *Business Week*, under the heading "Catch 'Em Young," reports that even department stores are paying more attention to kids, "realizing the importance of instilling loyalty in consumers as early as they can."

A corollary of catching them young is using them as shills to draw in parents. "Sell the kids, sell the parents," advises *Broadcast Advertising,* and explains that children remember names of all kinds of products and ask their mothers to buy them. "Nine out of ten mothers grant these requests," beams the magazine. Many advertisers completely outside the kid field are finding ways to use children to woo grownups. An agency executive says, "Several years ago, Texaco learned the value of offering premiums to children—not adults—so that the youngsters would wheedle their parents into shopping at the Texaco stations." A marketing man at a large frozen food company told the late *Herald Tribune,* "Few people are aware of the depth of children's influence on food buying." He estimated that school-age children influence 15 percent of all family food buying. Jules Henry calls this using of children an invasion of the judgment of our kids and terms the advertising world "an insolent usurper of parental function," which makes parents "mere intermediaries between their children and the market." Henry concludes, "This arrogance is terrifyingly reminiscent of another appeal to children over the heads of their parents: that of the Nazi Youth movement."

To understand the real, the important effects of what is happening to our kids in the name of selling and consumer building, we have to examine not only the products and people involved. We have also to understand our children and, more important, ourselves. I'd like to make it clear now this book is not going to offer a master plan for coping with every specific of the mass society. Neither will it advocate government control of television, censorship of comic books, outlawing of toy weapons, or prohibition of soft drinks. Solutions don't start out there but in here, with you the individual parent and with the individual child.

We should consider, too, the reasons we allow the mass media and the mass products to take over part of the rearing of our children. Our reasons are often legitimate. In his nostalgic anthology of comic book heroes, Jules Feiffer makes the point that for the kids of the 1930's and '40's, comic books, though junk, were a place to escape to and be safe from the adult world. "Comic books were our booze," Feiffer explains. So today we'd like our kids to be able to relax away from pressures, to be entertained by comics, television, toys. We find we have to use the mass media, particularly television, as the baby-sitter of last resort. As consumers of a medium like television, we have the right to be concerned with it. We'll expand on the uses, good and bad, of the mass media and mass products throughout this book.

The manufactured objects of the kid world, the dolls and guns and breakfast foods, can, like the blind men's elephant, be different things to different people. So it is necessary to consider these various objects from the point of view of the child, the parent, and the manufacturers. I've tried to deal with this last group as fairly as possible, keeping in mind philosopher Alan Watts' injunction that it's important never to approach "in a spirit which fails to honor the opposition, or which regards it as entirely evil or insane. It is not without reason that the formal rules of boxing, judo, fencing, and even dueling require that the combatants salute each other before the engagement." Kid business, we salute you.

Now to see one of the fundamental ways in which kids are processed and passed on to the next stage in their careers as consumers, let's turn to the world of Barbie.

2. The World of Barbie

We don't talk about just Barbie. We call it the World of Barbie.

ROBERT C. WILL
public relations man

Advertising pushes kids to act beyond their age. If a little girl plays with these teenage dolls she's looking forward to late adolescence. A child experiences himself by living in the now of his childhood. Many late teenage delinquents were never comfortably seven-year-old kids.

DR. JOHN LANGDELL
child psychiatrist

The signs said "Official Trade-In Program" and "All New Features" and "Supply Is Limited." They weren't stuck up in an auto row salesroom or flying over a discount warehouse; they were on display in the front window of a shopping center toy store. It was a mild spring day, the first after a week of rain, and Mattel, Inc., was introducing its new 1967 model Barbie dolls. You could find the same posters, plus the new Twist 'N Turn Barbie and assorted promotional sales materials, in thousands of toy shops and department stores in the United States. If you didn't notice them, your 5-to-12-year-old daughter would be sure to.

The fact that children's toys are now sold and promoted with all the gimmicks, intensity, and, often, lack of ethics once limited to used car dealers is one of the unsettling things about the late '60's. The World of Barbie is a good place to start try-

18

ing to find out how this has come about. Why pick on Barbie? She's not the sole begetter of the excessive and seductive advertising aimed at children, not the only enforcer of the passion for possessions. Barbie is, though, the most pervasive and observable symbol of what's happened in the kid industries in the past ten years, the decade in which money and leisure increased and the whole country grew younger. And the great and obvious success of the Barbie doll and the Southern California-based Mattel Company has influenced many of the businesses that exist by selling products made for children. The techniques developed and adapted to sell Barbie have been widely borrowed.

Equally important is the effect of Barbie on the millions of little girls who own the doll. Acquiring a Barbie doll can be the beginning of a big habit for a child. To buy all the clothes and props Mattel offers to go along with Barbie would cost several hundred dollars. While dolls are as old as time, Mattel is one of the pioneers in creating a doll that actually lives better than a good 30 percent of the real children in this country. Besides the obvious materialism of Barbie, there is an entire philosophy connected with the doll—a mystique built up by the doll, the advertising of the doll, and the innumerable Barbie byproducts. The World of Barbie is a carefully conceived joint creation of a large group of advertising people, public relations men, Mattel executives, staff psychiatrists, and researchers. Nothing about Barbie is accidental or unplanned, and nothing as old-fashioned as affection goes into the product. "People like to think you make toys with a bunch of cute little elves," some of Mattel's public relations men told me. "But you don't sell five million units with elves."

The largest toymaker in America, Mattel, Inc., doesn't consider itself merely the inventor of the Barbie doll. Mattel likes to emphasize the diversification of its operations. Diversification, as in any large industry, is one good way to keep growing and prospering. Mattel, with its headquarters plant twenty free-way minutes south of Los Angeles, produces over 400 different toys each year, several of which will show up in later chapters. First Barbie.

The initial admission charge into the World of Barbie is between $3 and $5. That buys your daughter the doll. Like the entrance fee at Disneyland, all this gets you is in. Everything else costs extra. The 1967 Barbie, the one with the new Twist 'N Turn waist "that creates a horizontal dimension of graceful movement," is just under a foot tall, with measurements of 5¼-3-4½. Her body, actually manufactured in Japan, is made of vinyl and can be bought with any of four shades of celanese hair, Summer Sand, Chocolate Bon-Bon, Go Go Co-Co, and Sun Kissed. Not quite naked, Barbie comes with a net swimsuit and no shoes. "We work like Gillette Razors," a Barbie PR man explained to me. "You know, first get them sold on the basic unit, then keep selling them the accessories."

In the 1967 spring push, Mattel introduced nearly twenty brand new costumes for Barbie. Ranging in price from $1.50 to $4, these included Pink Moonbeams, consisting of "an Alencon-type peignoir and tricot negligée with lace top"; Caribbean Cruise, "lounging pajamas with backless bodice"; and Underprints, "print bra, half-slip, and panty with garters, Princess phone, mirror, comb and brush." Two dozen of the older outfits are still in stock and also available. Among them sleeveless sheaths, a skirt-suit for wearing to club meetings, a fur-trimmed deb ball dress, corselet with sheer trim, and a lunchtime homemaker ensemble offering a print dress, a saucepan, a kettle, a toaster with toast, and no shoes.

Your little girl doesn't get off the hook simply by acquiring a major part of the Barbie wardrobe. For one thing, there are ten other different dolls in the World of Barbie. There's Barbie's boyfriend Ken, added—says Mattel—at the request of the little girls themselves. Ken is an inch taller than Barbie, looks something like a department store dummy who shrank. In 1967 he was available only with blond molded hair. You can't buy him as many changes of clothes as Barbie, and he doesn't have a Twist 'N Turn waist. At the right hand of Barbie is Midge, until recently labeled "Barbie's Best Friend." Midge can wear the same clothes bought for Barbie. Nudging Midge for second banana honors is Francie, Barbie's MOD'ern Cousin. Francie in turn has a Fun Friend named Casey. Mattel has even added a token Negro to the Barbie world. Actually it's only Francie with a new skin shade, politely called Colored Francie. A Mattel executive says the colored doll is not advertised much and admitted sales had not been "in proportion to the size of that segment of the population." Completing the group are Tutti and Todd, Barbie's Tiny Twin Sister and Brother; Chris, a friend and playmate of the twins; and Skipper and Scooter, who are also friends or relatives. Whatever the exact relationships, all these littler dolls have clothes to be bought. Until recently Midge had her own boyfriend, Allan, but he has quietly dropped out.

The child who becomes a real Barbie completist will naturally also want the peripheral Barbie products Mattel makes, or allows to be made under various licensing agreements. There are Barbie wallets, Barbie carryalls, Barbie coloring books, Barbie thermos bottles and lunch boxes, Barbie and Francie Color Magic Fashion Designer Sets, Barbie and Ken costume trunks, Barbie's queen-size beds, Barbie's fashion shops, Barbie's Dreamhouses, Barbie's Family Houses, Barbie dollcases, Barbie and Francie dollcases, the Barbie Hair Fair full of wigs, wiglets, and hairpieces, and there's even a Tutti doll which comes equipped with her own scaled-down Barbie doll.

In 1959, the year the youngest of the war babies became teenagers, Barbie made her first appearance. Ruth Handler, vice president and one of the founders of Mattel, had been thinking about the doll for several years. She'd noticed her daughter liked to play with paper dolls, liked to dress them up.

Mrs. Handler felt existing three-dimensional dolls didn't lend themselves to this kind of make-believe. "They were clumsy and weren't meant to wear clothes that had any real style," she has said. "I thought, 'Wouldn't it be nice if there were a three-dimensional fashion doll?' " It's also probable Mrs. Handler and her husband Elliot, who own Mattel, had noticed that little girls were looking to new idols as the 1950's ended. The increasing amount of time and money being spent on winning the growing teen market was spilling out of the mass media onto a lot of 5-to-12-year-olds. "Through toys the child enacts scenes from his imagination of the grown-ups' life," says Elliot Handler. "Or of his life as he envisions it will be when he grows up." By 1959 middle-income family children were becoming convinced that what they wanted to be when they grew up was a teenager. Sensing the early tremors of the youthquake, the Handlers put Barbie on the market. They named the doll after their daughter.

One of the disadvantages of your little girls, from a business point of view, is their lack of much ready money of their own. "We don't think of little girls as having any disposable income," says Robert C. Will, who heads the Mattel public relations team. "We have to work through parents." In introducing Barbie, Mattel saturated the media with ads and commercials. Explaining the Mattel formula, the *Wall Street Journal* said, "They use heavy TV advertising that bypasses the middlemen, such as retailers and even parents, to appeal directly to the kids, who are supposed to practically order their mothers and fathers to buy." If Mattel did not introduce the concept of the TV toy, the toy that's so strongly advertised on television that millions of kids will demand it, they definitely perfected its successful use. "The sales history of Barbie," pointed out a recent Mattel press release, "is a classic in the toy industry. Barbie became the most successful doll of all time." By the early '60's the Handlers were selling several million Barbies a year.

Any doll with a large advertising agency (Carson/Roberts of Los Angeles, where they answer the phone with "Have a happy day!") and a public relations firm (currently Harshe-Rotman & Druck, one of the largest, located high up in one of L.A.'s many Tishman Buildings) is going to attract attention outside the kid world, and not just with the parents who are financing her. In 1963 a *Life* spread helped introduce Barbie's newest wardrobe, which the magazine said would cost $136. In 1964 *The Saturday Evening Post* profiled her. Barbie now had her own comic book, magazine, and fan club, and she was writing a newspaper column. A couple of years earlier *The New Yorker* had admitted Barbie into its On And Off The Avenue section, saying to readers, "If you surrender to what is put forward as the inevitable, you may as well start with Barbie. . . . One can, if one is absolutely crackers, fit her out with a wardrobe that comes to $247.60." That particular before-Christmas issue of the magazine also had 98 ads offering clothes and accessories for real girls and women.

There is always some disagreement as to the cost of Barbie and her clothes. One of the reasons is that Barbie, along with several newer TV toys, is used by many toy shops and department stores as a loss leader. Even some toy dealers are not happy about this. "We sell a lot of Mattel's merchandise," says one. "But the trouble is we don't make anything on it." When I asked a Mattel vice president how much the basic doll should cost, he said, "It depends on where you buy it."

Little-girl money, while it may not be disposable by industry definition, is certainly there to be spent. Every year the mothers of little girls are persuaded to spend about 320 million dollars on dolls and doll clothes. After the Barbie revolution, the toy industry decided to get much of this money with teenage fashion dolls and wardrobes. Among the most successful have been Tressy, whose hair grows when you press a button in her stomach, and Tammy, made by the Ideal Toy Company. Ini-

tially Ideal didn't quite comprehend the motivations, and conditioned responses, of children. They introduced a Mom and
Dad for sale along with Tammy. Even though these parental
dolls were fully articulated and could bend their legs, they
didn't sell at all. Barbie herself has spread to Europe and there
are imitations there, too. In Italy there is Sophia, and the most
popular variation in England is Sindy. Her boyfriend's name
is Paul and her apparel equals Barbie's, running from Undie-
world lingerie to Leather Look casuals.

The imitations who have come too close to Barbie in name
and patented parts were taken to court. Mattel is extremely
careful about its patents, trademarks, and copyrights. "We're
always in litigation," says Theodore Horwith, secretary-
treasurer of Mattel. Outside the courtroom Mattel does not
dignify its competition by mentioning any of the rival dolls by
name. The only comment I got on the subject of Sindy was,
"What English doll?" According to the *Wall Street Journal*,
the makers of a German doll named Lili claimed certain features of Barbie were quite similar to those of their doll. Mattel
bought the company. Despite vigilance and lawsuits, Mattel
hasn't been able to keep its less obvious competitors from doing
well. Some 20 million non-Barbie teenage fashion dolls are
sold every year, many of them as expensive to maintain as the
original. One characteristic most of the dolls share is size.
Therefore it's possible for your child to dress Barbie in Tammy's
dresses or Tressy's negligees.

In advertising the Barbie doll, Mattel, Inc. today makes
heavy use still of television, adding print for a split-level attack
that hits both adults and children. To introduce the new Twist
'N Turn Barbie, two separate kinds of television and print ads
were used, those aimed directly at children and those meant to
talk straight to mothers. The biggest kid-directed push was on
the Saturday morning television cartoon shows, where "Mattel
dominates all three networks, all year long, with the biggest

Saturday morning schedule of any advertiser in any industry." In May of 1967, a good part of this time was devoted to full-color commercials about the new Barbie and the special trade-in offer. Meanwhile, in magazines like *Family Circle*, Mattel was already at work pre-selling young mothers.

The television commercials for children mixed hard sell, broad flattery, and polite plastic sensuality. Focusing on an incredibly cleaned, scrubbed, starched, and polished little girl, the commercial set out to convince little girls that the new Twist 'N Turn Barbie surpassed the old model in every way. It had a new face, new real eyelashes, new hairdo, and a new net swimsuit. Best of all it could twist and turn. This last advantage was illustrated with a closeup of the doll torso doing a conservative grind. "But what do I do with my old Barbie?" asks the little girl. The same thing your family is supposed to do with old cars, old electric razors, old TV sets, and old refrigerators. Trade it in. While the announcer's voice, obviously influenced by Robert Preston in *The Music Man*, chants about the new doll, a cleaned and scrubbed line of skipping little girls descends on a fantasy toy store and takes advantage of the Barbie doll offer while the supply lasts. Mattel has managed to convince your little girls that they are in complete control of doll buying and are free to junk their old obsolete Barbie, to rush out with it and a dollar and a half (the special trade-in price). The entire Barbie commercial doesn't show a parent, and the only adult figure visible is a toy store owner, made of cardboard.

Mattel has something to say to parents, too: Give up. Mattel's full-page color ad in the May issue of *Family Circle* was headlined "Don't say 'No' just because she already has a Barbie doll." The large photo presents a cute little girl, a sort of midget Julie Andrews, with one shed tear on her cheek. The accompanying copy assures young mothers they don't have to refuse their daughters a new Barbie doll on the flimsy grounds that they already own one. No, you can "dry your little girl's tears" for only $1.50, by trading the old doll in on the new one. Then, with a straight face, Mattel says, "As any little girl will tell you, this new Barbie is something wonderful." Sure, she'll tell you that, because Mattel has been telling it to her in the middle of *Bugs Bunny* and *Space Ghost* for the past three weeks.

When talking directly to the toy trade, Mattel is more direct, less modest. The headline on a two-page ad in the April issue of *Playthings* announced the Barbie trade-in as "the most important toy promotion for 1967." Mattel told toy store owners and department store buyers the Barbie Twist 'N Turn doll was going to be introduced with "a massive television campaign" and promised they'd sell not only unexpected quantities of dolls but "a heck of a lot of costumes besides." As in the parent-aimed ads, Mattel pretends a carefully created need is an inherent one. "This new Barbie doll is the one all the kids want," dealers are assured.

Among the major implements, other than direct advertising, that have made Barbie well-known and a salable celebrity are the Barbie Fan Club and the Barbie Magazine. The club is free and the magazine costs $1 for six bi-monthly issues. Mattel's 1967 press releases say that "more than 1,300,000 youngsters have become members of the Official Barbie Fan Club." If this figure is accurate, it means Mattel has recruited nearly 10 percent of the entire little-girl population of the United States. What is more "a European Barbie Club has brought almost 200,000 girls to membership, and is growing rapidly." The American Barbie Club is a plainclothes Camp Fire Girls founded by Mattel in 1963. Its several thousand chapters have monthly meetings, presided over by a grownup. Each girl must bring her Barbie doll to the meeting with her. The membership applications and the letters your little girls write to the club's Southern California headquarters are one of Mattel's best sources of information on the little-girl market. From such letters, for instance, it was discovered that girls are moving out of the World of Barbie at an earlier age today, around age 12 as opposed to 13 or 14 in the early '60's.

Thin and pale, the Barbie Magazine is issued every other month and is not for sale on newsstands. Of the 24 pages in the average issue, from four to six are given over to advertisements. Apparently little girls aren't protected by the same standards of publishing that govern adult magazines, and so no warning as to what is an advertisement and what isn't appears in the magazine. A two-page spread devoted to selling the Barbie and Ken Little Theater, in the September–October 1964 issue, is laid out and illustrated in the same style as the real fiction and news stories. On the inside back cover of the same issue, Standard Plastics offers to sell the by now, hopefully, stagestruck readers a Barbie and Ken Costume Trunk. Possibly a few little girls sense the mercantile motives behind the publication. In a recent suggestion section of the letters page, a kid told how, using a matchbox, "you can make your own cash register for Barbie."

The joy of acquisition is the cornerstone of the magazine's philosophy, but there are other precepts given stress. There is an emphasis on grooming which suggests a compulsion shared by the assorted advertising and public relations personnel who manufacture the Barbie literature. In an eight-page pink insert, Barbie puts forward advice on beauty and charm for the 5-to-12-year-old. "Hi, do you know how pretty you are?" begins Barbie. "Pretty is shiny hair and sparkling eyes and liking people." The booklet gives ten rules for care of the hair, including "Don't use a cream shampoo or those containing eggs if your hair is oily. Buy the kind with an alcohol base," and "Color a box with pretty paper to keep your bobby-pins, rollers, barrettes, and hairbands in." The exercise page gives instructions for little girls who want to keep slim and trim to better show off their clothes. "Walk like a movie star . . . wear clothes like a model." For pretty hands your daughter should buy "emery boards, orange sticks, cuticle remover, and baby oil for softening cuticle." Barbie's insert ends with a twenty-question checklist mothers and big sisters are to help fill out every day for a month. Most of the questions could be asked during a barracks inspection, but on the aesthetic side there is "Did you notice a pretty sunset, wild flower, or raindrop?"

In the stories and articles Barbie champions keeping a bright surface no matter what, even if it means lying for awhile and managing the news. But it's often easy for Barbie's mother to sense when Barbie is having an ethical crisis. "Today I offered to take her shopping with me . . . and she wasn't the least bit interested." Barbie's relationship with Ken is growing more shadowy and vague, and even at his best Ken was nothing more than another prop for Barbie. One Barbie story explained him this way, "Ken is an exciting adventurous boy who loves sports cars, sports of all kinds, nice clothes, and of course, Barbie."

After reading several issues of the Barbie Magazine, reporter Donovan Bess asked, "Just what is the character that Mattel and its affiliated corporations are molding? Do they want a nation of power-mad girls bent on establishing an all-female government? Or do they hope for a nation of narcissistic matrons who live only to dress (never to undress)?" This puzzlement about who Barbie is and what she represents comes about because she is not simply a teenager anymore. She is a composite, part consensus teen and part woman's magazine ideal consumer. She is part feedback and part guide. Mattel has rooms in their Hawthorne, California, plant where they watch children playing with toys. From hours of observing behind one-way mirrors and listening over concealed microphones, Mattel has learned much about what little girls want. Not necessarily what they should have, but what they really want or what they can be made to feel they want. This they get from Mattel, along with a strong shove into the buyer's world.

What sort of little girls is Mattel interested in, what sort is it helping to create? In a study of suburban children across America, Dr. Alice Miel of Columbia University found that "the child of suburbia is likely to be materialistic and somewhat of a hypocrite . . . often conspicuously self-centered." Kids felt "there was a single norm of behavior. . . . They were confined to a narrow view of what people are and should be like." Dr. Miel also feels that suburban children have an "obsession with neatness" and tidiness and reject anyone whose social and economic position doesn't allow him to be neat and tidy. "Parents thank us for the educational values in the World of Barbie," says Ruth Handler of Mattel. "They say they could never get their daughters well groomed before. . . . That's where Barbie comes in. The doll has clean hair and a clean face, and she dresses fashionably, and she wears gloves and shoes that match."

A study of girls in their teens found that in their dreams about the future "the little white home with the picket fence has been replaced by a $60,000 suburban ranch or colonial house." In commenting on this notion, Grace and Fred H. Hechinger, in their book *Teen-Age Tyranny*, notice that "while the dream houses are specific, the younger generation's acquaintance with the economic facts of life appears sketchy." Most of the girls questioned, though yearning for a $60,000 home, expect their husbands to earn only about $12,000 a year by the time they're middle-aged. "The likelihood that such advertisement-inspired dreams, coupled with such appalling economic ignorance, will lead to disillusionment, or marital disaster . . . is uncomfortably great."

Certainly Barbie is not the chief cause of these values and beliefs. But after living in the World of Barbie for a protracted period, being exposed to its paraphernalia and philosophy, your little girl can't help being pushed toward the tidy conformity Barbie represents. Not only does Barbie help set a

standard of conduct now, she is an important tool in the long-
term conditioning of your child. "With Barbie girls learn to
expect to be valued by an ever-increasing wardrobe and their
ability to manipulate their fathers and, later, husbands, into
buying clothes and more clothes," psychiatrist Alan F. Leveton
told a recent child-study symposium. "Through her, both boys
and girls are introduced to a precocious, joyless sexuality, to
fantasies of seduction and to conspicuous consumption. This
reflects and perpetuates a disturbing trend in our culture, which
has serious mental-health complications."

Dr. Leveton, who has daughters of his own, is director of
the Pediatrics Mental Health Unit at the University of California Medical Center in San Francisco and also heads his own
family therapy center. He told me, "We've also noticed kids
coming into the clinic who are using the Barbie doll in mastur-
bation situations. This is only with a relatively small number
of children. The really bad thing about the Barbie doll is the
way it heightens the consumer motives in children, in a lot of
children." Dr. Arthur Jersild, veteran child psychiatrist at
Columbia University, has also attacked the fantasies of adult-
type consumption Barbie encourages. "Superimposing adult
fantasies on children at such expense," he has said, "is un-
realistic."

Barbie works continually at slotting your little girl into a
predetermined future, a future which has simplified in the past
decade. The ideal role seems to be that of a suburban matron
who rarely leaves the house, changes clothes frequently, and
uses a lot of convenience products. Betty Friedan, in *The
Feminine Mystique*, quotes a woman's-magazine profile of a
Texas housewife which sums up fairly well what can happen
to grownup Barbies. "Even at this hour of the morning (it is
barely nine o'clock) she is wearing rouge, powder, and lipstick,
and her cotton dress is immaculately fresh. . . . Sometimes, she
washes and dries her hair before sitting down at a bridge table

at 1:30. Mornings she is having bridge at her house are the busiest, for then she must get out the tables, cards, tallies, prepare fresh coffee, and organize lunch. . . . During the winter months, she may play as often as four days a week from 9:30 to 3 P.M. . . . 'Sometimes, I feel I'm too passive, too content,' remarks Janice, fondly, regarding the wristband of large family diamonds she wears even when the watch itself is being repaired. . . . Her favorite possession is her four-poster spool bed with a pink taffeta canopy. 'I feel just like Queen Elizabeth sleeping in that bed,' she says happily. (Her husband sleeps in another room, since he snores.)"

It's not far-fetched to say many advertisers see in this housewife the ideal consumer, that they dream of a world of queen-bee matrons in suburban cul-de-sacs. Of course, many women refuse to play this game, but after a child has been propagandized by Barbie from the age of 5 through puberty she may find it very difficult to think of breaking out of the pattern. Even the child who gets free and establishes her own identity has a more painful time.

To find herself, to not simply accept a part, is something each girl must eventually do. In the consumer society the pressures against ever making this discovery are large and powerful. Edgar Friedenberg has spoken of how these pressures can destroy the identity of young people and abort the birth of the self. What the World of Barbie and the creators of that world refuse to recognize is that the real world changes and that each generation must find an identity consonant with its own childhood and its own beliefs. Child psychologist Bruno Bettelheim, in discussing the growing-up girl and the sources of her self, says the more "the girl's psychological identity ceased to reside in childbearing and homemaking, or exclusively so, . . . the more her problems of identity and self-realization were compounded. By now, the female adolescent struggles not only with having to decide whether her place is in the home or in society at large, or in both, but to what degree and with what justification. Thus the problems of youth have become nearly the same for both sexes; the sexual differences count for less, because the conflicts of growing up are so much more psychological than sexual."

Bettelheim remarks further on the futile nature of many of the activities tradition still imposes on women when they grow up. "I do not refer only to gardening, which replaces the conspicuous embroidery of an earlier age, or to the bridge circle or country-club life. . . . I refer also to much that passes, unexamined, as more valuable pastimes, such as the PTA or the League of Women Voters. When used to cover up a vacuum of truly significant activities, of serious involvement, even these lose the genuine satisfactions they could otherwise confer." Bettelheim sees that even now, "a woman, no matter how gifted or successful in her work life, is judged a failure if she does not marry fairly soon. From adolescence on, therefore, the pressure to marry interferes with her ability to find self-realization in her own personal way."

To allow children to be constantly enticed to abandon their search for themselves, to allow them to accept a pre-packaged, ready to live life, is wrong. The arbitrary domestication of all young girls is wrong. To let ourselves be forced into thinking we can prove our love and concern with objects and goods is also wrong.

Meanwhile Mattel grinds on, and by the time you read this they will have introduced a new talking Barbie. A few days after the last year's Barbie, with $40.50 worth of new clothes, was introduced, the police of a New Jersey town apprehended two little girls, aged 8 and 11. The children had pulled off several burglaries and were nicknamed the Barbie Doll Bandits, since among the objects they swiped were two Barbies. They also took a total of $500 in cash and used it all up on "wild spending trips downtown." While a fondness for Barbie won't lead to a life of crime, there's no doubt the World of Barbie is helping condition a large portion of our young girls to think one of the essentials of the good life is an endless succession of wild spending trips downtown.

3. War Toys

The advent of nuclear war has brought about a fundamental change in the very nature of war itself. . . . Actually the nature of conflict being what it is, and the danger of nuclear holocaust being ever present, it is compelling that solutions less than total war be found.

LT. GEN. JAMES GAVIN

G.I. Joe is everybody's hero, is every boy's dream come true.

HASBRO TOY AD

Like undertakers who never mention death, the makers of toy guns and weapons don't like to be associated with violence and killing. Complaints about violent toys and war equipment are misdirected, the toy industry feels. "They're just what they are—toys," says William McLain, the 1968 president of the Toy Makers of the USA, Inc. "This whole thing is being blown out of proportion." There are many things that contribute to the violence in our society, the Toy Makers' president believes, and cites television as one real cause.

Shortly after the assassination of Robert F. Kennedy, two Southern California toy companies announced to the press a change in policy on weapon items and war toys. The companies were Mattel and Eldon, and what they actually did was not to change policy at all, but simply to undertake public opinion surveys. Walter Ross, a Mattel vice president, told the *Los Angeles Times*, "We are trying to get a cross section of opinion." He said Mattel would interview psychiatrists and parents

34

and devote several months to going into "the whole proposition of toy weapons." As I'm writing this, the results of Mattel's and Eldon's surveys have not been made public. Settling a moral issue, or a psychological one, with a public opinion poll, shows Mattel and Eldon to be in line with at least one main current in American thought. While Sears and Montgomery Ward have begun eliminating, or at least down-playing, war toys, most large toy dealers have decided to wait and see. "We will carry them until the manufacturers stop making them," said one Southern California toy store manager. In a country which has spent one trillion dollars for real armaments since the end of World War II, the outcome of the surveys can perhaps be guessed.

While planning for the Christmas season of 1966, a Philadelphia toy company, Amsco Industries, Inc., decided to make a peace toy. They held a competition and offered a prize for the best peace toy idea submitted. The winning suggestion was awarded a thousand dollars. But Amsco never went into production. They explained they'd found there wasn't any market for peace toys. The same has not been true for war toys. Every spring in New York, a small group of mothers protests the making of war toys by picketing the annual Toy Fair. It has no effect. "Anti-war pickets don't fret toymakers," reported *Advertising Age* after the 1967 demonstrations. That year's president of the Toy Makers, Mrs. Min Horowitz, explained to the press that military toys account for only 5 percent of the industry's yearly sales. Mrs. Horowitz didn't add that 5 percent of all the toy sales in America amounts to well over 100 million dollars a year. More money is spent on buying our children war toys than many small nations spend on real weapons and war equipment.

The yearly proliferation of toy weapons and guns and the large amount of television time and print space devoted to sell-

ing them are becoming matters of concern to many profes-
sionals outside the toy trade, to psychiatrists, and to legislators.
For example, in the spring of 1967 a group of California As-
semblymen, led by John L. Burton, attempted to introduce a
bill that would have caused all toy guns and war toys sold in
the state to be labeled "Toy depicting violence or war. May be
harmful to children." The psychiatrist who testified in support
of the bill at the committee hearings in the state capital said,
"When parents buy such toys for children, they give tacit approval to resort to violence. We encourage them to play at
violence and war."

Since Burton's Assembly Bill, No. 911, involved a psychological judgment rather than a medical one, it never had much
chance of passing and it was voted down in committee as being
unenforceable. John Burton did succeed in focusing attention
on the war toy problem and it's likely one of his prime inten-
tions was exactly what a toy executive told me he thought it
was. "He's just baiting us," the Southern California toymaker
said. "He wants us to take some action ourselves. We don't intend to." Then he added, "We don't make any of the really bad
war toys anyway. Not dangerous things, like some companies do."

Psychiatrist Fredric Wertham was one of the strongest opponents of the continuing and growing emphasis in America
on violence and the implements of violence. "Toys of violence
teach disrespect for human life," Dr. Wertham said. "Children
learn the fascinating feeling of power that comes from aiming
even a toy weapon." He believes toy advertisers "have planted
in the child's mind, and that of his parents, the idea that hardly
anything is more important in a child's life than a collection of
guns, knives, and any conceivable variety of warlike toys."
Child psychiatrist Alan Leveton, introduced in the previous
chapter, is not quite so absolute in his stand. "I have kids coming into the clinic, kids 7 and 8, and they're afraid of getting

killed in Vietnam," Dr. Leveton told me. "With a toy gun they can work out their anxiety." What he does reject is the indirect war toy, the push-button, missile-launching kind. "It gives the kid no direct contact with anyone. Violence at a distance is always bad." Dr. Michael B. Rothenburg, a professor of child psychiatry, has said, "If children are conditioned to work out their aggressions with such things as atomic cannons, or if they are encouraged to think of all those who oppose them as subhuman, and that the proper way to deal with these opponents is with Polaris submarines, then we are developing an adult population which, some years hence, will find it relatively easy, if not even natural, to put such horrifying weapons to actual use."

"Make all-out war in your own home," suggests an ad for Strathmore Toys. "You get enough nuclear battle equipment for maximum-effort warfare and massive counter-attack," Strathmore promises. This company isn't listed in the toy trade directories, and all I know about them is that they had enough money to buy full-page color ads in comic books like *Batman* a couple of Christmases ago, and that for only $1.25 they'd sell your child enough plastic equipment to play *Missile Attack*, a game which allows "you to deliver the nuclear knockout."

In 1965 an outfit calling itself the Nuclear War Game Co. of Downey, California, introduced *Nuclear War*, a game that could conclude, according to the instructions, "with the world and most of the solar system destroyed." You'd like to think a game with directions such as "lethal doses of radioactive gamma rays kill another 10 million" is really a piece of black humor or veiled pacifist propaganda. Many better-known game and toy manufacturers have also introduced board games utilizing nuclear weapons (Avalon Hill's *Tactics II* is one such), assassination (*Stratego* by Milton Bradley), and nuclear brinkmanship (Bradley again, with *Summit*). Any middle-sized toy department is also likely to stock *Hit the Beach, Blitzkrieg,*

D-Day, Guadalcanal, Gung-Ho, and *Bombs Away* games.
From Pixie Toys kids can buy, at just 59¢, war pinball games
like *Machine Gunner* and *Battleground.*

Any boy who wants to work off a little steam by napalming
people has several sources for play equipment. Aurora Plastics
sells a Republic F-105 Thunderchief complete with napalm
pod. Monogram Models offers a kit for constructing a 1/72
scale A1-E Skyraider with two napalm pods. The Illinois-
based Monogram introduced "new Vietnam action packaging"
in 1967 and told the trade the war equipment in their Combat
Hobby Kits "has year-round appeal for youngsters and adults"
—appeal now heightened "with official new color and up-to-
the-minute Vietnam authenticity." Besides a wide assortment
of bombers and fighter planes, a boy can buy (from Revell,
Inc.) a "Herky Bird" for crop defoliation. Anti-personnel
bombs have also come onto the toy market.

Since the early days of Vietnam escalation, when Mattel,
Inc., splashed jungle camouflage on a batch of unsold Dick
Tracy machine guns and marketed them successfully as guerrilla weapons, the counter-insurgency theme has been popular
in the toy world. Aurora has a six-inch-tall Green Beret figure
with M-16 rifle and grenade. Marx, the most successful
privately-owned toy company in America, sells a Green Beret
Weapons Outfit, and there are jungle fighter weapon sets and
special forces weapon sets available from several other large
companies. There is even Green Beret bubble gum.

The annual directory issue of *Playthings,* the major toy trade
magazine, records over 40 companies who make toy guns.
Many of these guns are war guns, weapons such as a Special
Mission Tommy Gun, a Little Burp Guerrilla Gun, and a Gung
Ho Commando Gun. Barbie-maker Mattel is in the weapon
business, too. They have discovered, possibly as a result of
studies in their glass-walled test rooms and research by their
staff psychiatrists, that boys like noise. So noise gets as much

emphasis as war in their gun advertising. Comic book back-cover ads for Mattel's Vietnam-inspired M-16 Marauder Rifle say, "If you think this gun looks great, wait'll you hear it!" To make sure kids realize fully what an auditory experience the gun provides, Mattel put *Braap Brra-a-a-ap Brap Brap* in hot red letters over the drawing of the boy firing the M-16. It may indicate something of Mattel's opinion of the toy trade that they used twice as many *Brap's* in their ads for the retailers. Remco also practices the noise philosophy, making Screaming Mee-Mee guns and rifles.

Until recently your boys could join a real toy gun army. This was the Kadets of America, with headquarters and armory in Savannah, Tennessee. C. C. Parris of the Parris Manufacturing Company invented the group in the early Eisenhower years, with the uniforms, gear and cork-shooting rifles made by his company. The Kadet handbook stressed learning the manual of arms, with a Parris Trainerifle, and practicing close order drill with available friends. The Kadets claimed 300 official troops across the country by 1966, the year Parris sold his company. The kid-size army was dropped by the new owners. The guns are still available.

The prolongation of the cold war, the ascendancy of the CIA, and the advent of James Bond have made secret agents celebrities again. One result is a whole class of toy espionage weapons. True to Ian Fleming tradition, there is considerable gimmickry and furtiveness surrounding these weapons. Terrence Young, who directed some of the Bond films, thinks the push-button qualities of the picture appeal particularly to children. "They're quite cynical. . . . I think the brutality of these films is increasingly a response to what children want."

Thus far, however, toymakers haven't been able to equal the snobbish viciousness and smarmy sadism of the Fleming books and movies. At best the toy secret agent equipment appears to be designed for someone who is part assassin, part practical joker. The spy merchandise on hand for kids runs heavily to concealed guns. Usually the hidden weapon is a water gun, though the James Bond Shooting Attaché Case conceals a gun firing plastic bullets. The toy people's obsession with hiding guns in attaché cases is possibly an unconscious parody of the commuting executive life, but the open intent is to appeal to the mechanical oneupmanship real secret agents are thought to practice. An ingenious variation is Mattel's Zero M Pocket-Shot. When it isn't a cap pistol, it masquerades as a knife.

The increase in secret agent toys, weapons, and games doesn't always indicate a hangup with violence on the part of the toy tycoons. In some instances it only demonstrates again their great ability for slapping a new label on an old product to turn a profit. You can admire the quick thinking of manufacturers who can come up instantly with Man From U.N.C.L.E. Secret Print Putty, James Bond electric drawing sets, and Ipcress File board games. You may not, however, want to turn part of your children's education and conditioning over to them.

The commander-in-chief of all war toys is G.I. Joe. Between ten and twelve million replicas of the eleven-inch-high fighting man have sold since he hit the kid market in 1964. A product of Hassenfeld Bros., Inc., of Pawtucket, Rhode Island, the G.I. Joe doll represents the most successful effort so far in adapting the Barbie concept to the war toy field. Because of the success of G.I. Joe, Hasbro, the trade name of the Hassenfeld Brothers, is now in fifth place among the top ten toy companies and grosses about 50 million dollars a year. The doll, designed by a Hasbro product planner named Don Levine, looks nearly as bland as Barbie's Ken, though Hasbro maintains the G.I. Joe face is a composite of those of twenty Medal of Honor winners. The nickname G.I. Joe was coined during World War II, prob-ably by *Yank* cartoonist and correspondent Dave Breger. Who-ever invented the name, Hasbro owns it now. Because of the initial doubts among toy buyers and jobbers as to whether

5-to-12-year-old boys would take to a doll and his accessories the way little girls had, Hasbro was forced to spend considerable public relations money. The objective was to convince everybody that G.I. Joe wasn't a doll at all, but rather a "sophisticated toy soldier" and a "virile fighting man."

To do this Hasbro produced a gung ho pitch film for the trade and then went into test market television. G.I. Joe began to sell. By the late 1960's, when G.I. Joe was selling everywhere, his wardrobe and weaponry included the uniforms of several domestic and foreign services, plus M-1 rifles, bazookas, and flame throwers. It costs more to outfit Joe than Barbie, proving guns usually win out over butter. While the 1968 model G.I. Joe didn't twist 'n turn, he did have new exclusive features. For one thing, he could talk. You pull his plastic dog tag and he says "Man the machine guns!" or "Take the jeep and get some ammo!" or "Prepare to pick up astronauts!"—depending on the branch of the service your doll belongs to. Joe has another advantage over Barbie in that while no one has ever heard of a platoon of teenage fashion models, boys are quite aware of platoons of soldiers. Hasbro devotes considerable advertising to encouraging the platoon concept. A running series of strip-style ads appears on the inside back covers of many national periodical magazines (*Batman, Superman,* etc.). Besides romancing the idea of buying more than one G.I. Joe doll, these well-drawn ads extol the importance of being an expert at jungle warfare, bazooka use, counter-insurgency, and footlocker maintenance.

Hasbro downplays the use of the word *war* in their advertising to kids, though they opt for the idea that combat and military life is fun. "The more action, the more fun for you and your friends," reads the copy in one ad. An earlier page was headlined "Join the fun with G.I. Joe!" The accompanying text explained, "G.I. Joe is everybody's hero, is every boy's dream come true. . . . He takes every military position—run

walk, crawl, climb, throw grenades—he's tremendous! . . .
Equipment for every action in attack or defense—machine
guns, rifles, flame-throwers, sandbags, tents, communication
gear, scuba suits. . . ." For further fun, Hasbro has an official
G.I. Joe Club, whose members get a plastic dog tag, a certifi-
cate proclaiming that each boy is "a collector of equipment for
G.I. Joe, America's Movable Fighting Man," an annual "big 32-
page" magazine called the Command Post News, and a letter
from Commanding Officer Col. Pat Lawrence with the salu-
tation "Welcome Buddy."

The campaign to sell G.I. Joe in the first three months of
1967 cost Hasbro nearly one million dollars. The promotion,
called The Capture Hill 79 Sweepstakes, was "the first sweepstakes in toy business history." Hasbro explained it this way:
"The promotion is fun for children. Designed to involve them
and their parents. And that involvement will mean more profits
for retailers." To an adult, the words Capture Hill 79 might
suggest bloody battles in Korea and Vietnam, but Hasbro assured retailers that the idea was "tailored to the fantasy world
of children." For the kid who really got excited by the promotion, Hasbro made a special *Capture Hill 79* boxed game to
sell. The nicest blending of the mercenary and the military was
the first prize, a foot-locker filled with $2,500 in cash. Com-
mercials for the sweepstakes, showing boys in mufti and war
helmets charging up a pleasant green grass hill, saturated the
Saturday morning cartoon shows.

Hasbro promised "a total of over 400 million Hill 79 selling
messages" to hit 65 million children. These commercials had
been "scientifically *Pre-tested* with children and mothers. . . .
Your assurance of a winning promotion." Toy sellers were
guaranteed that the commercials had obtained the highest score
ever, using the eye-blink method "developed at the University
of Chicago." Behind the Hill 79 promotion was Hasbro vice
president Stephen Hassenfeld, who is in his middle twenties.

He is fond of saying to his salesmen, "Don't tell me that the dealers just love it, tell me how much they love it."

The *New York Times*, during a war toy debate in 1967, quoted a child psychiatrist, Norman Westland, as saying of the G.I. Joe doll that he is "a virile, masculine figure." Since both *virile* and *masculine* mean having the characteristics of manhood, and since Joe has no sex organs or secondary sex characteristics, Dr. Westland apparently means that the weapons and uniforms assure G.I. Joe's maleness.

A more recent war doll is Captain Action, actually a hybrid who is part G.I. Joe and part superhero. He is the creation of the Ideal Toy Corporation of New York, and he can change not only clothes but identities. The basic doll resembles a futuristic barge captain. He sells at the same price as G.I. Joe, between $4 and $5. In 1967, twelve alter-egos, celebrity superheroes, and soldiers from TV and comics were on sale. Each of the role changes involves a costume, face mask, and weapons, which Ideal prefers to call accessories or equipment. Each identity switch costs around $3.98. Captain Action can also be provided with a mortar set, an amphibious anti-crime car, and a boy companion. This sidekick is Action Boy, and he comes with beret, costume, knife, and black panther. So far Action Boy has only three identity shifts—Robin, Super Boy, and Aqualad.

Captain Action's preoccupation with weapons is so pronounced that even when your boy turns him into Steve Canyon or Captain America he carries one, if not two, guns. In his own comic book milieu, Captain America is strictly a punch-in-the-nose and thunk-with-the-shield hero. Steve Canyon hasn't done anything more violent in comic strips than public relations for the Air Force in years. When a kid buys the Lone Ranger identity for Captain Action, there's not only the famous six-shooter loaded with silver bullets but a rifle as well. One of the main points of the Lone Ranger's ethic during his decades on radio and television was that he never killed a man, never even wounded an opponent if he could help it. With the additional hardware Ideal has added, he's bound to be tempted. There's also a Tonto disguise in the catalogue, though unless a boy is very adept at miniaturized quick change two basic dolls will be needed for extended Lone Ranger and Tonto play.

All of this really shows that Captain Action is not twelve heroes at all. He's only one person: the man with the gun, the man whose weapons give him the edge. He is faceless and can only define himself with violence. Here's what the makers of Captain Action say about our kids: "We've got 'em: 97.7 percent of all kids in the United States. They'll be watching our hard-selling TV commercials every weekend."

If your boys wants to read war when he's not playing war, he can check the newsstand, where *War and Attack, G.I. Combat, Our Army at War, Star Spangled War Stories, Fightin' Marines, Sgt. Fury and His Howling Commandos, Our Fightin Forces, Army War Heroes*, and usually a dozen other combat-oriented comic books are on sale. So far Vietnam doesn't figure much in these comic books, and the vice president of National Periodicals says the Vietnam war is unpopular with kids and is also, as National found when they tried to sell it, unsalable. The popular war is World War II. The soldier hero of the comic pages is about as real as the cowboy hero of television, and World War II is usually presented in terms of locale and action rather than issues and beliefs. In a letter column of a World War II comic book, the editor apologized for accidentally leaving himself "open to the charge of being anti-German." While continuing characters aren't as common in war comics as they are in comics in general, there are several recurrent heroes. Among them the previously mentioned Sergeant Fury, plus Sergeant Rock, Lieutenant Hunter, Captain Storm, and Super Green Beret. Fittingly, the 1940's symbol of downtrodden enlisted man, Sad Sack, is also around in a comic book of his own.

Actual bloodshed is often off panel in war comics. There's a great reliance on the noise element of war. The writers and artists of war strips have exceeded even Mattel, Inc., in the onomatopoeia of violence. A glossary of hand-lettered war noises would include *Krak!*, *Blam Wham!* and *Pakka Pak Bap Bap Thakka Brakka!*, which are, respectively, the sounds of a Luger being fired, a 90 mm. gun firing on a German machine gun nest, and machine guns being used against the Gestapo. A bullet that misses you and hits a tree goes *Pting! Pshing!* and bullets hitting the dirt (as when you're being strafed) go *Vip! Vip!* Hand grenades flying toward a target make a *Whissh Ffwiss* sound, and when the target, including several German soldiers, blows up, it goes *Bwam! Whump! Whoom!* Hand-to-hand combat produces *Wok! Whump! Oooff!* When it gets really painful, or fatal, *Aaagh!* and *Ahhhhhh!*

The major defenses of war toys are that they help boys work out aggressions and are a sure route to masculinity. As to aggression, most current research indicates that violent shows and toys don't let off a child's violent impulses and may encourage and stimulate violent acting-out. Nor is there any proof that a gun or two, a plane, and a scattering of toy soldiers aren't sufficient for working out the everyday anxieties, and war fears of boyhood. Dr. Ernest Dichter, one of the two claimants to the title of inventor of motivational research, tells advertisers that fathers want boys to be men and "there is often a feeling that playing with guns will ensure male identification." This attitude Dr. Dichter labels as realistic. Our national preoccupation with masculinity affects mothers, too, and prompts letters like the following: "Dear Dr. Molner: I have a son, 3, and am concerned because he has some very feminine ways." Rather than insure masculinity, it seems much more likely that the 100 million dollars' worth of war toys, the napalm planes, missile launchers, and the rest, will help convince many boys that violence and aggression are normal forms of self-expression.

Some child experts feel, as does Bruno Bettelheim, that "children must be taught about violence so that they can learn to master it." This attitude can't be argued with, but we do have the right to object to the *way* our kids are taught about violence. In the intense war toy sales push, violence tends to get normalized and boys get put in the role of aggressor. The countless documentaries and reports and re-creations of President Kennedy's assassination caused Tom Wolfe, in an essay on violence, to comment: "I have been intrigued with one thing. The point of view, the vantage point, is almost never that of the victim, riding in the Presidential Lincoln. What you get is . . . the view from Oswald's rifle. You can step right up here and look point-blank right through the very hairline cross in Lee Harvey Oswald's Optics Ordinance telescopic sight and watch, frame by frame by frame by frame, as that man there's head comes apart."

Many of the war toys thrust kids into the same vantage point, that of the killer with the mechanical edge. Our kids are being persuaded that the gun is a talisman, a crutch, a magic implement to make them powerful and to make them men. They're being taught that those who oppose them can simply be wiped out, often from a safe non-involving distance. Some remarks Thomas Mann made in 1938 about the Nazi educational program seem to fit much of the teaching of violence our kids are receiving from the war toy people. "Its content is never confined to training, culture, knowledge," Mann wrote in 1938, "the furtherance of human advancement through instruction. Instead it has sole reference, often with implication of violence, to the fixed idea of national pre-eminence and warlike preparedness."

To criticism of war toys, the Toy Manufacturers president

has replied, "It is ridiculous to say that if we stop war toys we stop wars. . . . Toys are replicas of the adult world, anyway. Manufacturers make only toys people buy." Though Dr. Wertham agrees with the replica idea, he puts a different interpretation on it. "Mass media violence is not only a contributing factor to harm; the fact that we so profusely produce it and permit it is a symptom of the time." A look at the real world our children are growing up in will provide a few more symptoms of our time. They live in a country where a continuing and growing number of all crimes are committed by kids, where over 600 children a year are killed in gun accidents, and where the rate of suicide and suicide attempts among children under the age of 14 has doubled since 1957. Where sniping, not riot sniping but suburban sniping for fun, is becoming a serious juvenile problem, and where a young boy can be arrested for killing an old man he never met and say, "I just felt like shooting somebody." And our children are maturing in a world where reason must become as important as weaponry. In such a country and in such a world, it is, at the very least, negligent and irresponsible to offer so much vicious feedback of the real violence of our lives to kids, by way of the toy shop and the war gun commercial.

In the edition of *Baby And Child Care* we use, Dr. Benjamin Spock talks about toy guns as valid tools for a boy to "let off steam." That was in the late 1950's; today Dr. Spock's concern for children has moved him to protest against the spread of nuclear weapons and against America's involvement in Vietnam. He now says: "In an age when nuclear weapons are steadily being piled higher and disseminated to more countries, and when annihilation could come at any hour, through brinkmanship or mistake or madness, I believe that we must build into our children a horror of violence, a devotion to civilized ways of settling disputes." Unfortunately, child care in our time forces us to engage in such efforts.

4. Pandora's Toy Box

With rare exceptions it is foolishly pompous to get scandalized
and accuse manufacturers, advertisers, and vendors of dese-
crating Christmas by trying to sell what you or I may think is
silly junk. Obviously some people like it and buy it, and that's
their business. It's said to be the fault of the commercializers
that parents buy overpriced, unnecessary toys for children.
And that's a fancy alibi. If you don't like what's being hawked
this Christmas, you don't have to buy it. And if you're a sucker,
your problem isn't seasonal.

> APRIL OURSLER ARMSTRONG
> *The Saturday Evening Post*,
> December 18, 1965

If we could keep play and the desire to learn alive throughout
childhood and adulthood, we would release a force more
powerful for good than any physical force that scientists have
yet discovered.

> CREATIVE PLAYTHINGS, INC.

Out of the ceiling loudspeakers in the toy store come
commercials the owner has recorded himself and rigged to
play continuously and audibly. The store is big and long and
overfilled with toys and artificial light. This particular one is a
short drive from our house. But its hectic clutter, its crazy-
quilt of worthless mixed with valid toys, makes it typical of toy
outlets all over the country. There are specimens of every kind
of toy and game here. Barbie and G.I. Joe rub shoulders with
Raggedy Ann; Motorific Torture Tracks nudge Tinker Toys;
Flintstone coloring books, a little dusty, are crowded in with

48

Richard Scarry picture books. There are Flying Nun dolls, Mamas and Papas dolls, matchbox cars, Incredible Edibles, toy skin diving snorkels, Play-Doh, German Panther tanks, official Monkee jigsaw puzzles, Gumbys, Easy-Bake Ovens, and Mowgli lunchboxes. There's even a bin of intensely bright colored shaggy stuffed animals, which toy dealers class as Grandmother toys. A Grandmother toy is one that's so dreadful, and usually so expensive, that only a grandmother would buy it for a child. In this one toy store you can buy your kids toys that will provide real fun, fake fun, and no fun at all. Toys that can teach them and toys that may permanently injure them. Toys that can amuse them, or poison them, or even blind them. It's a complex carnival, and both the beneficiaries and the victims are the same children.

Before any further samplings of the specific products of the annual deluge of toys, a few thoughts about just what a toy is supposed to be. "The nature of toys," says historian Antonia Fraser, "is compounded of pleasure, fantasy, and imitation." A toy should give pleasure, inward and outward, be a sport and a pastime. A toy should be a tool that helps a child develop both physical and creative skills. A toy should teach a child, too, about himself and about the world and where he is in it. While many toy manufacturers agree publicly with the above basic definitions, and even support the American Toy Institute's research into the nature and value of playthings, many of the toys sold in America don't fulfill any of the basic purposes well. Some toys do such a bad job they can almost be called anti-toys.

Talking about toys as tools and educational devices may summon up visions of black frock coats, stiff collars, and rolled umbrellas, but it nevertheless has to be done. Fun is the most abundant ingredient in American advertising and can be added, by implication and persuasion, to any product. Sometimes it's really there, sometimes a reasonable facsimile. Toys, though, should be more, at least a little more, than just fun. For children, learning is continuous, not something done at specific scheduled times. Part of their learning experience is the toys they play with. Through toys a child learns first about himself, about how he works and how good it feels to move. Gradually he learns how other things function, what the world is like, and what people do and can do in it. "A child loves his play, not because it's easy, but because it's hard," Benjamin Spock has said. "He is striving every hour of every day to graduate to more difficult achievements and to do what older kids and grownups do."

Further, for children toys, and play itself, serve as a means of communication. Erik Erikson has written of "the language of play" that helps children "make up for defeats, sufferings and frustrations, especially those resulting from a technically and culturally limited use of language." If play is a language of childhood, then the toys we provide make up the vocabulary and can have an effect not only on what a child says but how he says it. "For the child, his body is an organ of expression, as well as of perception," says a study published by Columbia University. "His attitudes toward himself and the world about him are expressed in the ways he uses his body more fully than in his verbalizations." While most of us forget our earliest childhood, even forget the enormous efforts we made then to understand, to break through and communicate, we often remember some special toy. It could be nostalgia, or it could be because the toy was one of the things that helped us join the world.

"Kids are demanding—just demanding—realism," the president of a firm making toy appliances told the *Wall Street Journal* last Christmas. The demand for toy versions of consumer products is due only in part to the child's need to imitate the world of adults. The rest is caused by a colossal amount of advertising which persuades a kid to ask not only for what he wants but what he's made to want. Imitation of adult activities is an important part of play, but there is a difference between imitation and duplication. Surrounding a child with an exact replica of the grownup environment, fully functioning in miniature, doesn't allow any room for individuality and fantasy. At best highly sophisticated and coldly realistic toys make the kid into a shrunken adult. They have nothing to do with his needs as a complex and developing personality. Toys that do everything, toys structured to produce only inevitable results, reverse the essential relationship between child and toy. They play with him. Worse, they program him, force him to find not himself but a preconceived self built into the toy. "The nature of toys must be of extreme importance to children," says Antonia Fraser, "not only in forming their fantasies, but also in guiding what sort of fantasies they form."

The sales of toys during the Christmas season of 1967 were, according to the trade publications, "solid if unsensational." Even so, the retail toy sales for the year were expected to exceed 2.6 billion dollars. Though billions are spent for a wide range of categories, including games, bicycles, and guns, there is always a top ten in each toy year. Judging by *Playthings'* reports on the most wanted items of that year, automation and edibility were the most popular qualities a late '60's toy could have. Dolls that moved, talked, and ate did very well, as did various kinds of remote control space toys and workable appliances. Mattel's Incredible Edibles, and imitations, made *Playthings'* list of "glamour numbers." Pure noise is not quite so much in demand as it used to be. Henry Orenstein, whose Delux Topper Corporation makes Suzy Homemaker dishwashers, irons, and vacuum cleaners, saw a trend. "The scientific development and vast new technology of the space age have had an influence on even young children," he said at the end of 1967. "This means that the demand for modern, more sophisticated and complex toys that do many different things is increasing."

Emphasis on the supposed new sophistication of children has prompted toymakers to dedicate themselves increasingly to what Isaac Asimov used to call robotics. Companies like Mattel and Remco are frequently on the best seller lists with toys capable of walking, talking, and performing certain other functions that used to be the exclusive property of human beings and real animals. Two hot glamour numbers of the late '60's are Remco's Tricky Tommy Turtle and their baby Crawl Along doll. "Remco Industries baby Crawl Along, a battery-operated doll that moves with a wriggling derriere," reports the *Wall Street Journal,* "is 'the hottest thing we've seen for a long time,' an executive says." The motions of both the turtle and the crawling baby are remote-controlled. One technical journal sees in Tricky Tommy Turtle "a revolution in toymaking" because of his cheap transistorized power source.

Since Mattel is the current titan of the toy business, it figures they would lead in the number of robot and automated toys turned out. Mattel's Talking Baby First Step doll not only walks and talks, she can roller-skate. Their Cheerful-Tearful cries and smiles, and also wets. Top-selling Baby's Hungry's two "D" batteries enable her to chew and drink. The Mattel-O-Phone, a triumph of plastic electronics, talks back to kids who use it and provides "two-way talk with 40 friends." To tax children's imaginations even less, Mattel sells talking hand puppets with prerecorded voices. For the younger child, Mattel's technicians have created a wheel toy called See 'N Say Ride-Away. This plastic vehicle "becomes a roaring motorcycle, chugging locomotive, car, or fire engine." Not when your kid decides to make a noise like one, but when he makes a selection with the pointer and activates the talking ring. The noises are all inside, recorded on a plastic disc.

Besides toys which are self-operating and self-contained, children, especially little girls, can now be surrounded with fully operational toy appliances. These appliances are not make-believe. They are miniaturized versions of the real thing. The Kenner Products Co., recently taken over by General Mills, devotes considerable full-color television time to plugging its Big Burger Grill, which is a small home grill heated by a light bulb. Kenner also manufactures the Easy-Bake Oven (makes food "as good as Mom's"), Easy-Bake Cake and Frosting sets, Easy-Bake Kiddie Dinner sets, Whiz Fizz Soda Fountains and, as the logical follow-up, the Easy-Wash Dishwasher (at $12.95). Emenee Industries, a subsidiary of Standard Brands, pushes a candy maker and a peanut butter machine. The Delux Topper Company has a full line of microappliances, including Suzy Homemaker irons, clothes washers, and sewing machines.

All of the toy appliances, the result of extensive research in design and engineering, are not really toys at all. They are child-scaled versions of actual adult appliances. As such they can function only in specific, programmed ways. With the Suzy Homemaker clothes washer, your little girl does not pretend to wash clothes, she actually does it. This literalness may lighten the laundry bill, but it forces the child into a miniaturized and rigid adult situation, a situation wherein there is no room for experimentation or fantasy. Since the end results are known in advance, the only surprise a child can get is by failing, by causing the appliance to malfunction.

The toymakers are also providing children with miniature versions of equipment with which they can duplicate some of the more disturbing aspects of our society. There are now numerous surveillance and spying toys available. Not the make-believe 007 things of the last chapter—fully functioning eavesdropping gear. For $12.95 a kid can buy the Big Ear, a parabolic mike with earphones. It will pick up outdoor conversations up to 200 feet away. Concealed cameras are available, devices for looking through keyholes, even kid-priced tape recorders with microphones that can be hidden. A kid can purchase a real lie detector to complement his privacy-invading toys. Of the booming business in spying toys that really work, Alan F. Westin, attorney and author, has written: "The constant celebration of privacy-invasion on TV, in comics, and through toys cannot help but affect a child's attitude about privacy and the intrusion powers of government. Long before children learn in school about the Constitution and the Bill of Rights, they have learned well that methods of law enforcement that happen to be illegal and immoral are standard operating procedures for the heroes of American society."

A new variation in built-in obsolescence shows up in the toy you can eat. The leader so far has been Mattel's Incredible Edibles, which did well enough in the middle 1960's to inspire Hasbro to develop Cannibal Animals. Aimed at what Hasbro refers to as "the Now Generation," the Cannibal Animals involve a candy substance and plastic molds. Mattel's is a more complicated product, and more expensive. Their food substance is Gobble-Degoop, and when put in molds and heated in a 110-volt metal heating unit, then cooled on cooling trays, it turns into candy insects, bugs, and worms. Two kinds of accessory packs are available, one of which contains molds for baking edibles resembling Bugs Bunny, elephants, bats, weird eyes, and tortoises. The television commercials for Mattel's edible toy shows kids happily eating spiders and little snakes. Apparently Mattel believes young kids with a flair for imitation will always wait until someone buys them Incredible Edibles and not try to act out the commercial with real backyard bugs and insects. Even just eating the various eatable toys isn't too wise, since most of them contain artificial sweeteners of the cyclamate class, plus a variety of preservatives.

The most important toy in this country is the TV toy. It can take an infinity of shapes and names: Barbie, G.I. Joe, Suzy

Homemaker, The Monkees, Tubsy, Johnny Astro. The product is not as important as the fact that it's heavily advertised on prime kid-time television in full color. The effectiveness of a saturation attack on kids by way of television is not as automatic as it was four or five years ago. "The golden age of TV toy advertising was probably the period from 1959 to 1964," thinks one toy marketing expert. "In those years we had a far greater number of hit items coming out of TV promotions." This doesn't mean television is no longer potent. It means guaranteeing big sales with television commercials is now slightly more difficult. When asked what sells best, toy dealers still nominate the TV toy. "We could sell anything that appears on TV if we could get enough of them," says a Boston wholesaler. Stores in Miami, Chicago, San Francisco say much the same thing.

Among the side effects of the TV toy, as we'll see in detail in the next chapters, are the destruction of smaller toy companies, the narrowing of choice for kids, and the raising of prices for most toys. This last point is, obviously, the one toymakers spend the most time denying. "It's an unfair rap," the editor of *Playthings* says, speaking for his thousands of toy business readers, about charges that prices are much too high. "Between 1923 and 1967 toy prices rose, in sum, 63.3 percent. Meanwhile the cost of living, which encompasses *all* goods and services, increased 97 percent. . . . This is not to say that bows should be taken. Prices and profits haven't been kept down as a public service. It's competition of the keenest kind that's been responsible."

While the price of toys may not have risen as high as that of some other consumer products, there's no denying that millions of advertising dollars are needed to compete in the toy business and maintain any kind of large-scale position. Popular consumer authority Sidney Margolius cites the TV-advertised toy as one of the numerous items whose price is significantly raised by the cost of commercials. In his latest book, he quotes kid huckster Art Linkletter as having admitted that because of the tremendous expense of television advertising, "toys costing the manufacturer $3 or $4 to produce go on the market for about $18 to $20."

For the past several years the Federal Trade Commission and the toymakers have been contemplating, with varying degrees of enthusiasm, a trade practices conference. There is a possibility by the time you read this that some discussions will have taken place toward setting up industry-wide standards on fair packaging, safety, pricing, and advertising. No complete and universally accepted code governing all these practices exists, and there have been considerable abuses up to now.

For all their studies devoted to the feelings and needs of children, toymakers in general show little concern when it comes to taking advantage of kids. It is often only pressure from the FTC that halts deceptive packaging tricks. The surveillance maintained by the Federal Trade Commission is to catch such things as large boxes housing small toys, packages not plainly and adequately saying what is inside, and packages which feature exaggerated illustrations of the toy in use. In the summer of 1967, ten large toy companies entered into consent agreements with the FTC to cease slack filling on toy boxes, to begin using containers dictated by the actual size of the toy. Among the large companies signing settlements—which is not the same as an admission of guilt—in July 1967, were Ideal, Hasbro, Remco, Pressman, and E. S. Lowe.

In a decision three years before, the FTC had ordered the Ideal Toy Corporation to stop using commercials that gave the impression that one of Ideal's toys performed in a "manner not in accordance with fact." The toy in question was a robot commando, and the FTC said the TV commercials for the mechanical man gave children the idea it obeyed voice commands when it actually depended on push-button controls. "Obviously," the FTC commissioner said, "a toy that obeys spoken commands is more marvelous and thrilling than one that responds only to a combination of mechanical controls. . . . Since the fact of voice control appears to be an important element in the desirability of a toy such as Robot Commando to children and to adults who purchase toys for them, respondent's representation is an unlawful deception." The principle that shows through the FTC's formal language is simply that you shouldn't fool children.

The safety of many toys still depends almost entirely on the manufacturer, and the toymakers feel any further tightening of standards should be on a voluntary and cooperative basis with the government. Most government-imposed controls apply to the ingredients and components of a toy and not to the finished product. A toymaker is not supposed to use poisonous lead-based paint, unhygienic stuffing material, dangerous uninsulated wiring, etc. Whether he does or not is a matter often left to his discretion and integrity. Less obvious hazards are frequently not caught until the toy has been put on the market and has caused harm or injury.

The assorted seals and signs found on toy packages and in toy ads are valuable chiefly for their decorative qualities. Anyone who advertises in *Good Housekeeping* magazine can use their oblong seal. All it promises is a refund if the product is defective. This is not the same as guaranteeing safety and wholesomeness. All that *Good Housekeeping* is really saying with its seal is that if your child is electrocuted or poisoned with a toy, the manufacturer will give you your $12.95 back. The *Parents'* magazine seal isn't worth much, either. It reads "commended by Parents' Magazine as advertised therein." You may have the impression that everything with this sticker has been tested by *Parents'* in its Consumer Service Bureau, but this is not so. In fact the government, in 1967, asked the magazine to cease giving this impression.

Appliance-type toys are usually backed up by private testing organizations, such as Underwriters' Laboratories. Established in 1893, Underwriters' is a non-profit concern with four testing stations around the country. The government now requires that UL safety standards be met by several hundred products. The government trusts Underwriters' Laboratories and relies on them. As the organization's president points out: "Without our standards, they would have to have a company the size of Underwriters' to do the job adequately." UL doesn't test every toy that comes off the line, which would be impossible. They test specimens in one of their labs and afterwards their 200 field inspectors make occasional surprise tours of the actual toy factories. Lab tests and peekaboo inspection are not sometimes enough, and the UL initials, according to Consumers' Union, do not automatically mean a product is safe. The Consumers' Union has on occasion found what they believe is potential for "severe, even lethal shock" in electrical appliances passed as safe by Underwriters' labs. One such incident, as told by former CU director Dexter Masters, involved an electric toothbrush. "The advertising literature accompanying it featured a child happily cleaning her teeth with the device," says Masters. "But the device was so constructed that, if it were accidentally or playfully dropped into a basin of water, anyone attempting to retrieve it could be electrocuted if he happened to be touching a ground, such as a water faucet."

Another problem with guarantees and safety standards is their link with the adult world. A heating unit that is safe by adult standards isn't always safe for a child. An object that becomes intensely hot is more likely to burn a child because a child is more likely to touch it. Much of the research and design work done by toymakers puts emphasis on how to design toy products that will appeal to kids and attract them. There is not enough concern given to the special safety needs of children.

The favorite advertising place of the Daisy Manufacturing Company is the back cover of comic books. Their ads have appeared on the back side of funny books since before Pearl Harbor. Ostensibly this Arkansas manufacturer is selling BB guns, but to do this Daisy has to sell the concept that all guns are fun and that guns assure masculinity. The Daisy air rifle advertisements never miss a chance to show a young boy walking through the woods with his dad, both of them proudly carrying guns. "Great for hunting with Dad—or for fun *indoors*," Daisy says of its Model 26 BB gun. The Daisy rifles are interim weapons in the mind of the company, surrogates until your boy is old enough to graduate to the real thing. "This Daisy BB Gun looks like a real .22!" exclaims one red-letter headline. A representative of the company sums up their philosophy this way: "No matter how much you may want to turn your back on it, the yen for a gun on the part of a boy is as natural as his very growth. The ownership and use of a BB gun satisfies that yen, and with proper training helps produce a better citizen."

As we saw in the previous chapter, the belief that citizenship can be improved with a gun is not limited to the Daisy Manufacturing Company. More important here is the plain and simple physical hazard connected with the Daisy product and its competitors. The BB gun is a frequent contributor to the national statistics on gun injuries to children. In his study of the American preoccupation with firearms, Carl Bakal reports that such injuries occur all over the nation. For instance, "a poll of 400 Illinois doctors turns up 139 cases of children treated for eye injuries caused by BB guns during a recent year; at least one doctor reported removing an eye, and many commented that BB guns have an even greater danger to sight than fireworks." The thought that many kids will move up from a Daisy to a real gun is less than comforting. Bakal establishes, in *The Right To*

Bear Arms, that America has one of the highest rates of deaths by gun accidents in the world. A fourth of those killed each year in this country are children.

For parents who are aware of and concerned with the hazards and deficiencies of many of the mass toys, a hopeful alternative has seemed to be the educational toy. The two most relied-on manufacturers of educational toys are the Playskool Company of Chicago and Creative Playthings, Inc., of Princeton, New Jersey. Playskool concentrates on simple unoffensive toys for younger children, infants, toddlers, pre-schoolers. They handle crib exercisers, blocks, pull toys, and peg toys, and also sell, for older kids, Lincoln Logs.

Building on a similar foundation, Creative Playthings, Inc., became prosperous enough to be bought out by the Columbia Broadcasting System. When this happened, in 1966, CP executives assured customers the only changes in the enterprise would be ones for the better. "We are enthusiastic over being part of the very creative CBS Family," an editorial in the Creative Playthings catalogue announced. "Other CBS units have long been undisputed leaders of the fields of communication, entertainment, and the arts. Interchange of knowledge with them, application of their experiences and skills to our work will stimulate our energies and our imaginations." This particular catalogue, titled *A HEAD START For Every Child,* was sent out in large quantities.

Though they are opening up more store outlets, Creative Playthings does most of its business by mail. The Princeton toy distributor is not a mail order house in the Montgomery Ward sense. Their approach is closer, in style of copy and use and layout of color photos, to the mail order catalogues sent to bankers and executives by dealers in fancy fruit and gourmet food. And like the merchandiser who can romance a dozen pears into being worth $8.95, the Creative Playthings people have been able to bring off some impressive markups.

By calling corrugated cardboard boxes Play-Core Hollow Blocks, CP can ask $19.75 for a dozen and a half of them. Six boards and six poles, which you have to assemble yourself, costs $37.50 (plus postage) when it's named Ladder Exerciser. Just as breakfast food makers have grown affluent by finding new ways to sell and package corn and wheat, Creative Playthings has been successful, and most creative, in finding new ways to sell cardboard and wood. This isn't to say that many of their toys aren't useful and valid. But they are vastly overpriced. Not to mention oversold and overpromoted. CP's copy promises miracles of education and insight, all described in a style so smug and pompous that it seems to call for Edward P. Morgan with his chin resting thoughtfully on his thumb to read it aloud. "My quarrel with Creative Playthings is not with the playthings they create," William K. Zinsser wrote in *Life*, addressing himself to this latter point. "What I resent is the language that certifies toys as edifying. . . . Creative Playthings is leading us all into joyless new ground."

Creative Playthings has succeeded admirably in gaining acceptance from nurseries, schools, and even the United States government. Their toys were bought, at apparently full catalogue price, for the new Head Start Centers. Typically, CP used the Head Start theme in its catalogues and advertising and promoted *A HEAD START for every child*. Outside of the lower-income kids who could be squeezed into the centers, no child from a low-income family can afford the Creative Playthings toys. Creative Playthings are for the middle-income portion of America—for those in a position to pay $18.50 for a toy barn, $11.75 for the animals to stock it, and $18.75 for the firehouse down the road. One child psychiatrist I talked to said he uses the Creative Playthings catalogue regularly. He looks at the pictures and then makes the toys himself for use in his clinic. He says he saves money.

To educate older children the toymakers offer a variety of science kits. A long-time staple is the chemistry set. When *Consumer Reports* surveyed the chemistry set field two Christmases ago, they found many inadequacies and possible dangers. "Even while supervising a child who is willing and able to follow instructions in his chemistry set, and whose set fully conforms to FDA requirements," the magazine cautioned, "you should keep alert for possible dangers. The manuals sometimes warn inadequately or not at all about certain kinds of hazards for which there appear to be no specific regulations under federal law." The findings of *Consumer Reports* led them to conclude that even in the best of sets there were dangers of fire and even explosions from alcohol lamps, of eye injury from some of the rocket experiments, of dry ice and other types of burns. Many of the manuals outlining experiments that involve changing water into a jelly or milk-like substance "neglect to state within the instructions for the particular experiment that the mock foods produced are inedible." There was also evidence of overpricing and, even in the most expensive sets, badly made equipment.

Because of the rise of Playskool and Creative Playthings, Inc., many larger toy manufacturers have been stricken with me-tooism. Many of the gimmicky and electronically hyped-up inventions of Mattel, Hasbro, Ideal, and Delux Topper are now labeled and promoted as educational. The word *educational*, like the Good Housekeeping seal, can be affixed to most anything. All toys, actually, are educational. What's important is what the toy teaches and how well.

It's possible then to buy your child a toy in most any toy store that can cause internal or external physical harm. The bulk of the toys we've considered are not dangerous in this tangible way, though. Their danger is that they are often non-toys, objects that don't provide knowledge or real amusement or any help with the long, lonely process of growing up. All of these non-toys are simply produced to be consumed and, while they fail to serve as toys, they do, all of them, succeed in the mass process of turning individual children into conforming, consuming adults. In our era, as David Riesman says, we can afford "building up in the child habits of consumption he will employ as an adult." This is the basic lesson the TV toy teaches.

Every childhood now is in danger of ceasing to be a voyage of discovery and turning into a prearranged tour, with the destination plainly marked and the points of interest along the way unvarying. Increasingly children realize where they're being delivered and simply drop out. "The media have created a picture of what boyhood and girlhood are like," says Riesman, "and they force children either to accept or aggressively resist this picture of themselves."

The characteristics of toys, the basic functions that have remained constant for centuries, are being blurred and destroyed. The possibilities for pleasure disappear with gimmick toys that are as quickly obsolete as last year's refrigerator. The potential for fantasy and even magic is stifled by the electronic toys with the pattern of play already built in. The things a child wants to say with toys cannot be said with toys that speak for him. While these toys do not provide an adequate vocabulary for children, they do convey one further message. The message is from the adult world and expresses the feelings and values of that world. Using these toys as clues, it's not difficult for a child to figure out what the grownup world is trying to tell him. Objects are important, things. Consuming is more valuable than liking. Affection can't afford to be long-term. Anything goes as long as it sells. The adult world is ours, and this is what we are saying to our kids.

5. Disneyland

Disneyland will never be completed, as long as there is imagination left in the world.

WALT DISNEY

When Walt was nine years old his ambition shifted; he now wanted to become an actor instead of an artist. His first two roles were those of Abraham Lincoln and Charlie Chaplin. . . . Luckily for Disney, he soon became a better Chaplin than a Lincoln.

ALVA JOHNSTON
Woman's Home Companion,
July 1934

When Walt Disney died in 1966 they flew the Disneyland flag at half-mast and Eric Severeid told CBS news viewers, "Judging by the way it's been behaving in spite of all Disney tried to tell it about laughter, love, children, puppies, and sunrises, the century hardly deserved him. He probably did more to heal or at least soothe troubled human spirits than all the psychiatrists in the world." Probably most of us felt an odd twinge of loss. It was almost mandatory, since we've all grown up with Walt Disney serving us as an electronic uncle. We've been delighted by Mickey Mouse color cartoons, Donald Duck newspaper strips, Uncle Scrooge comic books, bright colors, broad gags, tricky animation.

Now, with our children growing up in the shadow of the still giant Disney empire, we are obliged to re-examine the Disney legacy. Years of careful and prodigious publicity and

64

public relations have built up Walt Disney until he is as solid and unreal as Lincoln in his memorial. Much of the writing and thinking about Disney, with few exceptions, consists of simply describing the long-standing effigy and rehearsing the accepted notions. Let us try to cut away the nostalgia and the sentiment and see what it is that Walt Disney Enterprises has been up to all these years.

Walt Disney was proudest of the fact that he was a business success. When asked in his last years to name the most rewarding experience of his life, Disney replied, "The whole damn thing. The fact that I was able to build an organization and hold it." The Disney organization is a gigantic sprawling mechanism, antiseptic and incredibly efficient, with the driving purpose of making money from children. The Disney machine may be bigger and cuter than a slot machine, but it thinks the same way.

Commenting on the machine in his unauthorized biography of Disney, *The Disney Version*, Richard Schickel says: "What made it superior to all its competitors was that it had the power to *compel* one's attention to a product it particularly treasured. All its parts—movies, television, book and song publishing, merchandising, Disneyland—interlock and are mutually reciprocating. And all of them are aimed at the most vulnerable portion of the adult's psyche—his feelings for his children. If you have a child, you cannot escape a Disney character or story even if you loathe it. And if you happen to like it, you cannot guide or participate in your child's discovery of its charms. The machine's voice is so pervasive and persuasive that it forces first the child, then the parent, to pay it heed—and money. In essence, Disney's machine was designed to shatter the two most valuable things about childhood—its secrets and its silences—thus forcing everyone to share the same formative dreams."

Walt Disney became the Henry Ford of fantasy, the king of the dream merchants, by being able to package and sell his particular dream of the world to more children than any man before him. What exactly were the components of the Disney dream? In describing Disneyland, the solid state of the dream, Richard Schickel's analysis is applicable to all the Disney products. "The quality of the dreams it represents is most peculiar—no sex and no violence, no release of inhibitions, no relief from real stresses and tensions through their symbolic statement, and therefore no therapeutic effect. It is all pure escapism, offering momentary thrills, laughs, and nostalgic pleasures."

Nobody exceeded the Disney factory at manufacturing the false dream, the escape to nowhere, and they spent decades getting kids excited about seeing the egress. The essential factor in all the variations on the basic Disney dream is denial. Denial that the world is what it is, that life is what it is, that the child is what he is—denial of the legitimate functions of dream and fantasy. Disney's greatest disservice to children was the persistent imposition of his lifeless dream on them. It does not start off true and then stray. The Disney dream goes wrong at once. "His universe is amoral; it contains only good," observes Professor Peter Michelson of Notre Dame University. "He has one aim, to sentimentalize and beautify. . . . His vision of nature is grand and harmonious rather than operational. Disney's art defines a world without the rigors of cause and effect."

The impulse in the Disney entertainments, in the feature cartoons, the wildlife documentaries, and the live action adventures, is toward improving on nature rather than accepting it. Many of the earlier cartoons show a Disney openly fearful of nature, and the animation of the 1930's is thick with brooding landscapes, dancing skeletons, entangling forests. He gets rid of this fearful aspect in the later films, not by coming to grips with it but by pretending it isn't there. So that all nature becomes stiff and pretty and touched, even in the daylight hours, with sparkling stardust. To the later Disney, nature had to be continually pleasant and, more importantly, clean. Disney seemed compelled to cleanse and tame nature, to put it in order, pave it over, and make it palatable. This attitude resulted in an overall view of nature that can contribute little to a child's real understanding and have an estranging effect.

What a kid requires is a sort of personal ecology, an awareness of the relationships between himself and his environment. He needs a working acceptance of the natural world, an awareness of the fact that he is a participating member of the whole community of living species. In discussing a widespread feeling of alienation from the natural world, psychologist Rollo May says: "This alienation has expressed itself for several centuries in Western man's passion to gain power *over* nature, but now shows itself in an estrangement from nature and a vague, unarticulated, and half-suppressed sense of despair of gaining any real relationship with the natural world, including one's own body."

The Disney inability to cope with, comprehend, and communicate about nature is more specifically illustrated by the Disney handling of animals. To Walt Disney, the beasts of the field and the birds of the air were just folks, and there is no acknowledgment in his work of the variety of life, of the individuality and special essence of different forms of life. All the animals in Disney are people pretending to be animals, their ambition to be cute and to be liked. To be picked up and hugged is not the sole purpose of life, though it may please a three-year-old child. To be yourself is important, be you human, alleycat, or fowl.

T. H. White, whose *Sword in the Stone* was transmuted into a full-length cartoon by Disney, observed after his only visit to Disneyland: "There is something wrong with Disney. . . . Why those awful mermaids encountered on the submarine trip? Why were they so saccharine, insipid, dishonest, unworthy, coy? Why was the sea serpent a babyhood dream, not grand or terrible or beautiful or even reptilian? . . . Why was everything a *pet*? It seems that to Disney women, animals, children, knights, dragons, and elephants are all pets. . . . Chaucer believed that animals must be true to themselves. He praised a horse for being 'right horsely.' Disney's horses are not; his mermaids are not mermaidenly, nor his sea serpents serpentine—nor are his humans human."

Anthropomorphizing animals can be used for humor, as with Mickey Mouse or two men inside a horse suit at the circus, but Disney's later realistic fake animals are not meant to be funny. Though he hired experienced documentary photographers to gather the raw footage for his live action nature films, Disney insisted on adding his own touches. "Anytime we saw an animal doing something with style or personality—say a bear scratching its back—we were quick to capitalize on it," says a writer who worked on the animal pictures. Disney's constant patronizing of animals—especially in the nature films, where incidents such as the mating of birds and the life-and-death struggles of lions were kidded with cute music and gimmick editing—illustrates his uncomprehending attitude toward the live world. "A child, with his innocent egoism, always invests the objects of his play and observation with the only qualities he knows—those of his own personality," Richard Schickel has said. "As he grows older he learns that there are other forces in the world beyond his own personality. . . . Disney never could seem to learn this simple distinction."

With human beings Disney was often at a loss, and those he didn't understand, or like, he turned into animals, reversing his favorite switch. Disney remained always moderately anti-Semitic, for instance, and in his early cartoons and strips he allowed Jews to be caricatured as large-nosed and bearded dogs or wolves. Negroes almost always appeared, in the 1930's and 1940's, not only caricatured but turned into monkeys and apes. To Disney, with studios a few hours away from Mexico, Mexicans were always bandits in the '30's, usually fat dogs with the stereotyped "greaser" trappings. Disney had an inability to sort himself out from the rest of the world, never reaching a place where he could say for certain who he was. "I'm not modest. I'm scared," he said toward the end of his life. "I'm not funny. I hide behind the mouse, the duck, and a lot of other things." It is hard, if not impossible, to teach what you do not know. The Disney school of natural history seems at best an inadequate place to send kids.

Walt Disney was promoted not only as naturalist and nature poet, but as the principal master of the fairy tale and children's fantasy in our century. Disney certainly had financial success with fairy tales, fantasies, and his versions of classic children's stories. Here again, it's important to figure out exactly what product he was selling. The first thing a child should get from a fairy tale is pleasure, enjoyment. Fairy tales and folk stories don't, however, survive for generations and even centuries because they're fun, but usually because they acknowledge a problem of childhood and present, in fantasy and symbol, a way to a solution. Just as Disney couldn't face up to nature as it is, he couldn't allow the basic meanings of the fairy tales he handled to remain intact. He began to falsify as far back as *Snow White*. In its original form, the story deals with some of the basic fears and desires of childhood. The fear of being abandoned, the awareness of the rivalry between generations, the sensed knowledge that growing up can be a threat to the parent because it means the parent has to accept that he himself is growing old and will die. The queen in the fairy tale decides to kill the maturing Snow White when the girl has supplanted her as the fairest in the land. Snow White's escape, her finding of sanctuary, and her eventual triumph is an acting out of the child's struggle for himself, for independence, coupled with the fear that the struggle may kill the child or the parent.

Disney started into this dangerous territory but never came out again in his filmed *Snow White*. He was sidetracked by cuteness, by rustic whimsy and animal behinds. This first full-length Disney fairy tale retains some of the values of the original; but as Disney prospered the cuteness and prettified nature scenes took over completely. The psychological meaning of a fairy tale shouldn't be put on top of the story. Yet some awareness of what the story means, what is beneath the surface, has to go into the creation of an effective version.

When he dealt with more sophisticated material, with classics like *Pinocchio, Peter Pan, Alice in Wonderland, Winnie the Pooh*, and *The Jungle Book*, Walt Disney most often distorted, or removed entirely, the meanings and values. "He made a young tough of Peter Pan, and transformed Pinocchio into a slap-stick, sadistic revel," says Frances Clarke Sayers, former director of Children's Services for the New York Public Library. "He shows scant respect for the integrity of the original creations of the authors, manipulating and vulgarizing everything to his own ends. His treatment is without respect for the anthropological, spiritual, or psychological truths."

It seems probable Walt Disney himself never decided whether it was better to be a child or an adult, and so he made nothing of J. M. Barrie's recognition of the sadness of Peter Pan's situation in never being able to grow up. Collodi's rambling, picaresque story of Pinocchio's struggles to find himself, to become a real boy, is blurred in the Disney version and loses much of its force under the weight of gingerbread and song cues. Even the posthumous *Jungle Book* throws away Kipling's notions and gives only the usual Disney human animals showing their rear ends. He even managed to get in the Negro monkeys and apes again.

Disney's most monumental botch was *Alice in Wonderland*. Lewis Carroll's book has caught perfectly, in fantasy terms, what it feels like to be a child, to know inside that many of the things adults tell you are false, and that being honest and being yourself can cause you trouble. The intricate odyssey of Alice underground leads to the satisfying point made at the book's end during the trial of the Knave of Hearts.

"Off with her head!" the Queen shouted at the top of her voice. Nobody moved.

"Who cares for you?" said Alice (she had grown to her full size by this time). "You're nothing but a pack of cards!"

This, no matter what Walt Disney tried to teach, is one of the things growing up means: to say that you are yourself and are not fooled by the masks and impersonations around you. Alice says this aloud and ends the dream. Lewis Carroll, locked into life as Reverend Dodgson, could only say it in fiction. Disney could not say it at all. Which is why there came to be such a frozen quality about Disney's work, such a waxwork perfection. The films go nowhere because they are afraid to admit there is anywhere to go.

The messages of the Walt Disney product are only part of his contribution to the world of kids. The rest is the commercial organization Disney built to sell his product.

Disney's early life has by now been recounted almost as often, and frequently with as much reverence, as that of Washington and Ben Franklin. The Missouri farm, where the boy Disney was inspired by the beauty of green fields, orchards, herds of dairy cows, flocks of chickens; the move to Kansas City, where Walt and his older brother, Roy, delivered newspapers; Disney's discovery of drawing. "What I liked to do best, as far back as I can remember, was to draw," Disney said.

"I don't know why; nobody else in the Disney family was at all artistically inclined. The other boys are businessmen, including Roy. My parents were not the type who delighted to show off their children's talents. Although I got no particular inspiration from my family, I could always count on sympathetic interest and encouragement."

During World War I, Disney, like Hemingway, was a volunteer ambulance driver overseas. Back in Kansas City he went into commercial art, got interested in animation. During this postwar Kansas City period Disney met a young cartoonist with the unlikely name of Ub Iwerks. Disney and Iwerks stayed together, except for a strained time in the late '20's and early '30's, for most of Disney's life, and it is Iwerks' style of drawing and approach to humor that are prevalent in much of the early product of the Walt Disney studio. "From Kansas City, Missouri, Disney followed his artistic star to California," is how the *National Geographic* describes what happened next. "His equipment: boundless ambition hitched to a fantastic imagination." Roy Disney came with Walt, and the brothers spent their first Hollywood years on poverty row, low-budget and hungry. Then came Oswald the Lucky Rabbit.

The creation of Oswald is described by Diane Disney Miller in her biography of her father. "The man back East . . . demanded a new series with a new character. 'So I came up with a rabbit,' Father told me. 'We wrote a lot of possible names for the animal. We threw them in a hat and asked the distributor to pick one. He drew out the name Oswald." The cartoon films were done for Universal, and that studio retained all rights. Though the Oswald movies sold well, Universal refused to give Disney the raise he eventually asked for. Disney quit, and in so doing he lost the Lucky Rabbit character. It was here, in the late 1920's, that Walt Disney decided never again to work on something he didn't own. This led to Mickey Mouse.

There are several versions of the invention of Mickey Mouse, often set down in a close approximation of Disney prose. One such appears in Coulton Waugh's history of American comics. "Walt just wasn't made to be stepped upon. . . . He decided to buck the system—with a new character, of course. It wasn't all inspiration; it was partly the memory of certain old days when a tiny, squeaking somebody ran along his drawing board in a charming, friendly way, and it was partly elimination; but as the legend goes, a little black and white party with big round ears popped out of Walt's head, ran down his arm, and waved a cute little white-gloved hand. It was Mickey Mouse."

What legend, and historians like Waugh, leave out is the fact that while Mickey Mouse may have vaguely resembled a real mouse that had infested Disney's old ramshackle Kansas City studio, he closely resembled most of the popular animated cartoon characters of the 1920's. Krazy Kat's paramour, Ignatz Mouse, had established himself in films over ten years before. The early Mickey also owed something to Pat Sullivan's well-known Felix the Cat, and much to the already-mentioned Oswald. The first Mickey, in fact, was really little more than Oswald with his ears bobbed.

In 1958, as part of the promotion for Disney's *Sleeping Beauty*, Simon & Schuster published *Walt Disney: The Art of Animation* by Bob Thomas. The section on the history of animation in this book, prepared with the cooperation of the Disney organization, gives the impression that nothing much happened in the field of theater cartoons until Disney. While acknowledging Winsor McKay, who did some of the earliest animation in this country, Thomas' Disney version of events entirely skips over men like Paul Terry, Walter Lantz, and J. R. Bray, who developed most of the techniques and approaches Disney built on. Thomas does allow Felix into his history, but puts Sullivan's cat down for not being enduring and not having a "well-defined personality." He neglects to say that when Disney was still back in Kansas City with mice run-

ning around on his drawing board, Felix was already one of
the most popular film characters in the United States, and the
young Walt Disney must surely have been impressed by the
Felix songs, Felix books, Felix comic strips, Felix dolls, and
Felix military insignia that flourished then.

The first screen adventures of Mickey Mouse looked like all
the other animated cartoons of the '20's, with the usual anal
barnyard gags and mallet-on-the-head violence. But Mickey's
film debut had one real distinction, sound. The sound was a
result of one of the lucky deals the Disney brothers were able
to bring off even in their non-affluent days. On a selling trip to
New York, Walt Disney met Patrick Powers, a former Universal Pictures executive who was now promoting a sound system
to rival Warner Brothers' new Vitaphone process. To Powers,
Mickey Mouse seemed like one good vehicle for attracting attention to the Powers Cinephone System. In return for using
Cinephone, Disney got distribution and advertising support as
well as financial backing from Powers. The agreement with
Powers, though it was to tangle the brothers in financial com-
plexities, did lead to *Steamboat Willie*, the sound short that
first drew attention to Mickey Mouse.

One of the peripheral effects of the crash of 1929 and the
growing Depression was the double feature. Showing two
feature-length films to pull audiences into the faltering movie
houses meant there wasn't time for the 20- to 25-minute short
comedy film anymore, for the Laurel & Hardy and Charley
Chase kind of thing. Cartoons, running usually under ten minutes, could still be fit in to brighten a program. And cartoons
didn't cost as much to produce, nor did salaries have to be paid
to their stars. The decline of the live slapstick film was one of the
things that contributed to the rise of Mickey Mouse. There was,
too, something in his brash, though falsetto, personality that
made him an acceptable fad object in the early years of the

Depression. The first voice of Mickey, for economy's sake, was Walt Disney's own. Later other rationalizations were developed. "Walt started squeaking out the Mickey Mouse dialogues in the early days and has stuck to it for a good reason," Alva Johnston reported after interviewing Disney in the mid-1930's. "If an actor or announcer were hired to speak Mickey's lines, the man might be hired away, and it would disturb fans to have Mickey's voice change from time to time."

Next after Mickey, the Disney brothers created Silly Symphonies, which used the synchronized motion and music techniques worked out for Mickey Mouse—techniques that eventually gave rise to the less than enthusiastic musician's phrase "Mickey Mouse music." The earliest symphony was *Skeleton Dance*, followed by such as *Springtime, Autumn, Playful Pan, The Merry Dwarf,* and *Mother Goose Melodies.* In these films, Disney's attitudes toward fairy tales, mythology, and all of nature began to lock in. In the early 1930's Technicolor's inventor, Dr. Herbert T. Kalmus, was having trouble getting anyone in Hollywood to try his color process. Another lucky deal for the Disney brothers resulted in their getting exclusive screen cartoon rights to the Technicolor process for a specified period of years. Disney used the color in a Silly Symphony titled *Flowers And Trees,* and the Disney studio won its first Academy Award for the cartoon.

The products of Walt Disney Productions, the name adopted by the brothers after forming a corporation in 1930, were good. The cartoons were entertaining and inventive and, despite the bare bottoms and dancing steamrollers, considerably more sophisticated than most of the competition. Still, at any other time but the '30's, Disney's reputation as a genius and a major artist would probably have had a harder time getting established. The linking of art and the machine, the idea that masterpieces could come out of a factory, was highly attractive to

many people in the Depression years. Writing on Disney in
the *New Republic* in 1932, Gilbert Seldes said of the Silly
Symphonies: "These pictures are the perfection of the movie;
they are the movie developing in its own field." Art critic
Thomas Craven called Disney "the most famous living hu-
morist," and was careful to explain that "his achievements are
the outgrowth of methods evolved from within the laboratories
of the motion-picture industry, not the results of theories borrowed from the arts." Harvard professor Robert Feild wrote,
"If we are to understand the art of Walt Disney, we must abandon once and for all the contention that the fine arts of music,
painting, sculpture, and architecture were the last word in
man's efforts to express with dignity. . . . We must awaken to the
possibility of entirely new types of creative activity more consistent with our immediate needs."

Equally prevalent were writers and critics who emphasized
that Disney was no highbrow, that his work was a people's art
that could also be enjoyed by intellectuals. "Mickey, like
Chaplin, was discovered by the mob before he was discovered
by the art world," Alva Johnston remarked in his women's
magazine article in 1934. "It was another case in which the
masses gave a lesson in art appreciation to the intelligentsia."
Disney would continue to fascinate anyone who wanted to get
off a little polite anti-intellectualism while praising him. In
acclaiming the educational and propaganda type of film the
Disney studios began doing just prior to World War II, *Fortune*
said, "The inspirations of mind and spirit that go into its making are as mysterious as those of any brilliant creative effort.
But the secret of Walt Disney's success as a teacher is easily
analyzed. It consists simply of the two essentials of good
teaching—essentials that have been all but forgotten in the
craze for scholarly research with which the German Ph.D. system has cursed American education since late last century. One
essential is clarity. The other is interest."

One of Disney's major gifts to the world of children was the concept of total merchandising. Though using established characters to sell products and toys was not new—Buster Brown had sold shoes decades before, and in the 1920's Felix the Cat and Barney Google had moved considerable merchandise—the Disney organization pioneered in character merchandising on a grand scale. "It was Walt Disney who first marshaled the forces of a character into a super-salesman," wrote child research expert Eugene Gilbert. The fad for Mickey Mouse in the early 1930's enabled Disney to begin turning his cartoon characters into commodities, a process that would eventually make Disney himself into a product. "Right after the mouse hit," Disney said in explaining his entry into merchandising, "I was in New York and a fellow kept hanging around my hotel waving $300 at me and saying that he wanted to put the mouse on the cheap tablets children use in school. As usual, Roy and I needed the money. So I took the $300."

By 1934 *Fortune* was able to report: "More than 80 U.S. companies employ Mickey Mouse or the Three Little Pigs or some other Disney character to push their wares, including General Foods, RCA Victor, International Silver, Ingersoll Watches, National Dairy Products. Their sales came to nearly 7 million dollars in 1933. . . . That brings him an annual gross of about $300,000." Besides being used as toys, premiums, and products, the Disney characters were now also available in comic strips, magazines, and books. The number two best selling children's book in 1932, the first year *Publisher's Weekly* kept track, was *The Adventures Of Mickey Mouse*. In 1933 *The Pop-Up Mickey Mouse* was in first place, and *The Three Little Pigs* was third. Whitman Publishing, a division of the giant Western Printing Company, was issuing Mickey Mouse Big Little Books, plus Mickey Mouse Wee Little Books, Mickey Mouse storybooks, Mickey Mouse paintbooks and coloring books, Mickey Mouse crayon sets, and Mickey Mouse *Old*

Maid cards, all to be sold in five-and-ten-cent stores. Mickey Mouse was even used in school books. The New York Superintendent of Schools said the mouse readers gave kids an extra incentive and "after they learn to read, it won't be difficult to center their attention on other books."

Back in 1932, Roy Disney hired a man named Kay Kamen, who had previously been a department store executive and advertising man in Kansas City, to set up a merchandising department and handle the licensing of the use of the Disney cartoon characters. According to accounts in business magazines of the '30's, where this aspect of the Disney operation was early admired, Kamen made it a policy to sell character rights only to major companies and only to one manufacturer in a category. Further, "the products must be legitimate and of good quality," and Kamen's licensing contracts gave Disney say over how products could be advertised and retailed. The usual fee for using Mickey Mouse then was from 5 to 10 percent of the manufacturer's net. Kamen's headquarters office was on Seventh Avenue in New York, and separate licensing offices were opened in Paris, London, Barcelona, and other European cities. With Kay Kamen working full-time on exploiting the mouse, Mickey and the other Disney characters showed up in hundreds of forms and on hundreds of products, from soap to sunsuits, from suspenders to neckties.

It was during the early Kamen years, too, that the Walt Disney name, the familiar signature, began to appear on products along with the likenesses of Mickey Mouse and Donald Duck and Snow White. This adaption of the patent medicine "none genuine without this signature" technique to kid products contributed greatly to making Disney one of the best-known men in America. Anyone whose name appears in the bottom of mush bowls, on glasses of cottage cheese, and on millions of books and comic strips, can't help picking up a certain notoriety. As the value of the Walt Disney name grew, Disney made increasingly sure his name would be the only one to be associated with the studio products. Disney artists and writers got little publicity, and it was a firm rule that any awards the studio won could be received in public only by Walt himself.

This policy was even for a time extended to the Disney cartoon voices, and the real identity of Donald Duck, for instance, was one of the minor puzzles of the middle '30's. Though the studio later admitted Donald's voice was done by Clarence Nash, they refused for years to acknowledge him and continued to plant rationalizations in the slick magazines. "If he gave 'screen credit,' he would destroy the illusion of those characters; and illusion is a specialized kind of reality that exists in the mind of the audience," said Hearst's *Pictorial Review*. Kay Kamen was killed in a plane crash in 1949, and his name is little remembered today because he was so good at promoting the idea that Walt Disney did everything at Walt Disney Productions.

The take from the merchandising in the '30's kept increasing, even while economic conditions grew worse in America. Commenting on *Snow White*, social historian Frederick Lewis Allen wrote that the film was "a godsend to the toy business. During the bleak first third of 1938, when the Recession was at its worst, over 3 million dollars worth of Disney toys were sold, and that summer, when the wheels of most factories were turning intermittently, the Sieberling-Latex plant near Akron was three weeks behind orders (after running twenty-four hours a day for months)—making rubber statuettes of Dopey and the other dwarfs!" During this same period there was also money coming in from the Mickey Mouse Theater of the Air, which featured Donald Duck's Swing Band and, supposedly, Disney himself as Mickey. Each subsequent Disney motion picture brought more new characters to be sold. Within three

years after the end of the Second World War, the net profits
to Disney from merchandising throughout the world were over
$1,900,000.

The realization that not only did the Disney cartoons and
features sell products, but that the products in turn helped sell
the Disney cartoons and features, led to the development of the
total merchandising concept. The current Disney vice president in charge of marketing and merchandising, Card Walker,
says: "Our approach has been characterized by new thinking
and new uses of old promotional mediums. . . . Since we control every facet of our business and handle only our own
product, we can select and schedule exactly how these activities will support and serve our overall effort." In talking, in
1966, about how the Disney version of *Winnie The Pooh* was
to be promoted, Walker explained specifically how the total
merchandising idea works. "The Pooh characters are taking
part in a 21-city tour, traveling on the company's turbo-jet.
The staff at Disneyland has prepared full-size costumes, and
specially trained people will wear them to depict the picture's
animated stars. . . . We have lined up television programs, local
advertising tie-ins, fashion shows and personal appearances.
. . . Through our licensee, Western Publishing Company,
3,500,000 *Winnie The Pooh* items will appear on retail shelves,
ranging from publications (19 in all) to games (14), puzzles,
and coloring books. Forty-two other Disney licensees will produce millions of toys, games, and other children's merchandise
which, in addition to generating additional revenue for the
company, promote the picture, too." The only time Walker
mentioned children, he used the word to go in front of
merchandise.

In the Disney-perfected total merchandising system, much
admired and emulated throughout the kid business, the child
is thought of only as the one who consumes and buys the

products. The selling of music from a picture before the film is even released, the offering of a stuffed replica of a cartoon character a child has not yet seen, all indicate that technique has taken over. The system goes round and round in a perpetual motion of selling with no real concern for children at all. Roy Disney has said: "All of the movies are geared to publicizing the final product, and making money while you do it." All of the things the Disney brothers put forth into the kid world were a result of this basic attitude: Mickey Mouse, Davy Crockett, Zorro. In the final years of Disney's life, whether he was unloosing a flock of pigeons at the Winter Olympics or riding in the Rose Bowl parade with Mickey Mouse, his existence was little more than one unending publicity stunt.

Though it was often promoted as a factory that turned out art, the Walt Disney studio operated just like a factory that turned out automobiles. Animation is a tedious production-line process, particularly the kind of full animation required in the 1930's. This method usually called for a separate drawing for almost every frame of film. By 1934 Walt Disney had 200 employees: some story men, gag men, and scenarists, 40 animators, 45 assistant animators, and 35 girls who inked and painted the drawings onto the sheets of celluloid used in animation. There were also sound men, electricians, film developers, lab chemists, and a 24-piece orchestra. Disney allowed all his employees to call him Walt. Some say he insisted. The days when the Mickey cartoons would flash a "Drawn by Ub Werks" credit on the screen were gone. Just as Henry Ford and all Ford cars were linked, so were Walt Disney and the Disney cartoons. It was to be assumed that anything coming out of River Rouge was somehow the creation of Henry Ford himself, and the same process was applied to Walt Disney.

Despite the first-name paternalism in force at the Disney studio in the 1930's, it wasn't always a place where you could whistle while you worked. As the '30's ended, many of the Disney employees were becoming more dissatisfied. Disney's basic attitude toward the majority of his workers is best exemplified by an anecdote his daughter recounts in her biography. When Disney still had a small studio, the animators worked sitting on old kitchen chairs and benches padded with old cushions and pillows. "One day, when the future looked a little brighter than usual, Father talked Uncle Roy into buying new rubber cushions for all hands and everyone was grateful. Then one man quit. That left an empty chair, and one of the other men grabbed his cushion. The next thing Father knew, everybody demanded two cushions. He thought, *They were happy without any cushions. Then I gave them one cushion; now they want two. I can't understand it.*" He seems to have reacted in a similar way to the strike that hit the Disney studio in 1941.

In the official Disney version of the nine-week strike it was a "jurisdictional strike." In telling of it to his daughter, who in turn told Pete Martin of the *Saturday Evening Post*, Disney explained: "Two groups of artists were competing as union organizers in Hollywood. One group claimed that they had the majority of my artists signed, but the artists in our studio who belonged to the other group said, 'don't believe them, Walt.' " Things were not that simple. The union that Disney objected to was the AFL Screen Cartoonists Guild and the union he favored was the Federation of Screen Cartoonists, encouraged within the studio in order to avoid outside union interference. The National Labor Relations Board had ruled in April of 1941 that this latter union was company-dominated, and a complaint was filed against Disney. He refused to give in and he continued to fight the recognition of the outside craft union. In the words of the Screen Cartoonists Guild, "the axe began to swing," and men who favored the SCG were fired. In May of '41, the SCG called a strike and the several hundred Disney artists who had joined it despite Walt went out.

Disney's was not the only cartoon studio to have trouble, not the only one to pay as low as $12 to $15 a week. But most of the others agreed to recognize the SCG. The working conditions in most of the cartoon factories were not good. "Layoffs were frequent, and often wholesale," said a later Screen Cartoonists account. "A worker could be laid off for any reason, or no reason. . . . Disney's had a fairly regular semi-annual 'ax-day.'" It was also a Disney practice, according to the Guild, to send "application folders all over the country to pick up aspiring young artists, to start training at $12 a week. Such was the magic of the Disney reputation . . . that each year the studio processed 3,500 applications. Of these, 60 lucky lads were allowed to pay their own transportation to Burbank to go to school. At the same time, layoffs and firings of established cartoonists continued."

Disney also had trouble getting his animators, inkers, and painters to work overtime for no money. In the rush to complete his first full-length cartoon, *Snow White*, there were extra hours of work but no extra pay, and Disney promised bonuses if the picture proved a success. The bonuses eventually paid to most of the artists were "barely enough to compensate them for the overtime they put in." Disney tried the same gimmick to get *Pinocchio* ground out. Bonuses were promised, though this time none were ever paid. The studio explained that the war in Europe was cutting off foreign markets and therefore money couldn't be thrown around. The SCG artists failed to appreciate this excuse. The strike, which began in May of 1941, according to *Fortune*, "so dismayed Walt Disney that he wept." He also jumped out of his car on one occasion, as reported in the *New York Times*, and took a swing at one of the pickets. Over half his employees were out on strike, and Disney is said to have had "all the automobiles of the on-the-job workers and the studio cars and trucks taken from sheds and garages and posed for the skyborne *Los Angeles Times* cameras." The strike went on for two bitter months. Disney then capitulated and a settlement was reached. But two weeks later the whole studio was closed down and Disney's 1200 employees were let go. When production began again, many of the strongest supporters of the Screen Cartoonists Guild were no longer working for Walt.

As it usually does, war work brought solvency for Walt Disney and his studio. Shortly before Pearl Harbor, Disney had been sent on a goodwill tour of South America by the State Department and given $270,000 to make films about the United States' good neighbors. The studio also began getting contracts to produce training films for the Army, Navy, and various governmental agencies. Washington had become in-interested in Walt Disney after noticing an employee training film entitled *Four Methods of Flush Riveting* his studio had made for Lockheed Aircraft. But the Disney brothers felt they had finally to sell stock, and the sales of Disney shares were another source of money. But it meant Walt Disney had more people to answer to.

The war, the strike, the bankers—all helped change Walt Disney, and after World War II he was never quite the same. As Richard Schickel says: "His films grew more and more sentimental as Disney grew more and more prosperous. The innocent, violent action of his early pictures gave way to the flat artiness of his more pretentious feature-length films . . . and then to the dismal live-action family comedies with which we have been more recently afflicted." The rigid sentimentality, the obsession with folksy virtues, the antiseptic nostalgia, and the growing conservatism that took increasing hold of Walt Disney are not uncommon among prospering businessmen, particularly in Southern California.

The Disney reputation and profits were helped immensely by early diversification into comic strips. The first syndicated strip, begun in 1930, was Mickey Mouse, and it developed out of the efforts of the Disney brothers to get extra operating money through merchandising. In thinking of "other ways to exploit characters like the mouse," Walt Disney decided, probably at the prompting of Hearst's King Features Syndicate, that a comic strip was the most obvious way to extend. By the middle 1930's the Mickey Mouse strip was one of King Features' most profitable and widely distributed items, exceeded only by *Popeye* and *Bringing Up Father*. Specific figures aren't available, but it's safe to estimate that the Mickey Mouse strip was bringing at least $100,000 a year to Walt Disney by this time. And it was only the first of dozens of strips to come, beginning with a Silly Symphony Sunday page and then a Donald Duck daily.

The Mouse strip has been drawn for almost forty years by one cartoonist. His name is Floyd Gottfredson, and he took over the daily strip from Iwerks in 1930 when he was 24. All the subsequent Mickey Mouse newspaper adventures—those with the Bat Bandit, the Blot, Peg Leg Pete, Robinson Crusoe —were drawn by Gottfredson. He works in a small simple office on the Disney lot in Burbank and he says, when asked if he minds having received no credit for his work, "It would only have confused the public." The Donald Duck feature, started in 1937, has also been done exclusively by another patient and anonymous artist named Al Taliafero.

The Disney organization was able to realize further profits from the strips by allowing them to be reprinted in comic book form. The very first regularly issued Disney comic was the *Mickey Mouse Magazine*, published by K. K. Publications, a partnership between Disney's Kay Kamen and Whitman's Robert S. Callender. This was succeeded in the early 1940's by *Walt Disney's Comics & Stories*. Although K. K. Publications still reprinted the newspaper strip backlog from the '30's, the new magazine used more and more original material. One of the long-time ghosts, specializing in covers, was Pogo's Walt Kelly.

Probably the most widely admired unknown artist to work in the Disney fold is an ex-gag cartoonist, ex-animator named Carl Barks. In the 25 years he served as "a sharecropper on the Disney plantation" Barks wrote and drew the lead Donald Duck adventure in each issue of the Walt Disney comic book. He also created Uncle Scrooge and did all full-length magazines devoted to the character. Allowed a much wider range than most Disney artists, Barks could say more and make fun of more things. But he was never allowed to sign his name to any of his work. During all the years the Uncle Scrooge magazine was among the top-selling Whitman titles, only Walt Disney's name appeared on the cover. In explaining why the Disney studio would prefer to see no mention of Carl Barks in print, a Disney executive said in 1966, while Walt Disney was still alive, "Comics are something special, and many young readers believe Walt draws them himself. So strong is this belief that studio executives prefer never to mention the men who write and draw the comic strips and comic books."

Not all Disney comic book ghosts accepted anonymity with grace. One of their best straight adventure artists insisted on inking his own name on the lead panel of each strip he did. This cartoonist insists that on at least one occasion Disney himself whited out the signature, though such erasures were usually handled by lesser studio and publisher employees. After giving up attempts to slip his whole name by Disney, the artist concentrated on getting his initials into print. He was successful for awhile at scrawling them on walls and unobtrusively on the spines of books and the sides of coaches. When the initials were spotted, he switched to a small monogram and managed to feature it prominently on uniforms, royal barges, airliners, and galleons until the day he was fired.

The Walt Disney comic book titles multiplied in the 1940's and 1950's, and both Whitman and Disney did well financially. Every million issues sold meant a gross take of roughly $100,000 for Walt Disney, and the most popular Disney titles always sell in the millions during their respective peak years. Costs were kept down by paying the artists from $28 to $32 a page for their art work, and the writers as little as $36 per complete script. The late Charles Beaumont wrote Mickey Mouse scripts during his lean Hollywood years before he began writing for *Playboy* and *Twilight Zone*. He felt the funny animal scripters were "a nervous and melancholy group," who occupied "the most insecure corner of a most insecure business." Another money-saving practice involves using the same original art work twice over a period of years and putting "Reprinted by popular request" on it. Since Disney usually acquired all rights to the drawings when paying for the first use, popular request reprints mean the artwork doesn't cost anything. Free art can survive for decades. The drawings in the 1967 comic book version of *Snow White* are the same ones used in the 1938 comic book version.

The success and the relative economy of production of the Walt Disney comic strips and magazines inspired other cartoon studios to start selling their characters to kids in strip form. The early '40's saw the comic strip and magazine debuts of Woody Woodpecker, Andy Panda, Bugs Bunny, Porky Pig, Tom & Jerry, Mighty Mouse, and even Oswald the Lucky Rabbit. There was some attempt to create a Walt Disney to front for each line of animals. The Warner Brothers' comic books displayed the signature of their non-drawing producer of Bugs Bunny films on all covers, but somehow Leon Schlesinger never became a household name. Today, with the sales of comic books based on television and movie cartoons nearly always guaranteed, most studios, especially Walt Disney Productions, plan the comic strips at the same time they plan the show or film.

In growing up in Hollywood, Walt Disney had to abandon many of the things he'd liked to do, including drawing. "I don't even doodle," he told interviewers in his last years. "I've never drawn anything for my grandchildren. I've got too many good artists around here." He grew so enormous his entire studio had to give up what it did best, making funny animated cartoons. Techniques and rituals had taken over, and their object was to make profits. Live action films were less costly and less liable—unlike *Fantasia* in its first release—to fail at the box office.

The partial conversion to full-length features was no doubt suggested by the stockholders the Disneys had to take on in the early 1940's. As far back as 1943, live actors had been used in *Saludos Amigos*, along with the cartoon characters. In 1946 came *Song Of The South*, a live action film with cartoon sequences. In the 1950's Walt Disney was releasing four or five live-action features to every full-length cartoon, and from 1960 until Disney's death only two full-length cartoons were completed. The earliest non-cartoons stuck to the timeless classics: *Treasure Island, Robin Hood, Rob Roy*, and *20,000 Leagues Under the Sea*. Walt's connection with most of the swashbucklers was only nominal, since they were produced and directed in Great Britain.

Eventually Disney returned to comedy. Making use of the perennially boyish Fred MacMurray, the studio turned out *The Shaggy Dog*. "I got to thinking, 'When it comes to making comedy, we're the ones,' " Disney explained. "So we did *The Shaggy Dog*. So far it's been seen by 55 million people." After the MacMurray hit, which has already earned over 11 million dollars at the box office, the Disney studio continued with a mix of public domain adventure, mechanical comedy, and spotless nostalgia in its live action films. *Variety*'s most recent annual listing of all-time box office champs includes 28 Walt Disney films, only a third of which are cartoons. The 1964 piece of Julie Andrews pastry, *Mary Poppins*, has already earned 31 million dollars, over twice as much as the frequently released 1938 cartoon *Snow White*. Disney professed to be puzzled about exactly what the films of his last years added up to, and said he wasn't able to answer a question as to what a typical Disney picture was. "Hell, I'm Disney and I don't know," he told *Newsweek* in 1962. "I've produced every type of picture except sick ones. The truth of the matter is, I try to make movies to please my own family."

Commencing in 1948, Walt Disney began applying his wholesome family notions about life to the world of real animals. The first of the True-Life Adventures was a two-reeler called *Seal Island*. It won an Academy Award and led to a new Walt Disney genre, with spin-offs into books, magazines, and a newspaper panel.

Walt Disney's engrossment with giving personality to animals and birds, the habit of patronizing nature, led him finally, in the later years of Disneyland, to audio-animatronics. The process, developed in Disney's robot factory, enabled him to build mechanical animals and birds for use in various Disneyland concessions, where live creatures had proved to be too much trouble. "We are using the new types of valves and controls developed for rockets," Disney told a reporter while displaying a group of mechanical parrots and mackaws. "That way we can get extremely subtle notions. Everything is programmed on tape." These particular birds, now located in the Enchanted Tiki Room, were programmed to sing Offenbach's *Barcarolle* and *Let's All Sing Like the Birdies Sing*.

Expansion into television, in 1954, gave the Disney organization opportunities for an even more total kind of merchandising. *Disneyland,* the *Mickey Mouse Club* and *Walt Disney's Wonderful World Of Color* allowed for further use of the Disney stockpile of old cartoons and shorts and provided excellent places to promote new productions and test new ideas. The shows also served to keep "the Disney name continuously before an audience in excess of 50 million," as Roy Disney has observed in several annual reports of Walt Disney Productions. These annual reports also emphasize the fact that the *Wonderful World Of Color* show "has played a significant role in stimulating color broadcasting throughout the industry and boosting color television set sales since its debut on the NBC-TV network in 1961." Certainly color pioneer RCA and the NBC network had this in mind when they took on the show, and counted on Disney-loyal kids' being useful tools in helping persuade adults to buy a color television set.

For the Disney brothers, television provided other, more direct, benefits. The Mickey Mouse Club and the Mouseketeers meant millions of dollars from the sales of club paraphernalia. Davy Crockett, portrayed by lumpish Fess Parker, was introduced in a three-part series on the Disneyland show in 1954 and caused the biggest television-inspired fad up to that time. All the Disney television shows are still airing somewhere. "Those who wonder where in the world the *Disneyland* shows have gone will find them (and often the *Mickey Mouse Club* and *Zorro*) on the air in 28 different nations," the annual report issued in 1967 told stockholders. "Today, Disney television shows are translated into a dozen languages, shipped to every continent, and even (beginning with the 1966–67 season) broadcast in color in Japan and Canada. . . . Some recent newcomers to Disney television are Uganda, Nigeria, Yugoslavia, Chile, Spain, and Trinidad."

Penetration by television is usually followed by increased doses of other Disney products. Roy Disney has estimated there are as many as 5,000 different Disney items on sale around the world. In outlining what a typical merchandising day around the Disney world might have been like, the 1967 annual report gave these examples: "RCA dealers throughout Canada offered Disney toys to build their in-store traffic and support sponsorship of Walt Disney's *Wonderful World Of Color* on the CBC network. Johnson & Johnson of England marketed its baby powder in a *Winnie the Pooh* contest wrapper, distributing it just before the picture's release there. Ron-Ron, a French cat food maker, bought a full-page color ad in *Paris Match* for an endorsement by (and for) *That Darn Cat*, opening in theatres across France. And Pepsi-Cola lined the California freeways with billboards backing its 'Win a trip to Disneyland!' contest."

Besides shifting into live-action motion pictures and television shows, Disney diversified into other areas. He became a builder. First there was Disneyland. "The germs of Disneyland was planted in my mind," Disney told his daughter, "when you and your sister Sharon were little and I took you to amusement parks and to zoos on Saturdays and Sundays. Those days were among the happiest of my life. At that point I was your number one date." To recapture the past and build his idea of an amusement park, Disney bought several hundred acres of orange groves south of Los Angeles, near Knott's Berry Farm. The orange trees were removed and, at a cost of over 5 million dollars, the original 61-acre Disneyland rose up.

Total merchandising saw to it that while Fantasyland and Frontierland were going up in Anaheim, Disney's television show was plugging them each week in an hour of prime time. "Disneyland will never be completed," Walt Disney said when the world's largest penny arcade was officially opened in the middle of 1955. "It will grow as long as there is imagination in the world." On the park's fourth anniversary, Richard Nixon, Art Linkletter, and 24,000 paying customers helped Disney celebrate. Linkletter said the only purpose of Disneyland was "the pursuit of happiness for all." Disneyland had grossed 48 million dollars by this time.

The magnetism of Disneyland has not diminished since. In 1966, 6,704,495 men, women, and children paid to get in: $2.50 admission for each adult, $2 for each child over 13, 75¢ for kids on down to 3. Disney's magic kingdom, with its half a hundred concessions and its big-smile huckstering, looks like a scale model of the entire kid business, a Las Vegas for children. The nearby Orange County airport handles chiefly two kinds of customers, those coming in to Disneyland, those flying out to Vegas. Just getting people to Disneyland is a major California industry. Western, PSA, and United will fly you there and arrange a tour (as low as $26.25 for three days, two nights) and Greyhound will bus you there ($109.95 tour cost per person from San Francisco). You can charge the transportation on a BankAmericard, pay for Disneyland concession tickets the same way.

Located a short monorail ride from the magic kingdom ($1 per person per ride) is the Wrather Corporation's Disneyland Hotel. And ranging around Disneyland, like waves around a dropped rock, are more whimsical motels than you're likely to find in a week's driving anywhere else in America. I noted the Candy Cane Motel, the Fantasy Motel, the Pixie Motel, the Princess Motel, the Jolly Roger Inn, the Space Age Motel ("Moon-level luxury, down-to-Earth prices!"), the Peter Pan Motel, the Musketeer Motel, the Little Boy Blue Motel and Rip Van Winkle's Motel. At the risk of offending reluctant grownups like Ray Bradbury, who attacked a critic of Disneyland for not being "man enough, or child enough, to admit" loving the place, I have to admit I find the magic kingdom and environs vastly depressing.

After Disneyland, the next inevitable step was the building of an even bigger and better Xanadu, Disney World. When completed, Disney World will sprawl over 43 square miles of land near Orlando, Florida. "Walt Disney Productions proposes to build not only a recreation and entertainment complex," announced the 1967 WDP annual report, "but a community whose impact on the quality of urban life will be measured for generations to come." This time Disney planned to build not only a Disneyland but an Anaheim to go with it. All profits from the hotels, motels, and all the additional activities that sprang up around the original Disneyland didn't go to Disney, but in Florida they will. Disney World will include as well an Experimental Prototype Community of Tomorrow. The new improved Tomorrowland in the Anaheim Disneyland, itself said to be a prototype for the tomorrow city in Florida, cost 23 million dollars to rebuild. Among Disney's partners in this were AT&T, General Electric, and McDonnel-Douglas. The idea of these giant corporations teaming up with the Disney staff to plan the future is not as heartening to me as it is to *Reader's Digest*, who call these projects "the living legacy of Walt Disney."

Nowhere did the contradictions between the Walt image and the Walt Disney Productions motives show more clearly than in the Mineral King project. Mineral King is in the High Sierras in California's Sequoia National Forest, and Walt Disney Productions plans to build an Alpine ski resort there. The plans were accepted by Secretary of Agriculture Freeman in 1965. The government land will be leased to the Disney organization for 30 years, and the profits from the 90 million dollar resort will go to WDP. The only problem is how to get through the wilderness. At the time Disney was given the go-ahead, the only way to reach Mineral King was "by a tortuous and steep mountain by-way."

The Disney brothers suggested the state of California build 25 million dollars' worth of high-speed access road to Mineral King. Though there was opposition from what Disney labeled "protectionist groups," the money will be coming out of Sacramento, with the blessing of Governor Ronald Reagan and Senator George Murphy. The feelings of reputable groups such as the Sierra Club that these roads would destroy the beauty of the wilderness, cause harm to the redwoods, and upset the life patterns of the animals who live in the wilds did not halt the Mineral King project. The same year, 1966, that the Sierra Club and others were trying to stop Disney from bulldozing the public forests, Walt Disney Productions re-released *Bambi*, "with all its wonderful woodsy characters and atmosphere."

After his death a woman's magazine wrote of Walt Disney, "He was 65 years old and he died of cancer. . . . Cancer is a harsh word. It's not the kind of word to be associated with the spinner of dreams. It's not the way in which Walt Disney should have gone. So let's imagine that *Mary Poppins* and *Peter Pan* flew down and whisked him off to some Never-Never Land . . . a place from which he can always look down and smile as he watches the children of tomorrow and tomorrow benefiting from the gifts he has left them."

Within a month, *Advertising Age* reported that "Walt Disney Productions, for the seventh re-release in June of *Snow White and the Seven Dwarfs*, has June-through-Christmas tie-in ad campaigns with National Biscuit Co. (Nabisco Rice and Wheat Honeys, $325,000) Procter & Gamble (Clorox, $325,-000) and Standard Brands (Royal Gelatin, $275,000). Disney's own ad campaign for the movie will total an estimated $925,000. Scheduled are 10 TV spots on 225 stations carrying *Wonderful World of Color*, 36 TV spots on each of 20 stations carrying *Mickey Mouse Club*, 10 TV spots on each of 49 stations carrying *Zorro*, 25 TV spots on 160 key NBC stations, and an estimated 6,000 co-op spots on 300 local TV stations." These two divergent quotes illustrate the two essential parts of Walt Disney, the Jekyll and Hyde of his favorite uncle front: sugary sentiment coupled with engulfing commercialism.

About Walt Disney's feature films, Wilfred Sheed wrote, in *Esquire*: "Those later affairs were foisted on millions of innocent children, yet they were children's movies mostly in the negative sense of not being adult movies. The noxious simplifications and falsifications were not suitable for any age, but children could follow the plots and the mechanical sight gags. . . . Disney's Philadelphia has even less flavor than Mary Poppins' London, and for the same reasons. It is a Sani-Flushed waxworks museum. . . . There are no smells in the streets . . . no flea ever landed on a Disney creature." Disney's daughter tells us, "It costs plenty to keep Disneyland clean, for Father insists that its restrooms be spick and span." The antiseptic preoccupation came to dominate much of Disney's last work.

Sheed's speculation that "anyone exposed long enough to Disney's serene myths would have trouble with reality" is an expression of a feeling shared by many teachers and child psychiatrists. As parents it is our responsibility to help counterbalance the tremendous pull toward falseness which the Disney enterprises exert. To do this we have to acknowledge not that we are still kids ourselves but that we once were, that we remember of childhood not just the safeties and the pleasantness but also the fears and doubts, the surprises and joys. Giving in to Disney, letting his philosophy carry kids off to a false world, will not make the real world go away. Which is good, since the real world is a much better place than the cold antiseptic magic kingdom Disney left behind.

Many of the problems of American life seem sometimes to rise out of the fact that America is not so much a sick as a childish society. Walter Elias Disney did much to encourage the retreat from maturity. For fun and profit, he was an affable bulldozer, and he worked mightily to convert the country into one vast Disneyland.

6. The Fad Makers

Something happens to people when they see a guy in that suit.

BOB KANE
Creator of Batman

Within the last century, and especially since about 1900, we seem to have discovered the process by which fame is manufactured. . . .We can at will (though at considerable expense) make a man or woman well known; but we can not make him great. We can make a celebrity, but we can never make a hero.

DANIEL J. BOORSTIN
The Image

There have been kid fads for everything from teddy bears to hula hoops. The most impressive and profitable crazes have been those built around heroes, real and psuedo, and popular characters. Like everything else in the kid business, the fads based on celebrity heroes have become systematized, and it is now possible to completely fabricate a notoriously successful hero. What has been done in the teen market with the deliberate invention of something like The Monkees is being tried increasingly in the children's world, too. The process of character merchandising, although it is sometimes dependent on the legitimate affection and admiration of children, is a coldly efficient one. The merchandisers have hung a price tag on practically every major and minor figure in our kids' echelon of heroes, and those characters who no longer turn enough tricks are hauled off to some sort of cultural glue works.

96

Characters who survive become shills, and their adventures on television and in books and other media are little more than advertisements for themselves.

Selling the rights to use children's favorite characters on toys and commodities has become a small but impressive industry within the kid field. Licensing and character merchandising were perfected by Walt Disney during the Depression, but of course it didn't stop there. Manufacturers in the 1930's found you could sell almost anything to kids by associating yourself with the right popular hero. As one market research expert puts it: "Children are wonderfully sensitive to characters, tending to identify with all the character's emotional upheavals, both joyous and sad. So intensely interested do they become in a character hero, fictional or real, that they will proudly quote his wisdom to their parents and friends. And on this knowledge, character and trademark licensing has proceeded to build up to the vast proportions of today."

Among the first real and fictional characters to follow Mickey Mouse in becoming commodities were Shirley Temple, Tom Mix, and the Lone Ranger. Shirley Temple, Hollywood's answer to charges that it was preoccupied with sex and machine guns, inspired innumerable sweet, curly-haired products in the middle of the Depression. In 1934 some 1,500,000 Shirley Temple dolls were bought. Tom Mix had been a real cowboy and soldier of fortune around the turn of the century, having been employed as a marshal and a sheriff and having fought in the Spanish-American War and on both sides of the Boer War. By the early '30's Mix, who had been playing fictitious cowboys in the movies since 1911, was a declining screen hero. He still had his Rolls Royce, he even had a cowboy-style tuxedo, but things were not as good as they once had been.

Then the Ralston Purina company bought the rights to Tom Mix. They created a Tom Mix radio show (which admitted on signing off that "Tom Mix was impersonated"), a Tom Mix

Sunday comic section advertising strip, and a club for kids called the Tom Mix Ralston Straight Shooters. All this brought a new popularity to Mix and he became not only the king of the cowboys again, but the king of the premiums. Nearly all the Tom Mix merchandise, the Simulated Gold TM Bar Brand Straight-Shooter Badge and the Tom Mix Periscope Ring and the rest, was the kind you had to send for with a box-top and a dime. Its main purpose was to boost sales for the Ralston cereals and not necessarily to make a profit. The Tom Mix premiums were so effective at moving Hot Ralston and Shredded Ralston that the radio show stayed on the air for a decade after Tom Mix himself was killed in an automobile crash.

An even more widely salable cowboy was the Lone Ranger, who was invented in 1932 by some people who worked for George W. Trendle's Detroit radio station WXYZ. The pulling power of the masked man was proved fairly early. To promote the program, before it had even moved onto national radio, Trendle offered a free popgun to the first three hundred kids who wrote in. The offer drew 25,904 responses. The Lone Ranger has remained one of the most valuable characters ever created. Though there isn't likely to be a Lone Ranger craze again, he can still sell cereal and toys. Toy catalogues still list Lone Ranger holster and gun sets ("Famed mask and silver bullet included!").

The advent of television caused a proliferation of merchandisable characters and fad objects. It is the theory of some television authorities, such as *Sponsor* magazine, that "every five or six years (clue: the time span between a child's birth and go-to-school age), a new tidal wave hits the 350-million-dollar field of character merchandising. In the early '50's, it was *Howdy Doody*; then, a toddler's age later, *Davy Crockett*." *Sponsor's* theory would explain the Batman fad, which hit about a dozen years, or two toddler generations, after Davy Crockett. From a parental point of view, children grow up too fast. For people in the kid business, five or six years is a long time between fads, and considerable attention is paid to increasing the frequency. A good fad can mean an enormous profit for everybody.

At his peak of adulation, Howdy Doody helped sell 30 million dollars' worth of kid goods a year. Davy Crockett, in both the official Walt Disney/Fess Parker version and the non-sched imitations, did even better. *Newsweek* reported the Crockett fad as "one of the most spectacular merchandising campaigns in history." Kids' admiration for and preoccupation with the fur-hatted Crockett allowed for an impressive range of exploitation. Davy Crockett was used in the middle 1950's to sell Betty Crocker waffle mix, Karo syrup, Green Giant canned goods, Libby deviled ham, Dryfast hair-styling lotion, Norge appliances, and even dog food and used cars. It's hardly necessary to point out that all this indicates more concern for moving goods than for encouraging children's legitimate need for heroes and mentors.

There are something like 50 organizations in the business of selling the right to reproduce established characters in merchandise form. The standard fee charged is 5 percent of the wholesale price of the goods sold. With a hot property, such as James Bond, this can mean as much as 2.5 million dollars shared fifty-fifty by the licensor and the owners of the character. Licensing companies range from Red Ryder Enterprises of Tampa and William C. Erskine of Amagansett, N.Y., who controls the use of Little Lulu, to King Features Syndicate, Harvey Famous Name Comics, and Mattel. A large part of character licensing is in the hands of the various television networks. CBS Films, Inc., in New York City will sell you just about anything that appears on the Columbia Broadcasting System: Captain Kangaroo, Gunsmoke, Petticoat Junction, Lost In Space, Hogan's Heroes, the National Driver's Test, and Walter Lippmann.

Radio Television Daily estimates that CBS makes in excess of one million dollars a year on licensing fees alone. Until 1967 the CBS operation was headed by Murray Benson, who first became involved with merchandising while an announcer on the Howdy Doody show. "Our job is to attempt to bring in prestige and profit to the CBS domain," said Benson, "in that order. The prime consideration in licensing products is that the product is always subsidiary to TV broadcasting and must reflect credit on both the program and on CBS." Benson has touched here on the total merchandising concept that so delighted Walt Disney. The Deputy Dawg balloon, the Beverly Hillbillies car, the Mighty Mouse coloring book, means not only a profit for CBS. These products, as long as they last, serve as a constant plug for the characters and the CBS shows on which they appear. To Murray Benson the visual impression of a licensed product could be almost as potent as a look at Medusa. Every visual impression reminds someone of a CBS show, and the number of these subliminal nudges "runs into the billions" in any good merchandising year. "This is a money-making operation," agrees Benson's successor, Arnold Lewis, "but the promotional value and the prestige are equally important."

To the networks, what is being sold to our kids is not so much a character-inspired toy or game as it is a long-playing commercial. NBC and ABC agree with CBS on this. In 1964 Eugene Pleshette, then vice president in charge of American Broadcasting Company merchandising, said of character toys and games, "This extra area of exposure calls attention to our TV programs in other advertising media, in stores, in markets." One of Pleshette's enthusiasms that season was a new ABC show, *The Addams Family*. In discussing how merchandisers must "find elements in their programs that appeal to the audiences each program is reaching," Pleshette told an interviewer of a Thing bank he'd thought up, inspired by the phantom hand that reached out of mailboxes and such on the Addams Family show.

The Thing bank, a simple variation on an old familiar novelty shop gimmick, probably dictated the inclusion of the Thing hand in the comedy program. That is, the toy was thought of first and then stuck into the show in some form. This technique isn't new, since radio serials and soap operas often build plots around the upcoming decoder or floral brooch. Today the content, the characters and props of a kid show can be changed to accommodate the merchandising department. In fact, as we'll see later, a whole show can be invented and then kept on television primarily for the sake of merchandising.

Screen Gems, Inc., who produce such shows as *Bewitched, I Dream Of Jeannie, The Monkees,* and *The Flying Nun,* have a New York merchandising office run by Edward "Hone$t Ed" Justin. Justin, who likes to tell clients his slogan is "Not needy, just greedy," tries to plant as much merchandise in the Screen Gems shows as possible. When in Hollywood he's been known during filmings to suggest that actresses and actors stand in poses similar to those struck by the character dolls and novelties he's promoting. Justin tours the country with actors dressed up in Yogi Bear suits. This dress-up element is quite important to merchandisers and publicity people. The day I was shown through the Hanna-Barbera animation studios, their public relations man was disappointed when I acknowledged I wasn't aware Los Angeles Mayor Sam Yorty had shaken hands with Fred Flintstone on the steps of City Hall the day before.

Networks and producers, incidentally, do well merchandising TV personalities and documentaries to adult markets. CBS' percentage of the profits from the hardcover book based on their TV special *Tour of the White House* with Mrs. John F.

Kennedy came to $100,000. They have been successful, too, with records based on musical programs and show themes and with books adapted from investigations of abortion and conversations with Walter Lippmann.

The largest licensing concern in the country does nothing but license. It's the Licensing Corporation of America, located in the Time And Life building. LCA is operated by Jay Emmett and Allan Stone. Stone entered licensing by way of merchandising Howdy Doody, which was produced for TV by his brother. The Licensing Corporation controls rights to James Bond, Fu Manchu, Sherlock Holmes, Star Trek, Superman, Gomer Pyle, Doc Savage, Arnold Palmer, Aquaman, Carl Yastrzemski, Bomba the Jungle Boy, Pat Boone, and Batman. Jay Emmett estimates the take from the whole licensing field as about 400 million dollars, higher than *Sponsor* magazine's estimate. Half of that money in 1966 came from two LCA-controlled characters, James Bond and Batman. The 150 million dollars grossed on Batman makes him one of the fad champs. "Everybody's wondering what the next Batman is going to be," says Allan Stone. "There ain't going to be a next Batman, not for a few years, anyway."

The craze for Batman, set off by television producer William Dozier's camp television version of the long-time comic book hero, brought hundreds of companies into the Batman business. "Every major toy and game company in the country," Emmett was telling interviewers in 1966, "will be involved." The images of Batman and Robin multiplied beyond toys and games and were used to move more merchandise and foodstuffs than Davy Crockett. There was Batman peanut butter, Batman soap, Batman wallets, Batman clothes. The joy and profits spread throughout industry. *Chemical Week* magazine, for instance, was able to beam, "Batman is a bonanza for chemicals. . . . Chemical products such as soap, pigments, synthetic fibers, and innumerable tons of plastic are going into Batman items."

For those who like to know what things are made of, I pass along the information that the kid-size Batmobile manufactured by Marx consisted of about seven pounds of injection-molded, high-impact polystyrene, and the Batman helmets were made of blow-molded polyethylene. Another advantage of a fad is that it allows for the conversion of a great quantity of otherwise unsalable items. One father I know noticed something oddly familiar about the Batman pilot in the plastic Batplane he'd bought for his two sons. He took a closer look and discovered that under the Batman paint was Fred Munster, whose popularity had waned the season before.

Stone and Emmett became so successful as a result of Batman merchandising that they were bought out, for 2.4 million dollars in stock, by National Periodicals, Inc., the publishers of Batman and Superman. In announcing the acquisition of LCA to its stockholders, National's president, Jacob S. Liebowitz, said the move was "a logical next-step in our corporate development. . . . Licensing, in fact, will continue to play an increasingly important role in our overall profit structure in future years, for we own . . . an inexhaustible supply of superheroes, all of whom are creatures of gadgets—and all of which can be profitably licensed." Licensing and merchandising considerations will also no doubt play an important part in the creation of all new characters National offers to children in its comic books.

The Licensing Corporation of America also profits from kids' interest in sports. Long involved with selling the merchandising rights to ball players, from Jackie Robinson to Yastrzemski, Allan Stone has recently added the United States Lawn Tennis Association and the Professional Ski Instructors of America to his list of clients served. The LCA arrangement with the tennis association allows them to license the product use of not only the USLTA name but those of the U.S. Davis Cup Team and the U.S. Federation Cup Team. "In return for royalties," reported *Time*, "manufacturers will be licensed to stick endorsements on everything from sweatsocks to sunglasses." Until Emmett and Stone got hold of him, admitted the tennis association president, "We never really knew how much our endorsements were worth." The Licensing Corporation also now controls the rights to merchandise French underwater explorer and diver Jacques Cousteau. Toy skin-diving equipment, thanks to Emmett and Stone, was on the market simultaneously with the airing of the first Wolper Productions documentary about Cousteau.

While crazes of a Batman magnitude are infrequent and it is difficult to predict exactly which character will next be able to push 100 million dollars' worth of goods, it is still possible to plan a relatively successful merchandising fad in advance. A good example is NBC's *Daniel Boone*. Since the basic notion here, Davy Crockett under another name, is so obvious we have to assume NBC hesitated so long only because they wanted to wait for a new crop of young children. The National Broadcasting Company even acquired Disney's own Davy Crockett, Fess Parker, to be their Daniel Boone. Because Fess Parker's lumbering talents shine only when he is wearing buckskin clothes and a fur hat, the Boone role has been the only other significant one in his career since the days when he was king of the wild frontier.

NBC, and especially its merchandising manager, Norman Lunenfeld, were so confident the miracle could be made to happen a second time they got all the merchandising deals together before the Daniel Boone show reached the screen. Months prior to the show's September 1964 debut, nearly forty character licenses had been issued and official Fess Parker/ Daniel Boone merchandise went into production. It included pajamas, hats, dolls, teepees, rifles, bubble gum, and lunch boxes. Four weeks before any kid in America had seen Fess Parker or heard him fire a shot, 168,000 Daniel Boone T-shirts had been sold. Ads for the Daniel Boone Trailblazer Club were already running by this time, and kids were being solicited to join.

Fearing that Parker as Boone would cause as many smaller toy makers and manufacturers to jump on the bandwagon, unlicensed, as Parker as Crockett had, NBC warned: "Please take notice that any companies which attempt to manufacture or sell merchandise which is in any way identified with our Daniel Boone television show or its star, Fess Parker, will be vigorously prosecuted to the full extent of the law." Since Daniel Boone had once been a real person and a historical figure at that, it was possible for unofficial Boone equipment to be made. At the time of the Davy Crockett mania, hundreds of manufacturers tried to trademark non-Disney Crockett items.

The creation of the Daniel Boone show and its attendant merchandise illustrates one of the many applications of the total merchandising concept. This is not the way children's entertainment should be created. Certainly technique has taken over and the process seems to be running away. Once the circle has been built, though, it's impossible to find its starting point many times. Do the networks put on a good kids' show and wait until it becomes popular to sell merchandise, or do they think up the merchandise first and figure whatever show they stick it on will automatically become popular?

Years ago the late producer Jerry Wald discovered that movies made from bestselling novels usually did well at the box office. Rather than buy the screen rights to expensive hit books, Wald took his own script ideas for pictures he planned to produce to less expensive novelists and had novels written to order. The books were published, Wald's publicity department helped them become bestsellers, and then he made his movies. It seemed to work in the adult world and so, as do many adult business ideas, this form of mercantile sympathetic magic filtered down into the children's world. A publicity man in Hollywood assured me that Daniel Boone has never done very well in the ratings but is kept on television because it helps sell millions of dollars' worth of Daniel Boone merchandise to kids. There's practically no children's character who can't be merchandised. A typical example is Dr. Dolittle, who first appeared in children's books in the 1920's. The 20th Century-Fox studios took "Hugh Lofting's beloved children's classics" and turned them into an overblown Deluxe Color musical. A full year before the film's Christmas 1967 release date, 20th's licensing corporation was peddling the character rights. As early as February of 1967 Selwyn Rausch, the licensing manager for 20th, announced that Aurora Plastics, Hasbro, Mattel, and Whitman were already signed up to produce Dr. Dolittle products. "Remco Industries has announced a spring 1968 line of Dr. Dolittle numbers," read an item in a November 1967 toy trade magazine, "including magic and craft sets, a Playhouse Office and two TV items—Fun Gum Animals and Animal Fist Faces." Most of Remco's Dolittle items were, as the item acknowledged, "variations on earlier Remco numbers." Dr. Dolittle merchandise included revised and newly written books (without Hugh Lofting's original illustrations), Dr. Dolittle marionettes, Dr. Dolittle paper napkins, and a Dr. Dolittle Merry-Go-Round Book, which *Newsweek* described as "flimsy and repellent enough to turn Doctor Dolittle himself into an enthusiastic vivisectionist."

Even expected fads that don't work can unload millions of dollars in merchandise. When the masked hero fever was still strong in 1966, ABC quickly scheduled *The Green Hornet* into its Friday television lineup. Competing in the 7:30 spot opposite *Tarzan* and *The Wild Wild West*, William Dozier's bland recapitulation of the old radio avenger's adventures barely made it through one season. This was sufficient time, though, to allow for the manufacture and sale of Green Hornet games,

Green Hornet toy cars, Green Hornet bubble gum, Green Hornet comic books, and a few shabby Green Hornet premiums. The radio Hornet, another George W. Trendle property, stayed on the air from 1936 through 1952, but television used him up in under six months.

The flop of a hero who looked to be a presold winner causes concern in the merchandising world. Trade magazines warn, repeatedly, that while merchandisers must keep "an alert eye out for new fads or gimmicks in which so many young people become interested," they must maintain flexibility and "be able to ride a rising trend or kill a downward movement on a moment's notice." Even though Davy Crockett was monstrously profitable, there were manufacturers who tried for just one more turn of the wheel and got caught with coonskin caps and frontier forts in stock when the fad suddenly died. They still think about it over a decade later. "One Monday morning the phones stopped ringing," a toy manufacturing executive says. "The orders stopped coming. Don't ask me why everyone picked that day. They just did." Eugene Gilbert, who knows more about kid consumers than anybody over voting age, warns all his clients, "It is important not only to know when to get into a particular licensing program, but perhaps more important, when to get out."

Kids need heroes and clowns, cowboys and funny animals. And objects to link them with their heroes, objects that have an almost talismanic quality, paraphernalia to aid them in the escape and let's-pretend that is necessary in coping with growing up. Unfortunately there is a diminishing place for children's admiration and affection in the realm of popular heroes. The prime consideration is what will sell. The heroes who survive in the efficiently run, and hardly sentimental, kid business are consensus heroes. There's no place for character qualities and concepts like "how you played the game" or even "striving to

win." If you are to make it as a popular hero, your central preoccupation must be with making children buy. You have to be
liked by many, not admired and loved by a few.

Even Batman was not above the ratings. When the television
show dropped from the top to the middle of the Nielsen list,
Batman was in trouble. *Variety* announced in the summer of
1967 that the caped crusader was washed up and would not
return on ABC's fall schedule. Finally, after a new gimmick
and potential fresh merchandising object was added in the person of Batgirl, the series was picked up for another season on
a once-a-week basis. The show got barely through a few more
months, its rating still low, before its final cancellation was
announced. Even former Presidential press secretary Pierre
Salinger's brilliant guest shot as a crooked lawyer named Lucky
Pierre couldn't save the doomed Batman.

The kid business is dedicated to maximum efficiency and
this, in the phrase of Jacques Ellul, "excludes spontaneity and
personal creativity." The shows kids will see and, increasingly,
the books and magazines they'll read, are going to be the ones
with the most universally marketable characters. And more
and more entertainments will be built around a set of exploit-
able props. Even access to a character is determined by merchandising. One reason why children can more readily find
Charlie Brown than Pogo is that until last year Walt Kelly had
steadfastly refused almost all offers to merchandise Pogo.
Kelly, by the way, is one of the few creators of a cartoon character to have much control over his work. The rights to nearly
all comic strip and comic book characters are owned by the
publishers and the feature syndicates. Usually, they don't even
need the permission of the artist to sell the merchandising rights
to his character.

The individuality of even popular characters is constantly
modified and blurred. Dr. Dolittle again: Hugh Lofting's
quirky, slightly jingoist, but essentially peace-loving books de-

scribed the doctor this way: "I suppose after hearing so much about him I had expected someone very tall and strong and marvelous. It was hard to believe that this funny little man with the kind smiling face could be really he." As far as the merchandising version goes, it wasn't really he. For the movie version Dolittle was played by, as one distressed British film critic put it, "funny little kind and smiling Rex Harrison." Rex Harrison because he'd been successful in a musical based on George Bernard Shaw's *Pygmalion*. The Dr. Dolittle movie was a musical, because a musical means record albums and song royalties. The chief instigator and promoter of the deluge of Dr. Dolittle merchandise has been the deceased Hugh Lofting's own son and heir, Christopher, an ex-*Life* magazine staff member in his early thirties. According to *Newsweek*, Christopher Lofting "sees no reason to be ashamed of his wheeling and dealing." He thinks Lippincott, who issue his father's books only in their original, illustrated form, "don't live in the twentieth century."

There is and has to be a profit motive in the kid business. But fad merchandising, character marketing, has gone so far in equating gross profits with survival that a sort of one-party system has come into being, and all heroes and kid characters are looking more and more alike. Loyalty to any of them is chancy, since your child's favorite may fail in the ratings or at the box office. Not only will a failed hero drop out, any future heroes with any of his traits or characteristics will just not be allowed to appear.

In his book on the radio heroes of the 1930's and '40's, Jim Harmon says those heroes "offered us a certain variety of standards in which to believe." Jack Armstrong, The Shadow, Sam Spade, Jack, Doc, and Reggie, The Lone Ranger. "There were some things believed in by all our heroes. . . . Radio morality said it was wrong to kill people, and right to help them. It was not a complex philosophy, only a standard interpretation of the basic Judeo-Christian ethic. As you grew up you learned that these standards had to be modified by reality, to be reinterpreted in the light of mature experience, but not completely demolished." When our kids are settling into their middle thirties and feeling nostalgic, will they be able to say anything like that about the mass media heroes they grew up with in the 1960's and '70's? I think what they're likely to recall, with a very few exceptions, will be only a crowd of interchangeable characters, shelved like a long row of cartons in a supermarket.

7. The New Improved Santa's Workshop

While it is pleasant to think of the elves of Santa's workshop magically building toys, most of the processes in a modern toy factory are performed automatically.

Parents' Magazine

Toy factories aren't sunny rooms filled with elves. They might be hot, particularly in August, but sunny they are not. And instead of elves, there are gigantic injection-molding machines, hot stampers, centrifugal plastic molders, and blow molders filling every inch of floor space.

Product Engineering

The toy industry, like the garment industry, is a competitive jungle.

Fortune

One thing observers of the toy industry agree on is that those involved in it are not elves. Even though elves, visions of Santa Claus to the contrary, are famous in folklore for being malign little people who roamed the countryside tricking the citizenry and stealing children. But they never became heavily industrialized. In this chapter we'll be concerned with the toy manufacturers, the toy wholesalers, and the toy retailers who make the business the great mechanized fairyland it is today.

While there are presently about 1500 toymakers in this country, the bulk of the business is done by the top 300. Among the

111

most successful of this elite are Milton Bradley, Louis Marx Co., Aurora Plastics, Tonka Corporation, Gabriel, Hasbro, Ideal, Remco, Wham-O, Topper, and Mattel. Mattel's stock was on *Newsweek's* late 1967 list of the "sweetest stocks" of the year. "Mattel's net is running 44 percent ahead of a year ago," reported the news magazine, "and its stock is up a fat 345 percent." Not all toy companies look as good as Mattel, and some financial experts warn that "the investor faces substantial risk in most toy issues." Even so, the bigger concerns have begun to appeal to investors, and in the 1960's more and more have gone public and offered stock for sale.

The toymakers, from giant to hardly noticeable, share the profits from retail toy sales estimated ˋat roughly 2.5 billion dollars a year. The dollar volume of toy sales has climbed steadily since the end of World War II, hitting one billion in 1954 and two billion just eight years later. Californians, according to *Playthings* magazine, account for over·10 percent of toy sales, and so do New Yorkers. New York City and environs is the best toy market within a state, followed by Los Angeles, Chicago, Philadelphia, and Detroit. If you live in Detroit you helped buy 62 million dollars' worth of toys in 1967, beating out San Francisco's 43 million dollars and Cleveland's 33 million dollars.

In the toy business, as the president of the Parker Brothers Game Company once observed, "The big get bigger and the small disappear." Plus which, the big get bought up by the even bigger. In 1967, after an unsuccessful attempt to acquire the Playskool Company, General Mills bought the assets and business of Parker Brothers. They also acquired the large Kenner Toy Company and turned it into a subsidiary. Playskool, meanwhile, merged with the publishers of the World Book Encyclopedia and a Cleveland department store to become Three Worlds, Inc. Smaller toy companies, as the *New York Herald-Tribune* reported just before it went out of business, "have been dropping by the wayside. Cruel competition has forced them either to abandon manufacturing or sell out to a larger corporation." Among the many smaller firms gobbled up lately is the S. L. Allen Company, which has manufactured Flexible Flyer sleds since the 1890's. It's now part of a Los Angeles conglomerate known as the Leisure Group, Inc.

In the twentieth century the toy business has never been a gentle business, though until after the end of World War II it was much smaller and much less influential. The transition from toys made by individual craftsmen to toys turned out by factories was made in the last century. By 1903 the toy industry was large enough to inspire an attempt at a toy trust. The attempt was made by The National Novelty Corporation, which gathered together over three dozen large toy and novelty manufacturers in an effort to cut down competition. The trust was strongly opposed by some leaders in the field and gradually failed and faded. One of the reasons for the failure was that many toys were still made by factories producing adult products and playthings as a sideline. These manufacturers were not interested in National Novelty's kind of monopoly. The history *Toys In America* describes the toy business of the period before the First World War as "vigorously cut-throat." The formation of the Toy Manufacturers of the USA in 1916 seems to have helped stabilize the ethics and tone down the more openly cut-throat practices. Strong tariffs against imports in the 1920's helped the American toy trade grow, to start becoming the flourishing giant it is today.

No one knows for sure, but after Mattel, Louis Marx & Co. may be the second-biggest toy manufacturer in America. Since Marx is privately owned, there is no annual report to stockholders to check for details on profits and expenditures. The *Wall Street Journal* acknowledges that Louis Marx & Co. is "believed to be the second-largest U.S. toymaker" and *Advertising Age* says the New York firm is "believed to produce the

largest variety of toy items." The company was put together
by the still extant Marx and his brother shortly after World
War I, and there are now Louis Marx & Co. factories scattered
across the United States and in Europe, South America, and
Asia. The Marx sales have been estimated at 80 million dollars
and upwards, and derive from a wide variety of relatively cheap
toys. Mechanical and battery toys, plastic and steel toys, games,
guns, doll-houses, slot-racing and train sets.

Initially a cost-cutting operation, Louis Marx prospered by
unloading millions of cheap toys on chain stores and mail order
houses. One of the chief Marx knacks is for providing cheaper
imitations of already popular items, with, as *Toys In America*
observes, "considerably less attention to realism, accuracy, or
detail." This history of the American toy business, in trying to
fix on Marx' contribution, says: "Louis Marx showed no particular interest in new ideas—he said there were none—or in
the psychological needs of children. He was interested in making millions and millions of toys at the lowest possible price—
and maybe that has been the contribution." Though the Marx
organization was long disdainful of advertising, the advent of
Mattel and the TV toy has caused them to become more contemporary. Their ad budget for 1967, a large part of which
went into color television commercials, was over 3 million
dollars.

Aurora, located in West Hempstead, N. Y., is one of the
conspicuous successes of the plastic age. The corporation produces plastic model kits, model motoring sets, and micro-gauge
trains. With Aurora model kits children can build bombers,
missiles, warships, warriors, monsters, and superheroes. Their
Gigantic Frankenstein kit costs $4.98, and for only 98¢ you
can get Captain America, Spider Man, the Incredible Hulk,
Tarzan, and Batman. Actually, with these dollar kits what you
get is a drab facsimile, since there is no paint included, although
Aurora's full-color magazine ads assure kids, not exactly un-

truthfully, that "models can be painted as shown." The Aurora Plastics Corporation pioneered in HO scale car-racing sets and the larger model cars used in slot-racing. The motor-racing sets have thrived to such an extent that makers of many of the traditional toy trains have gone into serious decline.

After helping topple the HO toy trains, Aurora, saying they sensed a comeback was due, introduced smaller toy trains of their own. When these 1/160th-scale Postage Stamp trains first appeared, Aurora's president, Abe Shikes, predicted they'd be an even bigger fad than model motoring. Aurora also owns Rowe Industries, makers of electric motors, magets, and anti-smog devices for real cars. The net sales for the whole Aurora complex in 1966 were over 27 million dollars.

One of the most aggressive companies in the kid business is Hasbro, and even its executive personnel has been affected by the youthquake. Shortly before the 1966 Christmas season, the Hassenfeld Bros., Inc., of Pawtucket, Rhode Island, installed a 27-year-old former GE ad man as advertising director and 24-year-old Stephen Hassenfeld, son of the president, as vice president in charge of marketing. Both replaced men considerably older. To further implement what a trade magazine called a desire "to emulate a typical consumer-goods approach, with revamped marketing program that includes new products, pricing, packaging, distribution, incentives, sweepstakes, test marketing, computerized market research, and advertising analysis," Hasbro added other, slightly older, executives from outside the toy field. They borrowed men from such concerns as Revlon and Morton Frozen Foods. "We didn't bring in all these new faces simply to impress the trade," the young Hassenfeld announced, "but to sell two where we sold one last year."

The majority of the other giant toymakers operate according to patterns and rituals similar to those of the companies we've already examined, sharing usually similar philosophies. The company that won't, or can't, adapt to the latest rules is courting extinction. One of the most monumental of recent collapses was that of the A. C. Gilbert Company. Gilbert had for nearly half a century been at the top of the toy business with its Erector Sets, American Flyer trains, and Gilbert chemistry sets. In the years from 1961 to 1965, the New Haven company lost over 10 million dollars. One of the principal troubles, according to marketing authorities, was that Gilbert had "failed to keep pace."

Alfred Carlton Gilbert, born in the 1880's, was an energetic and eclectic man. He was a proficient magician, an Olympic pole vaulter, and a medical doctor with a degree from Yale. He was able to indulge most of his interests through the toy business, and by the time of World War I, A. C. Gilbert Company in New Haven, Connecticut, was producing magic sets, chemistry and science kits, and Erector construction sets. The Erector, with its tiny metal girders, was really a variation on an earlier toy called Meccano, but Gilbert's energy and ingenuity enabled him to push the Erector Set ahead of all competition. The American Flyer trains were not an invention of Gilbert's. Until the Depression, the electric train's original manufacturer was operating the largest toy train plant in the country, producing 6,000 trains a day. When the American Flyer Company collapsed, it was acquired by A. C. Gilbert, who maintained the quality and fidelity to detail of the original owners. Gilbert helped found and was the first president of the Toy Manufacturers Association. He stayed personally involved in his company until his death in 1961. He insisted on high quality, and a high price, for his toys, and he liked to attribute his success to the fact that he had always remained a boy at heart.

The company was run after Gilbert died by his son, A. C., Jr., who had been president since 1954 and became chairman also in 1961. Things were already going badly by this time. "Today's booming market is vastly different from the one in which Gilbert thrived," reported *Sales Management* magazine in its detailed post-mortem on the company. "Now, television, and not catalogs and window displays, is the primary advertising medium, and because of TV's cost, the break-even point on toy sales goes even higher." The Gilbert Company found that most of its quality items were dropping out of the perennial class. Toy trains were no longer fascinating to as many boys. Slot cars were. Part of this was due to changes in the real world, but the model motoring sets had been much more forcefully promoted.

In 1962 Jack Wrather's Southern California Wrather Corp. bought a controlling interest in A. C. Gilbert. Wrather, who also owns the Disneyland Hotel, Lassie, The Lone Ranger, and Musak, wasn't able to guide the company out of its troubles. It lost 5.7 million dollars in 1963. Wrather had, on gaining control, stuck one of his own men in as president, while easing out A. C., Jr. Now he bounced his man and brought in Anson Isaacson from the Ideal Toy Company to take charge. The Gilbert organization lost 1.9 million dollars that year. In June A. C. Gilbert, Jr., age 45, died. The year 1965 brought losses of nearly 3 million dollars.

Besides failing to keep pace, the A. C. Gilbert Company had "made big mistakes in product planning, introduction, design, engineering, quality, packaging, distribution, pricing, and promotion." In the effort to emulate the new kings, Gilbert began putting 1.5 million dollars a year into television advertising. The toy line was expanded and diversified. Gilbert's 1966 catalog included auto racing sets, James Bond and Honey West dolls, and 300 other items. The company was no longer able to maintain the quality of its products, not even the Erector. "Gilbert had a natural in its Erector Sets," a New York toy chain buyer said. "They neglected it. They used to offer sets up to $75 packaged in metal boxes. Now the most expensive is only $20, the parts are flimsy, and it's in an oversize cardboard box. They did the same thing in their chemistry sets." At this writing the Gilbert Company is part of a conglomerate called Gabriel Industries. The entire factory stock of spare parts for the Gilbert American Flyer trains was bought by a Connecticut hobby firm.

A new immensity in the toy world, and an even surer sign than the decline and fall of A. C. Gilbert that things are changing, is the conglomerate being put together by General Mills. Starting in the mid-1960's, the Minneapolis grain octopus began diversifying, assimilating toy and game companies. In September of 1965 General Mills bought Rainbow Crafts, whose best-known kid product is the modeling compound Play-Doh. After the deal to buy Playskool didn't come off, General Mills bought the Kenner Products Company, a toy maker who'd been spending over 2 million dollars on television advertising for its wide line of toys. Next the Craft Master Company, makers of paint-by-the-numbers sets and the Airfix line of scale model planes, was bought up for 6 million dollars. This was followed by the acquisition of the veteran game-makers, Parker Brothers. All these companies are now under the control of General Mills' Craft, Games, and Toy Division, which is headed by vice president Craig A. Nalen.

Of the expansion into non-foods, Nalen says, "We are discovering that more and more consumers—children and adults alike—are seeking active involvement in their leisure time. We intend to offer products which will enlist active participation by the consumer." There have also been Wall Street rumors to the effect that the Columbia Broadcasting System, which already owns Creative Playthings, has been trying to add Mattel to its holdings. The rumors have, so far, been denied by both CBS and Mattel, Inc.

From the outside, one toy factory looks pretty much like any other toy factory, though the ones in Southern California sometimes have palm trees planted in front of them. Inside, the assembly lines look like those in most any factory. Instead of seeing auto bodies being put together, you're likely to see bald plastic babies getting blonde celanese hair stuck on top. The processes within most large toy factories have become increasingly similar. Mattel's annual reports outline these processes well, providing, too, an insight into their attitudes toward their products and customers.

"New product ideas are proposed to the Product Planning Committee for review and discussion. These may take the form of an initial concept or a design prototype. Following approval of a specific concept, the Research and Design Group is assigned to determine feasibility and develop working models. Next, child testing programs and market research studies are initiated, simultaneous with cost analysis. Concurrently, work is begun on package design as an integral part of the total marketing strategy. The next step is design engineering and quality assurance analysis. . . . The various financial aspects— ranging from fixed cost investment to production, promotion, and marketing budgets—are reviewed and approved. Tool design and fabrication are then undertaken. The manufacturing technique and the assembly line are planned. Simultaneously, the Domestic and World Marketing Groups develop merchandising programs and set them into operation. The new product then rolls off the assembly line and is shipped by rail and truck. . . . From concept to consumer, this process takes from six to eighteen months. . . . Through the effective cooperation of several thousand individuals, a new toy thus evolves."

With Mattel, as with several other large toy concerns, some of those thousands who help in getting the toy from concept to consumer are employees in factories in Europe and Asia. Because of variations in wages abroad, particularly in Hong Kong and Taiwan, and variations in the costs of materials and production, it is often difficult to establish what a toy retailing for $12 to $15 actually costs to make. Difficult, that is, for consumers. Toy manufacturers take it for granted that their wares are not in the same class with "some functional non-toy product." A Remco official says, "Toy manufacturers should be paid for their creativity and for the considerable time invested in research and development." The president of Gabriel Industries considers that when it comes to price "you'll find more value being offered in toys today than any other consumer product."

Mattel, Inc., took on a new executive vice president in September of 1967. His name is Seymour Rosenberg and his hiring, to quote one financial editor, "kind of symbolizes what is happening in toys as the industry and its product attain increased sophistication." Rosenberg's experience before Mattel was vice president for long-range planning and development for the giant conglomerate Litton Industries. Part of the new sophistication is the increased emphasis on design and research and development. Mattel's R&D staff now numbers over 300. A toymaking neighbor of Mattel's, Eldon Industries, doubled its Research and Design staff in 1965. And such a section is becoming an essential part of all large toy operations. Almost always with the tight security measures Mattel borrowed from the Southern California defense industries.

Toy manufacturers still rely somewhat on outside designers and idea men. Sometimes the outsider is a one-shot artist like the late Charles Darrow, who invented *Monopoly* in the early 1930's, sold it to Parker Brothers, and never bothered with another toy or game. But there are also full-time concept and design men. The most prominent of these professional toy inventors is Marvin Glass, an intense weary-looking man in his early fifties. Glass, who has characterized himself as being "an artist, genius, millionaire, sentimentalist, egomaniac, and a very lonely man," heads the biggest independent toy design firm in the country. His Marvin Glass & Associates in Chicago employs fifty artists, designers, and engineers.

Marvin Glass contributions to kids' toys include the *Mouse*

Trap game, the Kissy Doll, Time Bomb, Mr. Machine, Super Specs, and the Robot Commando. Though he believes "a toy must have a certain amount of fantasy that reawakens an echo in a child," Glass doesn't find that children are a good source of ideas. Kids have "secondary imaginations, are conservative and intimidated by their parents." To Glass one of the basic purposes of toys is catharsis. "The best thing for a child to play with is another child," he explains. "The next best thing is a toy, especially one that can play back." The various androids and robots he's designed have this play-back quality, plus what Glass believes is a satirical touch. Of the Kissy Doll he said, "Kids have been kissing dolls for thousands of years; it was about time they reciprocated." His purpose in building Mr. Machine was "to humanize and satirize the machine . . . to reduce it to Chaplin form." His Robot Commando was "the dream of every general." As for war toys of all kinds, "Kids don't object to a military toy in a world full of hydrogen bombs. If it's bad for them to play with guns, it's worse for governments to make them."

Glass charges his clients, which have included Ideal, Hasbro, and Milton Bradley, a flat fee for a design, and also gets 5 or 6 percent of gross sales on the toy. The *Mouse Trap* game did 5 million dollars' worth of business during its peak years in the middle 1960's, meaning at least $250,000 a year for Glass on that item. Furthermore, "games like *Mouse Trap* are becoming staples," according to Glass, and this means "long-term profits for me *and* the manufacturer." Marvin Glass and his staff submit nearly three dozen toy designs to manufacturers each year, and all but a few are accepted. Glass employs few women in his design firm, since he feels they are too opinionated and hence not creative. He prefers men over 40, and his staff includes men who thought up weapons for the Germans in World War II.

The whole toy industry is, in Glass' opinion, unimaginative. "The toy business lives with the psychosis that if Company A has a successful line, then Company B must rush out a similar toy," he says. "Why do they think a $2 piece of junk is better than a $10 quality toy?" Obviously Marvin Glass would rather be a toy designer than a toy manufacturer. He does sometimes, however, wish the members of his profession got more recognition. "As far as recognition goes, we have the status of Red China. . . . I'd like to be able to sign my own creations, but I've spent my whole life in an industry that would rather conceal my identity."

Research and development staffs and proven free-lance toy designers somehow don't seem sufficient insurance against a flop. Often toy manufacturers will try out a proposed toy in a sample market city, or group of cities, before going into full production and nationwide distribution. The attendant commercials and print ads can be tested at the same time, with time bought on local stations and space taken in regional editions of national magazines.

The toy business being what it is, test marketing can be risky. A prevalent item in the trade is the knock-off toy, a cheap copy rushed out by a rival or smaller firm to cash in on the advertising thrust of the more expensive big-name toy. Letting a toy into a test market means the knock-off meisters can get a head start on an item that looks to go national successfully. The large companies are willing to chance it because of the tremendous cost of a full-scale country-wide failure. "We're tired of having made mistakes because of not getting into test marketing," says a Hasbro man. "And we're not worried about knock-offs. We have a six-month tooling lead. The big companies won't copy a $2 or a $3 item. And we have tremendous advertising that small firms can't match."

Toy manufacturers' trust of each other is fine-spun at best, and their trade magazines often include cautionary statements such as this: "NOTICE. Notice is hereby given that Aurora Plastics Corp. of West Hempstead, New York, owners of

United States Patent No. 3,228,607 covering track for toy motor vehicles, intends to vigorously enforce its rights to said patent and to prevent infringements of its claim. All infringers dealing in or using our patent rights will be prosecuted to the full extent of the law." Comparable warnings of prosecution have also appeared to protect such imitable items as Wham-O's hula hoop.

The distribution system of the toy world has been termed, by *Television Age*, "a chaotic one in which jobbers, discount stores, and retailers ranging in size from tiny to gigantic vie for the big-markup, high-volume items from year to year, with virtually no loyalty to any manufacturer or brand." A toy outlet, depending on its size and situation, can get its merchandise through a wholesaler, a manufacturer's salesman, or the manufacturer himself. Toymakers on their side have to deal with buyers for wholesale warehouses, discount stores, department store chains, and toy shops. The newest element in this chaos is television advertising and "its ability to make national sensations of numerous toys." Television commercials, or the promise of television commercials, are now an essential selling tool for the toy salesman. A salesman for a large toy concern will make sure the buyer knows how much TV backing his company is giving its new line of toys. He'll hand out proposed commercial schedules that detail national plans and call for "18 network shows! All 3 networks! . . . *Plus* the heaviest TV campaign in our history!"

Increasingly, television ad time is bought through the advertising agencies, and this has cut down on the number of spots which can be bought by the toy wholesaler locally. This development, in the view of *Television Age*, is for the better, since the practices of local jobbers have "led in the past to charges of overcrowding (squeezing as many spots as possible into a half-hour), of virtual blackmail ('If you want me to handle your line of toys, you buy some spots on my show'), and other unsavory occurrences." While television advertising can be a distribution aid, the heavy emphasis now placed on it means the small manufacturer who can't afford a TV campaign may not be able to sell his product at all. Ever since Mattel and Hasbro helped make television essential, the number of lesser toy companies has diminished. Not always is it the junk dealer who goes under. Many exceptional and experimental toys have been forced off the market because they couldn't get distribution.

The president of one of the biggest toy companies insists his salesmen must accept all his policies and all his products, whether they believe in them or not. "The fact is," he says, "a truly good salesman has the *inhuman* quality of being able to love every item he's charged with selling." On his visits to buyers a toy salesman, inhuman or otherwise, may appear carrying the actual toys or mockups of them, elaborate display pieces and even small rear-screen film projectors for running off full-color commercials. Buyers exist in a rain of freebies. Gift cigarette lighters, gift calendars and memo pads and, quite often, such elaborate bribes as cash and girls.

Besides national, regional, and local wheeling and dealing, the toy manufacturers depend on a yearly sequence of toy fairs. The largest and most influential is the International Toy & Trade Fair, the eighteenth of which was held in the New York Hilton in the spring of 1968. The New York fair lasts five days, involves a thousand manufacturers, and ten times that many buyers and jobbers. The upcoming toys and the upcoming promotions and advertising are shown to the buyers. The public is not admitted. There is, as in most conventions, a certain amount of exaggeration present at the toy fairs. Toymakers have been known to make promises about their wares and their proposed ad budgets they had no intention of keeping. Buyers expect this and, says one toy executive, "The buyers know by now which companies tell the truth in their sales talks, and which don't."

Toys today are sold in department stores, toy shops, discount houses, supermarkets, variety stores, grocery stores, drug stores, luncheonettes, and bicycle shops. The burgeoning discount houses are getting a larger and larger share of the business, selling some 20 percent of all the toys sold in America. The five-and-ten leads the discount stores by a couple of percentage points, with department stores getting a 23 percent share. Toy stores trail with only 8 percent of total toy sales. In spite of year-round advertising campaigns, half of the toy sales are still made during November and December.

The volume of sales in department stores can be impressive. The toy departments of Macy's nine New York stores gross 6 million dollars annually. Almost three-quarters of this business takes place between the Macy's Thanksgiving Day Parade and Christmas Eve. Macy's 34th Street store in New York City employs a toy staff of 200 salespeople, 50 stock boys, three floorwalkers, a dozen pitchmen, and a half dozen toy buyers, during the peak period. Macy's likes to acquire much of its toy merchandise outside the country, in places like Japan, so it won't have to compete with discounters who use American TV-advertised toys as lures. Another reason for going abroad "is the willingness of foreign producers to make toys for us on an exclusive basis," says the head of the buyers. "Something the U.S. manufacturers aren't willing to do anymore, even for someone as big as Macy's."

Among the highly successful toy store chains is F. A. O. Schwarz, whose thirteen branches turn in total amount sales of well over 8 million dollars. Frederick August Otto Schwarz opened his first toy store in New York in 1862. A German immigrant, he had three other brothers who went into the toy store trade. His Baltimore brother is said to have been the first to install a live Santa Claus in his shop at Christmastime. All of this tradition is now in the hands of Parents' Magazine Enterprises, Inc., an 80 million dollar operation that bought F. A. O. Schwarz in 1963. "Schwarz adds a lot of glamour to our overall business," says Parents' chairman George J. Hecht. The New York Schwarz store stocks 12,000 items, selling for from $1 to $1,000.

Smaller toy outlets vary from the cluttered shoddy peddlers to the specialty importer. There are still toy shops where the owners and toy buyers have a concern for children and will stock only toys and games they believe in. During the writing of this book I got to know some toy store owners, and one in particular impressed me. His store is in a large college town and, though he handled name-brand toys, he would stock no war toys. He specialized in imported building and construction toys and in items that impressed him from the smaller distributors here and in Europe. It's the kind of toy shop you can actually enjoy, along with your kids. When we visited his store just before Christmas, he asked me if I'd seen a recent piece about the possible harmful effects of sodium cyclamate, one of the newer artificial sweeteners. Then he held up the top box in a new stack of one of the edible type toys. "These all have cyclamate in them," he said. I asked why he stocked them then. He shrugged and mumbled, "Business. People see it advertised, ask for it." When we left the store he called, "Don't tell anybody you saw that stuff here."

The fact that discount stores stock toys is viewed variously in the toy world. An executive at General Mills' Kenner Toy subsidiary feels, "The revolution in the toy industry that began 10–15 years ago was triggered primarily by TV advertising and mass merchandising. . . . Mass merchandisers (or discounters, as we sometimes call them) discovered that toys moved at a rapid clip and that promoting them at cut prices was a surefire traffic-builder. . . . TV and mass merchandising

transformed us into a low-markup, high-turnover business."
From the maker's point of view, low markup and high turnover
is good. He wholesales his toy to the retailer for, say, $2.37.
Whether the retailers sells it to the customer at $4.98 or $3.59
doesn't reduce the manufacturer's $2.37. However, because
many of the smaller retail toy stores can't compete on price with
the discount houses, they are having declining sales and some
have gone out of business.

The Christmas season is the only time newspapers and magazines pay much attention to children who aren't doing something wrong. This Christmas past there was a smattering of
optimistic articles and feature stories about a swing away from
heavily promoted television toys and back to simple old favorites. Actually, there is little reason for being optimistic, or
sighing with relief. No crisis has been passed. A slight drop in
the sales of TV toys, a mild revival of interest in staples like the
Raggedy Ann doll, won't stop the toy business. It's rolling like
a great plastic juggernaut, oblivious to minor impediments. The
smaller companies will continue to drop away, the giants will
swell to greater size. The kinds of toys available for children
will depend on the decisions of an increasingly narrower circle
of big companies. Toys are already much more consensus products than they ever have been. Competition and consensus will
be the two most important factors in determining what toys
will be put on sale. There will be fewer alternatives to the
mass product.

The way the business is now, each big company must introduce dozens of new items every year and weed out old ones. "An
active line of toys is 40 to 50 percent new each year," Elliot
Handler of Mattel says. "It's almost like changing one's field
of manufacture every twelve months." This leaves less place
for perennials, for toys that will be available season after season.
If you see a toy you think your child might enjoy when he's a
year older, there's no guarantee it will be around next year.

Just as you can't buy a new 1967 Mustang any more, you can't usually find yesterday's toys. Some years ago a critic of the mass-produced product remarked on how difficult it was becoming to find products that pleased you as an individual. You have to take things in the colors they come in, and there is little use looking for a particular shade of blue. Perhaps a particular shade of blue, a personal choice, no longer matters. The mass toy business is conditioning our children for a world where it doesn't. The child who has the best chance in such a world is the one who makes himself like what everyone else likes.

At a toy executives' symposium last year, one vice president predicted, among other possible inevitabilities, that industries outside the toy field would continue to acquire toy companies. The toy field would then become even narrower than it is. One of the results will be, as is already becoming the case with the complex holdings of General Mills and the Columbia Broadcasting System, that single large organizations will have complete control over what kind of toys children play with, what kind of food they eat, the commercials they see and the shows they see them on, the stores they buy them in. I can't help seeing the whole world of children being run by one vast conglomerate firm, somewhere in the future. A firm with a giant computer at its head. I can only hope that ultimate computer will think it is a boy at heart.

8. "When You Sell A Kid"

It must be said that without advertising we would have a far different nation, and one that would be much poorer—not merely in material commodities, but in the life of the spirit.

LEO BURNETT

Homer: What do Cornfucious say?
Jethro: Man with broken leg make no complaints.
Homer: No complaints?
Jethro: Can't kick.
Homer: Ooh, that's corny.
Sound effect: Bong.
Both: Corny as Kerrogg's Corn Frakes!
Jethro: The *real* corn frakes.

Kellogg's Corn Flakes
commercial
Prepared by Leo Burnett Co.

Which brings us to the advertising profession. To the agencies where the advertising for the toy, cereal, candy, and soft drink companies is created and dispersed. The destination of most advertising budgets. Mattel's 12 million dollars, Hasbro's 7.5 million dollars, Mars Candy's 10 million dollars, General Mills' 40 million dollars, Wonder Bread's 7 million dollars, and General Foods' 94 million dollars. It goes for commercials and ads, promotions and premiums, for testing and probing kids and for devising ways to deliver them sales messages around the clock in every medium from radio to schoolbook covers.

The companies in the kid business put a relatively high per-

129

centage of their profits from sales back into advertising, a tendency they share with the tobacco and malt liquor industries. The ad agencies help them spend their advertising budgets, creating the commercials and buying the television time and ad space. The giant kid concerns are usually handled by the giant advertising agencies. Since these agencies are well-known but anonymous, a review of their commercial credits outside the kid field will give an indication of the attitudes and creative philosophy of each. Topper Toys' advertising is done by Dancer-Fitzgerald-Sample, a large national agency that also creates advertising for Best Foods, Falstaff Beer, Schick Razor, Standard Oil, and most of the General Mills breakfast foods. Marx & Co. and Mars Candy are handled by Ted Bates Agency, a hardsell outfit that also does commercials for Viceroy cigarettes, Playtex Living Bras, Carter's Pills, Super Anahist and Anacin. Until the spring of 1967, all the Post cereals (Alpha-Bits, Honeycomb, Post Toasties, etc.) were in the Benton & Bowles office, along with accounts like American Motors, Beech Nut, Canada Dry, and Texaco. Then Post shifted to the Grey Advertising Agency, which handles advertisements for Kool-Aid, Bufferin, Ex-Lax, Kent Cigarettes, Revlon, and Erik Cigars.

Agencies with kid accounts are naturally preoccupied with children and young people and continually make statements about them. A couple of years ago the president of Young & Rubicam, whose agency promotes Jello, announced "American youth tends to think of itself as a faceless mob." The trade magazine *Media/Scope*, in reporting on the Young & Rubicam study which had prompted this remark by its president, suggested some ways to handle the youth market and its faceless problem. "Treat youth with authority; 'protect' them; 'control' them; tell them what to do. Basically they're insecure and afraid to take risks. Reassure them in advertising copy."

A vice president of the Leo Burnett Agency told a conference on advertising for children, "There is no real formula for good ads. Our primary goal is to sell products to children, not to educate them." At this same conference an advertising manager for Oscar Mayer said, "When you sell a woman on a product and she goes into the store and finds your brand isn't in stock, she'll probably forget about it. But when you sell a kid on your product, if he can't get it, he will throw himself on the floor, stamp his feet and cry. You can't get a reaction like that out of an adult."

One of the most frequently quoted advertising men in the kid field is Mel Helitzer. "There are do-gooders who feel that advertising to this young group involves exploitation," he has said. "True, the right kind of commercial sinks into their subconscious, but if the product is no good kids will never ask for it again. You can only fool a kid once." Helitzer ought to know. He is the president of Helitzer Waring Larosa, Inc., and HWL has more kid-oriented accounts than just about any other advertising agency. Helitzer is a former ad manager for the Ideal Toy Corporation, and his agency, founded in 1963, helps advertise such products as Tressy and Tiny Tears dolls, Spalding sporting goods, and *Jack & Jill Magazine*. The agency was originally called Helitzer, Waring & Wayne. Wayne was actually radio announcer André Baruch, who must be one of the few advertising men ever to have operated under an alias.

"As an agency," Mel Helitzer says, "we want to practically guarantee the client success, by offering—in this order—(1) research, (2) product development, (3) advertising created specifically for children, and (4) pretesting of the commercial's effectiveness." The creed of Helitzer Waring Larosa was handed down by Helitzer in the pages of *Sponsor* magazine and turns up frequently in other trade publications and in the office memos of other agencies. Included in his ten guideposts are the points: "Because children like 'fun things,' make the copy and presentation comply. Capitalize on loyalty, but deserve it.

Children love their heroes, and if a hero says, 'Eat Wheaties,' they will—for years and years and years. To be able to capitalize on a fad, a company has to be able to move in and out fast. Be honest with children."

Helitzer believes in psychology, too, and feels the Oedipus-Electra complex can sell kid products. "Show the child who's playing with the sponsor's product," he advises, "being approved by the parent of the opposite sex." Helitzer has predicted, and then created, major opportunities for adult products in the child market: commodities like meats, dairy products, soups, cameras, and color TV sets. It was while explaining this that Helitzer made one of his most frequently-quoted remarks. "Almost any product that is not morally, ethically, or hygienically wrong for children can be adapted to sell in the young market. We haven't even begun to scratch the surface yet."

And the president of the country's first kid-oriented advertising firm believes children can be used to get adults to buy adult products. Making car commercials which motivate kids to insist the family buy a Volkswagen or a Mustang not only sells cars now, it's "an intelligent investment. Even if it's a long-term investment, it's still a good one, because car manufacturers expect to be in business a long time."

The concept of the child as shill for grownup products is one advertisers find fascinating, and it inspires trade magazines to run articles titled *Sell The Kids, Sell The Parents* and *Woo Child, Win Mother*. Besides aiming commercials for family products at children, ad men are deft at devising gimmicks to make kids bring their parents into places of business. Discount stores, gas stations, and supermarkets have used premiums that have to be picked up, or bought at a bargain price, on the premises.

Reporting on a typical regional promotion, *Sponsor* told how McDonald's restaurants brought in customers by using kids. "During a six-week campaign on WCAV-TV Philadelphia, thousands of 6-to-10-year-olds 'drove' their parents to the 18 McDonald's restaurants." To get this accomplished, a "picture coloring contest was used to 'lure' the kiddies. The contest invited youngsters to obtain uncolored pictures of Gene London, a station personality, either by stopping at the station or one of the nearby McDonald's drive-ins. . . . McDonald's, also interested in getting merchandising mileage out of its advertising, offered distinctive countermen's hats to the children in addition to the coloring pictures." For the 1967 Christmas season, the McDonald's hamburger outlets across the country used Santa Claus to attract the family, promising personal appearances of St. Nick and free Schwinn "Sting Ray" bikes.

Tobacco is one of the large industries that expects to thrive indefinitely. The competing tobacco companies know children make up their minds about whether or not to smoke quite young, and most agree, though no longer openly state, with the Liggett & Myers' vice president who said of young potential smokers in the early 1960's, "When he does decide to smoke, we want to get him." To Dr. Fredric Wertham the philosophy of the cigarette manufacturers and advertisers shows a disrespect for the value of human life. After the Surgeon General's report and numerous other reports linking smoking with cancer, heart disease, and respiratory disorders, it seems irresponsible to advertise cigarettes at all. But, Wertham observed in 1966, "more than half of the cigarette commercials appear in young people's viewing time, before 9 P.M. . . . They are presented with false images of male virility and female glamour. The idea conveyed is that every manlike, adventurous occupation needs the smoking of cigarettes: mountain climbing, athletics, every sport, piloting an airplane. . . . The message for girls is that attractiveness and romance require the help of cigarettes."

This view is shared by many of the pediatricians and child psychiatrists I've talked to. Dr. Hulda Thelander, of the Children's Hospital in San Francisco, has worked with children for more than two generations, and one of her major concerns now is to try and stop all cigarette advertising. "I've written letters to the networks," she told me in the spring of 1967, "and to the local stations, but it doesn't do much good." Protests about cigarette commercials have, at this writing, caused some outside restrictions to be placed on what can be said about cigarettes and when it can be said. Supposedly a show that has an audience of more children than adults cannot feature cigarette advertising. Football and baseball players can no longer say they smoke, and no children or obviously young people can be featured in cigarette commercials. There are still plenty of middle-aged cowboys in evidence, plus assorted lovely matrons and enough flowing streams and pounding surf to make everybody, even the cigarette companies, feel clean.

While many of the things advertising people say about children seem to indicate a detached and mercenary attitude, the people who write most of the kid commercials have children of their own. As they are anxious to point out. A Mattel advertising executive fended off a criticism of his company's commercials by saying, "Don't be so sure all our stuff is junk. I'd like to point out that I view these things as a parent also. I'm a father of four." And a Leo Burnett creative director assured an advertising conference, "Bad commercials rile me as a father and an advertising man." The ability to think of yourself as a parent and an advertising man leads as often to creative schizophrenia as it does to honest commercials. One advertising writer I talked to asked me to sample a new flavor of soft drink his agency was preparing a campaign for. I tried it and observed the drink wasn't much good. "I know," he said. "I tried it on my kids and they don't like it either." He shrugged. "But the client wants us to sell it."

The cost of reaching children in a massive way is sizable. One minute of network time during the Saturday morning cartoon marathon sells for as much as $8,500. Producing a one-minute color commercial can cost anywhere from $10,000 to $100,000. And usually an advertiser will want his commercial to air more than just once. Three times every Saturday for thirteen weeks means he pays over $300,000 for his time slots alone. That plus production and talent costs can mean as much as half a million dollars is involved in a one-minute commercial. This causes a strong need to feel confident about the commercial and its results. One way to create confidence is with research and testing.

So, to come up with concepts which can be turned into kid commercials and advertisements, agencies and manufacturers usually feel they must rely on a bulk of gathered data and research material. "Several advertising agencies," says *Sponsor* magazine, "have spent a great deal of money researching the child market, and a number have permanent departments devoted to finding out what makes Johnny tick (sales-wise)." Typical of the agency-based child study group is Batten, Barton, Durstine and Osborn's Children's Marketing Opportunity unit, set up three years ago "to supply a package of services and advice on selling products in a market comprised of 40 million American consumers between the ages 4 and 12."

Besides investigating how to move kid products, CMO also explores ways and means of turning existing adult products into child-oriented commodities. "Research tells us parents will buy up to 80 percent of all products under $1 that their kids ask for," says a Children's Marketing Opportunity spokesman. "So what we say to clients is that they will buy your product if you ask the kids to ask them to buy it." BBDO's favorite instance, in 1966, of this sort of switch was Alberto-Culver's Mighty White toothpaste, "a fluoride toothpaste like any other except that it is aimed at children." CMO has been exploring the idea of directing dog food commercials at kids, since they "often are keepers of the dog anyway." Included on their staff is a consulting psychiatrist whose job it is to test-run sample commercials on groups of children.

Influential and often quoted is the Developmental Research department in the Benton & Bowles advertising agency in New York. This is the kid study group headed by Rutgers professor William D. Wells. The research done on children by Wells and his interviewers, who call their agency facility P.S. 666, enabled him to break down the responses of children in the 5-to-12 age range. "As TV viewers and as recipients of TV commercials," Dr. Wells has said, "5-year-olds are just beginning to be critical of what they see; by 12, sophistication has set in." Extensive probing and questioning of kids resulted in Wells' drawing up a set of "general observations about their influences on purchases, and their reactions to advertising on TV."

The P.S. 666 gang learned that "for attracting and holding children's attention, moving pictures are much better than still pictures, and pictures of any kind are a lot better than words. . . . Children are especially reactive to certain 'motivating scenes'—scenes which announce an extrinsic reward for using the product, which feature genuine news about new products, which endow the product with magic power, which show someone wanting the product, which show someone enjoying the product and saying 'it's good,' which demonstrate the product's attributes in motion." *Sponsor* paraphrased the rest of the general precepts of Professor Wells as: "Show the product, show it big and show it doing something."

Wells has developed numerous techniques for using children "as respondents in advertising research." Establishing rapport is important, and since many of the P.S. 666 interviews are conducted during gatherings in private homes, Wells feels the first essential is to "get the mothers out of the room." Then the interviewer and the kids can relax while the interviewer "conducts a pre-interview" which will gradually lead up to actual questions about product and commercial preferences. Even with rapport, some children are "struck dumb by the presence of a strange adult. It is sometimes possible to draw such children out by patient and cheerful cajoling, but sometimes all efforts fail."

Worse yet is silliness, a symptom most frequent among groups of 5- and 6-year-olds. This renders them "nearly useless approximately half the time." Not only are these youngsters silly, says Dr. Wells, but they "won't answer questions sensibly." Dr. Wells finds 10-to-12-year-olds much more cooperative. I find myself siding with those silly 6-year-olds. Dr. William D. Wells, with his staff of smiling interviewers and his batteries of questions about Benton & Bowles products, doesn't have the right to an answer. It's too bad that by the time we reach parental age we're as cooperative as Wells' 12-year-olds with the probers and the pokers. Indeed, Wells found some of his quizzings of older children were spoiled because the kids were "too eager to please" and answered everything in the affirmative.

Advertising agencies without a built-in marketing research department must rely on intuition and outside help. While smaller agencies are satisfied if a copywriter has tried out a new product or a new concept on his son's Cub Scout pack, many large ones prefer the security of an established independent research group. The investigators work in much the same way as their agency counterparts, querying and collecting information wherever they can. Schools across the country have allowed pupils to be quizzed in class, and so have many boys and girls' organizations. *Boys' Life* itself, the official Boy Scout magazine, freely provides the results of its own market data surveys of boys to any interested agency or research firm. The publishers of the school periodical *Scholastic* are also known to be "excellent sources for material on the youth market."

Even research done in parochial schools by the *Young Catholic Messenger* has found its way to ad men. Why the *Young Catholic Messenger* wanted to determine that 40.8 percent of the 1600 quizzed students have Coca-Cola in their homes and 25.2 percent have Pepsi is not clear, but the beverage trade magazine that reprinted the findings had some use for the figures. Besides interviews conducted in schools and neighborhood gatherings of kids, the research people like to ask questions in the vicinity of supermarkets. "Interviewers were stationed in parking lots of high traffic centers in Dayton, Atlanta, and Boston. A total of 151 interviews, 50 per city, were conducted with women who had two or more children and who had purchased a fruit drink within the last month," reads a typical research study.

Motivation people frequently remind advertising people how essential they are. "Billions of dollars in sales are being lost because of an advertising and marketing fallacy," the president of one youth research institute told a gathering of Dallas ad men recently. The fallacy was in thinking that youth from 5 to 25 had the same attitudes, whereas research would show "each group must be reached by its own media, influenced by its own appeals." This is worth doing, because all youth is "eager to spend money."

Among the largest independent research organizations is the Gilbert Marketing Group, which consists of Eugene Gilbert & Co., Gilbert Youth Research, Inc., College Marketing, Inc., and the Student Marketing Institute, Inc. The Gilbert complex promises its clients innumerable testing and research services and information on kids' brand preferences and buying behavior. Gilbert will arrange copy testing and taste testing, and guarantees clothing manufacturers it will "get student leaders to wear and promote approved styles." It will help in "preparation of text material for special school use as part of supplementary teaching . . . pamphlets, charts, and film vehicles directed toward faculty acceptance and complete student understanding." The Gilbert group has twenty years' experience in studying the youth market, not to mention the wisdom gained from "the accumulated results of over 10 million interviews taken among youth and adults" and "8,000 representatives and faculty supervisors in 500 cities."

The founder of all this is Eugene Gilbert. Gilbert is in his early forties, and it is certainly true, as one of his clients has said, that he has "done more to create interest in young people as a market for business than any other single force in our country." Gilbert invented youth research while he was still a member of the youth market himself. "While Gilbert was still in high school, he had begun to grasp two propositions," wrote Dwight Macdonald in his *New Yorker* profile; "that his contemporaries had a style of life that was fast becoming *sui generis*, and that manufacturers and merchants, practically all of whom labored under the disadvantage of being adults, were ignorant of this special world." In college Gilbert created the Gil-Bert Teen Age Services to provide research information on high school and college students. He was soon earning $10,000 a year.

By the time he reached his early thirties, Eugene Gilbert was grossing roughly a million dollars annually from the entities in his Gilbert marketing group; had written *Advertising and Marketing to Young People*, the definitive book; and was producing a *What Young People Think* column for the Associated Press. The column is today signed by his sister Nancy and appears weekly in about 300 newspapers. Gilbert quite early expanded the range of his research beyond teenagers and now offers "consumer research among the 5-to-25-year-old market." Representative clients for whom Gilbert has researched include Borden, Coca-Cola, AT&T, Johnson & Johnson, Ford, GM, ABC, and Time. Gilbert feels this way about children: "The youth market is of enormous value to industry. . . . Every year this market has many billions to spend on itself. It represents another great financial potential to manufacturers."

Research provided by advertising agencies and motivation study groups is not infrequently supplemented by material gathered by the kid business companies themselves. At Mattel, for example, there is a research and design group which not only develops working models of toys but carries out child testing programs and market research studies. Mattel's R&D wing employs psychologists along with its artists and designers. "A number of playrooms, therefore, are included in the main Mattel plant in Hawthorne," reports Parents' Magazine's Consumer Service Bureau. "Each room has a one-way mirror and microphone pick-up system so that company specialists can observe children playing and monitor their conversation." *Parents'* further explains that Mattel, Inc., tests its toys in "homes, orphanages and nursery schools." I assume that Marjorie B. Keiser of the magazine actually saw the testing facilities she depicts in her consumer column, though on my own visit to Mattel's Southern California factory I wasn't allowed in the R&D wing. There is a uniformed guard in the lobby, and no one without the proper pass is admitted. My guides, a public relations man and a vice president, also wouldn't tell me how Mattel recruits the children it uses in the test rooms. When I asked to see one of the rooms the vice president shook his head. "They're just like any other little rooms," he said. "Except for the one-way mirrors."

How motivational research on children is done, and the uses the material is put to, are presently matters of individual and company ethics. The most broad and obvious excesses, and the out-and-out illegalities, of the actual advertising aimed at children are usually caught by such bodies as the FTC, FCC, and FDA. On a quieter level, there are several self-regulatory bodies to look after commercials and ads. The American Association of Advertising Agencies, for instance, makes some effort to police and censure.

For radio and television there is the National Association of Broadcasters and its code. To the NAB, "children, especially pre-schoolers, are highly dependent on the guidance and direction of the adult world around them—television included—for their individual development." Therefore "since younger children are not in all situations able to discern the credibility of what they watch, they pose an ethical responsibility for others to protect them from their susceptibilities." Included in the advertising guidelines of the National Association of Broadcasters is a series of directives to assist toy manufacturers and their agencies in preparing and evaluating commercials. Theoretically advertising agencies who don't abide can't have their commercials aired on any station displaying the NAB seal of good practice. Stations who use commercials that break the rules will be reprimanded and could conceivably lose the right to display the seal. The toy guidelines forbid presenting "the toy in a manner that is not authentic."

Also to be avoided are "demonstrations suggesting attributes not inherent in the toy as purchased. . . . Dramatizations from real life staged without clearly qualifying their relationship to the toy. . . . Unfair glamorization of the product via large displays, dazzling visual effects, sounds of the toy's real life counterparts. . . . Dramatizations which could frighten or scare children. . . . Demonstrations of a toy in a manner that encourages harmful use or dramatizations of children's actions inconsistent with generally recognized standards of safety." The NAB further requires that advertisers avoid "presumptions that a toy requiring a material investment can be had for the asking . . . appeals that, if a child has a toy, he betters his peers, or, lacking it, will invite their contempt or ridicule. . . ." Avoid "employing irritating audio or video techniques to demand the child's attention" and "any implication that optional extras, additional units, or items that are not available with the toy accompany the original purchase . . . demonstrations which create the impression that a toy comes fully assembled when such is not the case."

Keeping the above standards of conduct in mind, sit down with your children and watch an hour of cartoon shows next Saturday. You'll find that all these NAB precepts on what to seek and what to avoid in kid commercials are sometimes ignored, and often very liberally interpreted by advertisers.

Advertising to children doesn't stop with radio and television, magazines and comics. Most everyone now agrees that the Quaker Oats Company went too far when, in the early 1960's, they dressed an actor up like the Quaker on their oatmeal box and sent him around the country to lecture schoolchildren on the dangers of Communism. Even so, Mr. Quaker was able to plug the virtues of Quaker Oats and a conservative way of life with over 2 million public school students before any school official complained and stopped him. That was in San Francisco, and the then Superintendent of Schools, Dr. Harold Spears, took a stand against any appearances of the oatmeal man. "My main objection is that I think the subject deserves more serious treatment," said Dr. Spears, and then added, "The commercial aspect of it gets me down."

A man dressed up like a box of breakfast food is a fat and obvious example of what is known as sponsored material and instructional advertising. Numerous subtler forms of advertising and industry propaganda saturate most of our schools, and nothing much is done about it. Instructional advertising, in the shape of booklets, filmstrips, movies, teaching kits, and comic books, isn't restricted to those manufacturers who are involved directly in selling kid products. The entire business and advertising community wants a crack at children. While each state has codes that govern what kind of material can be introduced into the classroom, the final decisions are made by local school districts and boards and even individual schools and teachers. The attitudes of many school officials and instructors toward sponsored material is usually one of awed gratitude.

"Literally thousands of individual companies throughout the United States, and scores of industry and trade associations, publish materials of special interest to schools," says one widely-used text on audio-visual materials. "Although the special interests and aims of industry and its associations are usually reflected in the materials, this does not necessarily reduce their usefulness in schools. It is a tribute to American business that many items available are widely accepted and highly valued by educators."

Millions of dollars' worth of sponsored material is available. Free pamphlets, booklets, and comic books from AT&T, Alcoa, U.S. Steel, General Mills, du Pont, Bristol-Myers, Swift. Free films from Bell Telephone, Shell Oil, General Motors, United Airlines, Ralston, the National Association of Manufacturers. A study done by Eugene Gilbert on 3000 students showed "four out of every five had received some kind of printed literature through the school. . . . The most significant fact in the study was the finding that a great deal of the material had been used and remembered by students. . . . Educational material does get through to the student, and he remembers enough about it to identify either the advertiser or the product."

With films, Gilbert found advertisers had to be sure to work their product and company name into the body of the feature because "the teacher may stop the projector before it reaches the end of the film where the name of the sponsor is mentioned." Some more recent research on the sponsored film is less pessimistic. The Modern Talking Picture Service of New York, a large film distributor, tells its clients that films are an ideal way to reach children, specifying that the YMCA has 2,349,649 members, the Girl Scouts 3.5 million, the Boy Scouts 4.5 million, and the 4-H Clubs 2.2 million, all of whom will watch films. "When used in schools, business-sponsored films gain added conviction," the service notes, while telling us that almost all schools accept free films. "Students accept as fact what they are taught in school." That couldn't be plainer. The Modern Talking Picture Service arranges nearly a million showings a year for sponsored films in schools and clubs.

Education is further helped by the distribution of large quantities of samples in schools—free packages of breakfast food and soap, free bottles of soft drinks, free toothpaste. "A healthy child is eager to try something new," says Eugene Gilbert. "Granting that the child is both acquisitive and inquisitive, who is to say that these instincts are not the first steps toward brand loyalty?" Whatever the audio-visual beneficiaries of sponsored material may feel about the "more colorful, more exciting, more interesting" teaching that such material makes for, the principal intention of the advertisers is to get their names into children's minds as soon as possible. There is nothing an advertising man gives a school that he isn't hoping will win him customers, present or future. In discussing the free schoolbook covers his client was providing 180,000 Catholic schoolchildren, an advertising account executive explained to me, "The book covers score points with schoolkids. They also gain wide exposure with nuns, parents, and grandparents."

Free instructional material can often serve a secondary purpose, that of persuasion and quiet propaganda. A documentary film produced by an oil company is obviously going to take the industry view; the alternatives to things as they are will simply not be mentioned. One local school board officer I talked to acknowledged that sponsored materials are frequently biased. To compensate for this, he said it was his policy to use the biased material and then have the teacher present the opposite view. Whether an often overworked and sometimes only partially informed teacher can always counter $200,000 worth of full-color propaganda the school board man wouldn't comment on. That many educators don't see anything odd about letting much of the consumer education of children be done with materials prepared by the large consumer product manufacturers is also unsettling. There has to be something better than using booklets on nutrition prepared by breakfast food companies and pamphlets on how to shop intelligently written on order for the giant food corporations.

In their book *Overcharge*, U.S. Senator Lee Metcalf and Vic Reinemer discuss another variation of the sponsored instruction aid. The American Economic Foundation is a tax-exempt organization that disseminates economic information by way of seminars and training programs for workers, corporation executives, and teachers. It also distributes educational pamphlets, books, and films. A.E.F. films have been permanently placed in more than 7,000 high schools. In the view of Senator Metcalf, "The American Economics Foundation introduces children and teachers to an America somewhat different from the country in which they live." The A.E.F. is basically against the income tax, increased wages for workers, and any further controls of public utilities. Senator Metcalf discovered that the foundation and its school program received considerable financial aid from utility and power companies. Power companies sometimes help the foundation distribute its materials, and such help results, according to an A.E.F. official, in school coverage which reaches "the saturation point."

As long ago as 1950, David Riesman stated that the young in America were consumer trainees, that the only frontiers the mass media was preparing children for were frontiers of consumption. Riesman said, "It has become worthwhile for professional storytellers to concentrate on the child market; and as the mass media can afford specialists and market research on the particular age cultures and class cultures involved, the children are more heavily cultivated in their own terms than ever before. But while the educator in earlier eras might use the child's language to put across an adult message, today the child's language may be used to put across the advertiser's and storyteller's idea of what children are like. No longer is it thought to be the child's job to understand the adult world as the adult sees it. . . . Instead, the mass media ask the child to see the world as 'the' child—that is, the *other* child—sees it." ⚹

A dozen years later, Jules Henry observed that man "trains his children for the roles they will fill as adults. This is as true of the Eskimo 3-year-old who is encouraged to stick his little spear into a dead polar bear as it is of an American child of the same age who turns on TV to absorb commercials; the one will be a skilled hunter, the other a virtuoso consumer. In contemporary America, children must be trained to insatiable consumption of impulsive choice and infinite variety. These attributes, once instilled, are converted into cash by advertising directed at children. It works on the assumption that the claim that gets into the child's brain box first is most likely to stay there."

If the advertising profession were to deny these kinds of charges it would be comforting, if not completely convincing. But, as we've seen, most advertising and research people agree with Riesman and Henry. They believe children can be taught to be consumers, can be manipulated to buy and ask for kid products now, and conditioned to store up loyalty for adult products that will pay off in the future.

The advertisers and testers believe their primary responsibility is to serve the interests of their clients. I don't advance this as a startling new insight, though I do think we forget that the kid business has the same concern as adult business: to sell the product. The kid products may be cuter or sugar-coated, but they're all merchandise to be sold. The men who write and produce the toy commercials, the men who ask schoolchildren which soft drink they like best, the men who watch kids through one-way glass. There is a familiar pattern to the way they talk about children, particularly when they talk among themselves, to how they study children and collect information about them. The terms and many of the strategies have a military, counter-insurgency ring. It seems quite possible that many of the men who are involved in selling things to children think of them as their enemies. In searching out the enemy, advertisers intrude everywhere, and there isn't any sanctuary in school, at home, or even in church.

We not only accept this advertising encroachment, we finance much of it. That 40 million dollars General Mills spends on commercials and ads, the 12 million dollars from Mattel, all represents a percentage of the sales of these companies. So while the advertisers are the invaders of the children's world, we have been made, however unwillingly, into collaborators.

9. Kids' TV: or, I Guess That'll Hold the Little Bastards

Uncle Don broke new ground in radio broadcasting. His many "firsts" include personally checking out sponsors and their products before accepting them for the program, sampling sponsors' products on the air, and accepting free merchandise for his own use from non-sponsors in exchange for free plugs. The one story about Uncle Don that has been told the most never even happened. The story alleges that Uncle Don signed off the broadcast one night and then, thinking he was off the air, said, "I guess that'll hold the little bastards."

FRANK RUXTON and BILL OWEN
Radio's Golden Age

Whatever the rewards, programming for children must be a labor of love, of caring about children and what happens to them.

RALPH GARRY
Television For Children

The difficult and confusing process of growing up forces kids to improvise, to grab tools and teachers where they can, from their entire environment. Their most constant teacher now, their most trusted mentor, is television. Children in America spend more time watching television than they do attending school. More time confronting the TV screen than riding bicycles, jumping rope, flying kites, playing touch tackle, or trying to talk to their parents. Our kids consume between 12,000 and 15,000 hours of television a year, which

148

comes to as much as four full hours a day in the company
of programs which are usually either strident and vicious or
dull and patronizing. Between what television should be providing children, what they are looking for, and what is actually
given them, there is a distressingly wide gap.

The uses to which children put television are many, all important to them. Most obviously, children want entertainment
and amusement. Children want to learn from television, to
learn what the world is like and what they are like. Incredible
things are happening to a child during the years he is most
involved with TV. "Physically, a child is maturing. Socially,
he is in the process of preparing and being prepared to take
part as an adult in society," says the Stanford University study,
Television In The Lives Of Our Children. "He is learning the
skills, such as reading and counting and getting along with
people, which he will need for adult life. He is mastering the
norms, the values, the customs of his society. . . . He is in the
process of discovery and goal-seeking. He is trying to form a
picture of his environment, and trying to separate himself from
his own environment so as to form an image of his own identity.
. . . For a child, these are difficult experiences, often productive
of hard blows, fears and frustrations. He can turn to television
to escape from the conflicts and frustrations of the real world
or, perhaps, to seek aid and enlightenment on his problems."

The "perhaps" isn't necessary. Kids do look to television for
help and advice, for more than simply amusement. "We know
a great deal about children's viewing habits," writes Boston
University professor Ralph Garry. "We know something of
the effects of television on children—not as much as we need
to know, but enough to say that facts are learned, attitudes
acquired, and behavior patterns adopted by means of television." For kids TV does function as teacher, arbiter, and
guide as well as entertainer.

Unfortunately, television is most often not a good teacher,

not a helpful guide, and not even always the best of clowns.
"If one accepts the premise that a child should be able to come
to television and find satisfying experiences available at his
level of comprehension," says Professor Garry in *Television
For Children*, "then a diversity of programs is needed. . . . The
daily kindergarten strip and the Saturday morning cartoon-
adventure combination doesn't satisfy these requirements.
Over a period of time, one should ask what has been offered
of news, of history, of art, of adventure, of short stories, of
science fiction, of reflections and reactions of children, of
sports, of persons, of vocations and hobbies, of games and fun.
. . . The overriding criterion is whether or not the child is better
for the experience. And 'better' includes the entire range from
sheer enjoyment to serious thinking."

With the three major networks offering hundreds of child-
hours a year of roaring apes, screaming vultures, exploding
Martians, vigilante heroes, monsters, torturers, boots in the
face, aliens buried alive, girls slapped, and animals maimed
and killed and ripped apart, the answers to Garry's questions
seem obvious.

What television is now it took almost a quarter-century to
become. Plenty of time for a generation to grow up with it.
During a seminar on children and television, a network executive said, "Children will watch anything, good or bad." A perfect epigraph for any history of kids' TV in America. A common attribute of all early kid shows, good and bad, was a low
budget. From the mid-1940's on, as the number of TV sets
quickly grew from 100,000 to over one million, children were
offered such shows as *Mr. I. Magination, Captain Video, The
Singing Lady, Time For Beany*, and *Howdy Doody*. Howdy
Doody, one of the first of innumerable puppets, was created by
Robert "Buffalo Bob" Smith and survived for thirteen years.
The frenzied Western-style puppet inspired the earliest TV

character fad, and Howdy Doody established that original television shows could generate merchandisable heroes.

While Howdy Doody specialized in noise and seltzer, the puppets of Burr Tillstrom provided a quieter kind of humor. *Kukla, Fran and Ollie*, with Tillstrom hand puppets and actress Fran Allison, went on live every weekday in Chicago and was kinescoped for local broadcasts elsewhere, as were most of the other national kid shows then. *Kukla, Fran and Ollie* was one of the exceptional children's programs that was able to appeal to adults as well. Though the show is gone, the puppets and Fran are still on television, most recently hosting a series of children's films on CBS. Though the trio is slightly dulled from having done too many commercials and guest appearances on incompatible programs, they are still entertaining. And *Variety* reports they still earn a good rating.

Along with puppets came cowboys. Television served as the dumping ground for hundreds of B Western movies, and kids in the late 1940's could enjoy two decades of Hollywood cowboys at once. Tom Mix, Buck Jones, Tim McCoy, Tex Ritter, Tim Holt, Hoot Gibson, Ken Maynard, Roy Rogers, Gene Autry, Rod Cameron, and Bill Elliott were all contemporaries to the children of the period. The Hopalong Cassidy films made by William Boyd in the '30's and '40's also got on television and generated another kid fad, complete with toy guns, Western clothes, comic books and comic strips. Boyd, an actor since silent films, had starred in the Hopalong movies for Paramount and later United Artists. The last of the films, produced by Boyd himself, had not done well in theaters, and Boyd was approaching bankruptcy when TV rescued him. Unlike many performers, Boyd owned the rights to his films and was able to participate in the profit-sharing more directly than most cowboys.

The first filmed series produced for kid television viewing

were also Westerns. Shrewd Gene Autry formed Flying-A Productions and turned out shows with himself as hero. He later produced *The Range Rider, Annie Oakley,* and a series about his horse. *The Lone Ranger* and *The Cisco Kid* transferred from radio to television as the '40's ended, and Roy Rogers left movies to appear in a TV show one critic recalls as being filled with both brutal action and deep religion. No one had yet heard of an adult Western.

One bright spot in early kid television was *Crusader Rabbit,* the first animated series done especially for television. The show dealt, in a fresh and funny way, with the adventures of the aggressive Crusader Rabbit and his timid, dense tiger associate, Rags. It came on the air in 1949 and was produced not in Hollywood or New York but in a garage in Berkeley, California. The garage belonged to a young cartoonist-animator named Alex Anderson. His partner was a young business school graduate named Jay Ward.

Anderson is a tall, quiet-faced man. His uncle John Terry was a political cartoonist who later created an adventure strip called *Scorchy Smith,* and his uncle Paul Terry was the animator who founded Terry Tunes. After serving in World War II, Alex Anderson worked in the Terry Tunes studios in New York and then came home to Berkeley. He got together with his old high school friend, Ward, and the two men decided to go into the animation business. "I talked Jay into it," Anderson recalls. "He'd planned to go into real estate. But the day he opened his office a truck crashed into the place and broke both his legs. We used the settlement money, and some I had, to start *Crusader.*"

In the late '40's, Hollywood studios and Hollywood animators were still depending on theater bookings and didn't want to offend anybody by going into TV. This cut down on the competition, and Anderson and Ward were able eventually to interest NBC in taking on *Crusader Rabbit.* Since the two partners were working on a low budget, they didn't try for anything like full animation. "I thought there were other ways to tell a story," Anderson says. "There wasn't much new about it. A lot of the simplified techniques we used on *Crusader* had been used in animated cartoons in the '20's, then abandoned after Disney came along." Equally important to Anderson and Ward were the story lines for the show, which were a combination of action melodrama and slapstick satire. "The show caught on pretty well," says Anderson. "Kids liked it, but we also got a lot of mail from high school and college students."

To get the *Crusader Rabbit* show into production, Anderson and Ward, at the suggestion of the National Broadcasting Company, entered into a series of complex agreements with the network and an independent producer who the network felt had the experience in television production that the two Berkeley men lacked. Over the next few years 195 five-minute segments of *Crusader Rabbit* were produced, segments which could be dropped into various local kid shows on NBC. Though *Crusader* was a confirmed hit, his success didn't do much for the partners. When their independent producer went bankrupt, Anderson and Ward found he'd put up the 195 filmed segments of *Crusader* as collateral on a loan and that these now, due to releases they'd signed, no longer belonged to them.

After law suits and negotiations, Anderson and Ward finally gave up and sold all their remaining rights in *Crusader Rabbit*. "We were too damn poor to do anything else," Anderson says today. He dropped out of animation and into advertising, became a vice president. Today he has his own advertising consulting service and no desire to do any more kids' series.

Jay Ward went back into real estate for awhile, emerged to team up with a former UPA animator named Bill Scott. Scott and Ward revived some of the abandoned Anderson and Ward projects, notably a series built around Rocky the Flying Squirrel and Bullwinkle Moose. They've been in television ever since, and now produce *George of the Jungle,* a show which, like *Crusader* twenty years ago, can be watched by adults and kids together. "You know," Alex Anderson told me when I talked to him, "I went with a friend of mine when he picked up his daughter at her college dorm a few weeks ago. It was Saturday morning, and all of a sudden the den started filling up with college kids. Packed in, to look at Jay's show on TV. When it was over they all trooped out. I'm going to have to start watching it myself."

What followed *Crusader* on television were more simply-done cartoon shows, many lacking the sense of pace and story of the original. Bill Hanna and Joe Barbera, after twenty years with MGM doing fully animated *Tom & Jerry* cartoons, ventured into TV with *Ruff 'N Reddy.* This mid-1950's show about a small aggressive cat and his big dumb dog sidekick was a combination of *Tom & Jerry* and the more simply drawn and more completely plotted *Crusader Rabbit.* Before going into production with *Ruff 'N Reddy,* Hanna and Barbera had been negotiating to take over the *Crusader Rabbit* property, and their early TV was obviously influenced by Anderson and Ward.

In the years between the debut of *Crusader* and that of the Hanna-Barbera series, television had offered children mostly vintage theater cartoons, even animated films made in the silent '20's and dubbed with sound for new TV showings. In 1958 Hanna-Barbera got *Huckleberry Hound,* the first all-animation half-hour series for kids, on the air, and its immediate high ratings caused networks and studios to pay more attention to cartoon shows. Established characters—Bugs Bunny, Porky Pig, Woody Woodpecker, etc.—were given shows, mixtures of old movie cartoons with newly animated introductions. Eventually most of the famous movie cartoon characters would be deposed by shows and characters animated specifically for television.

Currently, television meets the important mutiple needs of

children with an impressively narrow range of programs: in-finitely similar cartoons, formula adventure and violence, a scattering of MC's in funny suits, and a few soft-spoken docu-mentaries, mixed in with this season's brand of family entertain-ment. This is what fills up the long hours kids give to TV. In Ralph Garry's study, *Television For Children*, based on re-search and seminars with educators and television producers, he asks: "Do we have anything to say to children about what to believe in and how to be? About that which we treasure so-cially, the goals we strive for and the behavior we adopt as a group to achieve them, and what we stand for as individuals, believe in and defend?" If our culture does have something to say to kids about itself, the kinds of shows we'll examine now are the language it is being said in.

For cartoon shows, 1967 and 1968 were years of monsters and superheroes—most of whom held forth in the crowded Saturday morning hours. The chief reason for the animated existence of *Birdman, Spiderman, The Fantastic Four, Super-man, The Herculoids, Aquaman, Sampson and Goliath, King Kong, Shazzan, Space Ghost,* and *Super President* is the night-time success of *Batman* two seasons earlier. The live-action *Batman*, aired at an early evening hour heavy with child view-ers, earned an incredible rating immediately. While it was lead-ing the top ten for all shows in the country, advertisers, network executives, and cartoon producers began retooling for masked men and super-villains, hoping superhero mania could be made to spread. "Ratings generally are the be-all and end-all of whether a program for children is selected for networking," ob-serves *Variety*. "The same wild scramble that accompanies the pursuit of ratings in the adult night-time hours prevails Satur-day mornings."

Many producers will tell you, sometimes sadly, that monsters and superheroes is what the kids want. Actually kids have no advance say. The decision to turn Saturday morning into a

superhero ghetto was made months before any of the shows
had been aired, or, in some cases, had even been thought up.
"The networks control our material," says the head of one
animation firm. "Do you think we put into story boards what
we want?" Norman Prescott, producer of *Superman* for Fil-
mation Animators, is much less depressed. "*Superman* has
pulled animation out of its barnyard rut," he says, "where lovable little animals have been running wild pulling gags and
playing pranks and making funny sounds." As to why the
lovable little animals have been replaced with crazed mutants
and roaring monsters who are equaled only by the superheroes
in the amount of murders they commit, another producer explains, "Kids have to have a little hostility to survive."

These are not the best of times for a live children's program.
On the weekend, at this writing, the networks will have little
to do with real people. "Live action is *out* now, according to
all three networks," *Sponsor* magazine reported a season ago,
"though they admit that TV is a mercurial business." The few
live-action programs to appear in the early hours of Saturday
and Sunday are spoken of apologetically by network sales
people. "We have to serve everybody. Kids watch this type of
program," said NBC's daytime sales manager in explaining
The Smithsonian and *Animal Secrets*. "Sometimes they're
asked to see it in school, sometimes their parents want them to
see it, and sometimes they *want* to see it."

On the entire broadcast schedule, the full week of network
offerings, there are few live-action shows intended exclusively
for children. In fact, once the weekend is over there are few
shows of any kind on the networks especially for kids. In the
weekday hours when children are not in school and before both
parents start to watch, the hours from three to six, there is no
network-produced children's show at all. What's available are
reruns of *Popeye*, soap operas, and MC-fronted hours wherein
tired and openly cynical men pretend to be Captain Satellite

or Mayor Art or Bozo the Clown between commercials and old cartoons.

When prime evening time arrives, at 7:30, there still aren't many shows basically for children. The usual network policy is to take a show intended for older viewers and make it a bit more childish. This results in *I Dream of Jeannie, Lost in Space, The Flying Nun,* etc., and later in the evening the flock of shows, such as *The Beverly Hillbillies, Bewitched,* and *Green Acres,* known as family programs. What the networks are trying to do, and succeeding at, with the family program, is to catch the three most important audience segments in one trap. "The No. 1 target is the young adult," wrote middle-aged TV columnist Dwight Newton in a piece demonstrating that the networks considered viewers his age dispensable, "the No. 2 target is the inbetween teenager." No. 3 is the child. The older viewer, Newton observed, is a nuisance to networks. "Collectively he is inclined to be conservative, watch his pennies, use his own judgment, be wary of commercials."

Evening programs specifically made for children are always about animals: *Flipper,* about a dolphin; *Lassie,* about a collie dog; *Maya,* about an elephant; *Gentle Ben,* about a bear; *Tarzan,* about a whole jungle-full; *Wild Kingdom,* about nonfiction animals and birds. A good many of these animal shows are produced by Ivan Tors, who is responsible for the one about the bear and the dolphin, plus *Cowboy In Africa* and *Daktari.* Tors maintains animal farms in Hollywood and Florida and says he believes in training animals with affection rather than force. His shows emphasize the humane treatment of animals.

The only flaw in the Tors programs is in the human area. "Even admitting that these programs are produced for children," Cleveland Amory said in *TV Guide,* "there is no excuse for the prevalence of scripts that would bore a baby." Amory admires Tors for his quiet and non-violent presentation of animals. Unlike ABC's *American Sportsman,* where, Amory feels, "They continue to produce a show which every week assassinates grizzly bears, leopards, elephants, and other animals in danger of extinction. If the men who run ABC themselves find enjoyment in such 'sport,' it is sad news."

Children who would prefer to see people, rather than animals, assassinated and inhumanely treated have a wide choice of programs. Conveniently scheduled in the hours before bedtime are such shows as *Rat Patrol, Gunsmoke, Cimarron Strip,* and *Garrison's Gorillas.* With the life of a TV series as precarious as it is, none of these last-named shows may still be on by the time this book reaches print. But their equivalents certainly will be. "Television is the medium whose nervous executives ban scenes of love but tolerate brutality," the *San Francisco Chronicle's* Terrence O'Flaherty wrote in a column devoted to the Garrison opus. "*Garrison's Gorillas* is a reflection of this preference for sadism, and it is important to note that the time is early in the evening so the kiddies can get their lesson in bloodlust while their Jello is digesting."

For many parents and critics there seems to be one oasis in the desert of children's television—a plump, soft-spoken oasis named *Captain Kangaroo.* Aimed at the younger children, the *Captain Kangaroo* show is the only program being offered kids by the networks on an everyday basis. "FCC Commissioner Nicholas Johnson has said that short of teaching kids to read, TV should at least be as good as any kindergarten," wrote the *New Republic's* television critic last year, "and *Kangaroo* comes very close to filling this prescription." *Newsweek,* in a piece otherwise putting down kids' television as a mini-wasteland, singled *Captain Kangaroo* out for praise and wrote him up in a paragraph with the boldface heading GENTLE. Actually, almost everything that's wrong with children's television in America, and certainly what's wrong with the way the kid business treats children, is evident in the *Kangaroo* hour. But since the

Captain is so gentle-looking and soft-talking, the hard sell and the exploitation don't glare as much as usual. At best, since he doesn't kick Mr. Greenjeans in the face or bury Bunny Rabbit alive, *Captain Kangaroo* is a lesser evil.

The Captain is in reality Bob Keeshan, a man in his early forties who used to be Clarabel the Clown on the Howdy Doody show. Out of uniform Keeshan looks a little like a balding Pierre Salinger; dressed up as the Captain, he resembles Walter Cronkite going to a costume party. There is about the show the same monotonously calm, don't-make-waves drone CBS affects on Cronkite's evening news.

Keeshan, whose own production company puts together the *Kangaroo* program, defines his show as "a visit. It depends on the human relationships of children with their father—or, most usually, their grandfather. A child has to learn about consideration in his relationships with others. Our characters are very gentle." Of the Kangaroo side of himself, Keeshan says, "So many of the heroes displayed to children are without flaws. That's ridiculous! It's unhealthy, for a child not to feel he can live up to a hero. He finds admirable qualities embodied in a hero; he would *like* to be like him—and then he must realize that he *can't* be like him. Captain Kangaroo would *never* be a hero to a child. He does bumble. He has feet of clay. This is a healthy thing." Unheroic and bumbling he may be, but clay-footed Captain Kangaroo does one thing perfectly. He sells. He wouldn't stay on the network if he didn't.

Using the same gentle voice he uses in urging children to say their prayers, Captain Kangaroo pitches breakfast food, toys, cupcakes, candy, and any other kid product he's hired to sell. Thanks to the CBS Licensing Company, there are even Captain Kangaroo products to buy. The captain's kindergarten, in its dozen years on television, has made its primary lesson how to be a consumer. Everything else, from the live animals to the glimpses of the UN, is almost incidental.

After watching *Kangaroo,* M. J. Arlen, the *New Yorker's* television columnist, wrote: "I don't think children's programs should always be true, beautiful, inspirational, or spiritually enlarging. I'm a great advocate of trash for young and old—good, honest, forthright trash. But this empty, empty, prissy, bumbling, singsongy stuff is something else, and I can't see that it adds up to much of anything. Grown men ought to speak in their own voices when they speak to children." But its very dullness and monotone patronizing help *Captain Kangaroo* win awards and prestige, and bring in advertising money to CBS. The show impresses people who think the only alternative to excessive violence is excessive non-violence.

"Many adults find it difficult to allow children full enjoyment of play situations," writes Ralph Garry. "These feelings extend to television, for a large share of television is a form of play in the entertainment it provides. Some adult criticism of television may spring from their feelings that work is good, play is not; that television would be better if it offered more 'wholesome things.' " *Captain Kangaroo* certainly has a wholesome don't-play-until-play-period surface. It's interesting, too, that a show produced as cheaply as *Captain Kangaroo* can be praised as a high spot. Lavishness and layers of fad technique can be deadly as well, but the bland tackiness of the *Kangaroo* set seems intended not as a spur to a child's imagination but simply as a concession to a low budget. Except for less tripping over cables and more commercials from large national sponsors, *Captain Kangaroo* could be a television show produced at any local station in the country, produced as long ago as ten or fifteen years, at that. If *Captain Kangaroo* is the best television can give, or rather sell, to younger children, its prestigious position is held only by default.

Since there are times when even the best of parents refuse to understand why children can't have fun quietly and calmly, and since many worthless television shows are nothing more than packaged noise and aggression, any kids' program that is quiet and calm is automatically viewed with relief and praised for being better than the usual run of stuff. And so *Romper Room*, which exploits children in the gentle Kangaroo style, has survived for nearly fifteen years and regularly shows up in critics' lists that ask, "Why aren't there more shows like these?" Certainly *Romper Room*, with its patronizing version of nursery school, avoids violence, aggression, blood and thunder, and nearly everything else that's obtrusive in life. It's safer to use as a babysitter than many shows. What's wrong with it, aside from its continual talking down, is the fact that it's, as Ed Dowling said in the *New Republic*, "in reality an hour-long commercial touting Romper Room toys. . . . Toddlers watching the kids playing on the show can't participate at home unless they have a Romper Room punchball or Romper Stompers, or whatever is being plugged."

The toys plugged on *Romper Room* gross something like 5 million dollars a year. This amount, combined with the profits from licensing the show in some ninety station areas in the United States, places its proprietors among the more successful people in kid show business. *Romper Room* was invented in 1953 by Baltimore TV producer Bert Claster and his wife Nancy, who operated a nursery school in real life. After one season on WBAL-TV in Baltimore, *Romper Room* was doing well enough to prompt CBS to offer to buy it. "We turned them down," Claster says. His wife adds, "One reason was because Romper Room believes in the personal touch." Today, with the program done live in ninety different areas with ninety different Miss Nancy substitutes, the personal touch is achieved by training each teacher in Baltimore before letting her solo, and by providing rough scripts for each day's broadcasts. "We wear two hats," Nancy Claster says when questioned about the heavy amount of selling done in her TV nursery schools, "and I think we wear both well. If we didn't, educators would have told us about it by now."

Nor is National Educational Television the answer, since it isn't doing much for children, either. NET's broadcasts for adults have been slightly more courageous and eclectic than those of the commercial networks, offering a broader view of the arts and entertainment and of life and opinion in America. For kids, however, the educational channels are providing programs whose chief virtue is that they are not violent. Intended mainly for the pre-school and early-grade child, they are almost all variations of the familiar kindergarten format.

That in twenty years the non-commercial broadcasters haven't moved beyond what was being done on the networks in the late 1940's would seem to indicate either lack of imagination or a deep-rooted conservatism. According to NET, though, what holds them back is a lack of funds. Still, it should be possible, even on a relatively low budget, to provide more than a procession of teacher/MC figures in front of dusty backdrops. Figures saying things like, "I have lots of fun on rainy days with a big lump of clay, boys and girls, and I just bet you will, too," or "My, boys and girls, did you ever wonder why the moose looks the way he does?" *Kukla, Fran and Ollie* was done simply. To hold kids you don't necessarily need $100,000 to spend. Kids don't know about production values, but they know dullness and talking down. The attitude implied on educational station shows like *What's New?* and *Kindergarten* (a title that can only appeal to kids who've never been to one) is "Take this, it's good for you."

Of the fantasy shows, the Canadian-produced *Friendly Giant*, with its miniaturized props and animal puppets, is the best of an overly cute and tacky lot. *Misterogers' Neighborhood*, which mixes fantasy and kindergarten, has a loyal kid and adult following and there are protests when it is dropped from local schedules. The show is inoffensive enough, but it illustrates a frequent misconception held by people who are trying to avoid the excesses of network kid shows. The producers of *Misterogers* have mistaken blandness for gentleness. Weakness is not the opposite of brutality, either.

Taken altogether, what do the kids' shows, and all the other television children have access to, offer? In terms of lessons learned especially, what is taught by a standard season of television? After contemplating the 1968 season, the National Association for Better Broadcasting said: "Television for children, 1968 style, is a mass of indiscriminate entertainment dominated by some 40 animated program series which are in turn dominated by ugliness, noise, and violence. . . . There are endless, easy, violent and noisy solutions to all problems."

Restraint is, obviously, no longer a necessary quality of heroes. If you have superior strength, use it. "We carefully train our children to have certain values about cruelty and aggression," says psychiatrist Francis J. Rigney of the University of California Medical Center, "but then we allow the 'might makes right' television heroes to undo this training." Reason and intelligence play little part in the problem-solving methods of most of these heroes. The problem usually revolves around the destruction of something, of someone. The solution, therefore, is simple. There is no due process on television. Villains are killed for crimes—jewel theft, robbery, grand larceny, world conquest—which do not carry the death penalty in most courts. The head villain is killed at the end of the show, his sidemen can be dispatched at any time.

If a hero's opposition happens to come in large quantities, the killing can be wholesale. On all of the Hanna-Barbera superhero shows, for instance, the enemies are usually alien invaders or savages. They are identical in appearance, no matter how many there are, and they can't speak any coherent language—much like a racist's view of all foreigners. The very difference is enough to justify killing. In Saturday morning segment after Saturday morning segment, Space Ghost, Sampson, Mighty Mightor, Moby Dick, all kill the aliens without even an attempt at communication. And in filmed shows in the evening hours, Indians and natives are still being slaughtered for the crime of being Indians and natives. "People are dying all over the place and no one mourns," observes one TV producer who is not yet completely numb.

The message in all this killing is easy to understand. Anyone not like us is a babbling and unintelligible creature, hostile and, if we stopped to ask him, probably stubborn as well. Don't even bother to ask him to reason together with you. Zap him. "In an age in which the stars themselves have become the most exciting frontier of all time," adds the Better Broadcasting Association, "TV teaches our children that outer space is populated by the most powerful evil beings ever to threaten mankind."

The average television hero, live or cartoon, has other traits that are not particularly admirable. There is a notable tendency not to fight fair. This may be the new realism, but after seeing your son's favorite hero—James West on *The Wild, Wild West*, for one—kick his opponent in the face, it's difficult to talk about fair play. The boot in the face is a growing favorite among heroes and, as we'll see in the next chapter, it's one of the favorite sports in comic books. When not using a weapon to kill, the television hero uses it to hurt, and as a tool to dominate. Dr. John Spiegel, who has been involved in a long study of violence, says, "Any weapon is a last resort." Yet for most television heroes it is the first resort.

The TV hero's reliance on and need for weapons has a metamorphic effect on his world. He is able to convert anything into an implement for violence. Unfortunately, the automobile is often used aggressively, with the continual implication that it is heroic to be fast. Certainly the fact that traffic accidents are the leading cause of death for young men between 16 and 24 in this country (over 12,000 were killed in 1967) has several causes, but television's glorification of the auto as a tool for aggression and a symbol of tough masculinity has made a contribution. The television hero's most consistent visible response to any physical show of force is pleasure: a smile after killing, a grin after kicking someone in the head, and a relaxing sigh after seeing a band of Indians exploded by dynamite.

The best-selling mass hero of our time has been Mickey Spillane's Mike Hammer, and the titles of the first books he appeared in illustrate the ethics and philosophy of a high percentage of television heroes: *I, The Jury* and *Vengeance Is Mine.* The TV hero, rigidly confident of his righteousness, passes judgment and hands out punishment, unconcerned with law or morality. On a *Mission: Impossible* show, for example, one of the team of heroes beats a confession out of a criminal. When the criminal mentions that his rights have been violated, the questioning hero replies, "Rights aren't for rats like you. They're just for decent citizens."

The use of surveillance equipment is as prevalent on television as is illegal intimidation. "Surveillance devices . . . are regularly employed by television's police departments, sheriffs' offices, and district attorneys' offices, as well as by such private eyes as Honey West and Mannix," Alan F. Westin wrote early in 1968. "What children never learn on TV is that the private eye's telephone taps are flatly illegal under Federal law, that their room bugging is forbidden in many states, and that their deliberate trespass onto private property to plant spying equipment is a crime. Of course, no private investigator is ever shown being prosecuted for such conduct. . . . Since the suspects whose privacy is invaded on TV are always guilty, what children learn is that only the guilty or their hired spokesmen complain about violation of Constitutional rights."

Possessing even less rights than criminals, suspects, and master villains, are minorities. On the cartoon shows it is the symbolic minority, the Martian and the Venusian and any other outlander who can be labeled an alien. As recently as a generation ago, the term alien was used to denigrate anyone in America who seemed different because of his background. Immigrant, foreigner, alien. Now prejudice is expressed more cautiously, and the alien who gets all the hate and frustrated aggression is from another planet.

In the night hours, and with live action, it is still possible to be direct—to wipe out or otherwise put down Indians, Mexicans, Negroes. While black people are now increasingly allowed to be on the hero's side without being his servants, Negroes are still being featured as crazed tribesmen and unthinking savages. Nobody even cares about the Indians enough to insert a token good Indian into most shows, and for most children the American Indian exists only to be a target for cowboys. The Mexican bandit is still much in evidence, and is almost the only frequently-seen representative of an entire country. The only Latin Americans who show up are vicious dictators. The lesson of all of this is that if anyone is too different he's probably dangerous—a kind of narrow imperialism that was supposed to have died with the last century.

The responsibility for what children see on television is diffuse, shared by Hollywood producers, network officials, and New York advertising agencies. While shows are usually manufactured on the outside, it is the networks—often under pressure from the sponsors—who control the content of kid programs and say what kind will be put on. None of the networks, NBC, CBS, or ABC, has a division or department devoted exclusively to children's programming. The cartoon shows are under the jurisdiction of the daytime program people, who are, in many cases, burdened with soap-opera-and-games mentalities. The networks' take from the Saturday morning cartoon shows alone is an annual 50 million dollars. "The networks, having convinced themselves that it's all right to abandon other forms of children's programming," wrote Richard K. Doan in a recent *TV Guide* piece on the cartoon shows, "are enjoying a heyday commercially. Cartoons are the sort of 'candy shows' that reap Nielsen numbers, and that's what the packagers of cereals and the makers of toys want."

Many inventors and innovators, especially in the entertainment world, go unsung and never get the credit due them. Such is not the case, however, when it comes to pointing at the man responsible for turning Saturday morning into cartoons: Fred Silverman, age 30, a CBS vice president who is in charge of daytime programming. In the early 1960's CBS only had two cartoons in the whole Saturday slot. Silverman, prompted by Kellogg and General Mills, added more cartoons. "We went to a two-hour block of cartoons. NBC and ABC took a look at what we were up to and began moving in the same direction." CBS currently throws four and a half hours of cartoons at kids on Saturdays, and Silverman is still, at this writing, the leader in the ratings. This has moved *Variety* to report that he "apparently feels as strong as Mighty Mouse." Silverman is more concerned with ratings than content. When I asked one animation executive what kind of control Silverman exercised over how much violence goes into the monster and superheroes shows, he answered, lowering his voice, "Silverman couldn't care less. If anything, he'd like to see more violence. It would get better ratings."

Most other opinions held about children at the networks are not heartening. The network official who said, "Children will watch anything, good or bad," remains anonymous, as does the one who said, "You can't make money and entertain children." Robert Klein, a vice president at NBC and an admirer of Marshall McLuhan, says openly, "There's no need to tell a story on TV with a beginning, a middle, and an end. Events are

not connected in orderly fashion in true-life situations. . . . Kids
who have grown up with TV fill in the gaps of disjointed plots
and understand them much better than older folks. Word-
oriented people find the experience of the moment, with no relation to what comes before or after, a difficult concept to
accept."

The producers of live-action shows are many, but the most
successful maker of animated shows is Hanna-Barbera Productions. They are, in *Variety*'s words, "the kings of the weekend cartoon world of networking." Bill Hanna and Joe
Barbera's company takes up two and a half acres in Burbank
and is said to be, by their public relations man, the world's
largest producer of filmed animation. For all their activity,
Hanna and Barbera have never acquired the household
charisma of Walt Disney. This doesn't seem to bother them,
and with their several hundred employees they proceed to grind
out whatever it is that's selling this season. H-B is quite open
about its sources of inspiration. Many of its earlier cartoon
series were based on existing adult shows. "*The Flintstones* is
just a caveman version of Jackie Gleason's *Honeymooners*,"
I was told, not apologetically, while being shown through the
Hanna-Barbera facilities. When monsters and superheroes became popular, H-B assimilated them and dropped *Yogi Bear*,
Huckleberry Hound, and the rest of the menagerie. They are
now responsible for *Space Ghost, Fantastic Four, Moby Dick,
The Herculoids, Birdman, Sampson and Goliath*, and *Shazzan*.

All their shows resemble each other, every frame of the
thousand feet of cartoon film they make each week looks like
every other frame. This is not because of any real style, but a
lack of it. At Hanna-Barbera the Disney art factory concept
has been taken about as far as it can go without replacing the
artists with machines. In order to turn out as much animation
as they do, usually in six-minute segments, Hanna and Barbera
can't use the complete animation used in theater releases.

"Disney-type full animation is economically unfeasible for television," Bill Hanna explains. "We discovered we could get away with less. We only animate fully where it's necessary. The old theatrical cartoons kept characters moving constantly—no holds, no heavy accents. Free-flowing stuff is harder to watch because of all that tedious detail."

There are in Hollywood producers who are still fond of all that tedious detail, though. One is Chuck Jones, who did *How The Grinch Stole Christmas* for television and created the Roadrunner while at Warners. "Illustrated radio. That's what it really is," Jones says about the Hanna-Barbera kind of limited animation. "The only value is quantity." To critics outside the business, such as the *New York Times*, there is a "cut-rate quality" about the Hanna-Barbera product. Comments on their second-rate art work, tired plots, and high-frequency horrors don't disturb Hanna and Barbera much. In fact, the highly unflattering *New York Times* piece quoted above was given to me, after his secretary had made a photocopy, by the Hanna-Barbera public relations man.

After surveying current television and some of the people involved in it, the unavoidable conclusion is that the needs most thoroughly served by the medium are those of networks, producers, and advertisers. Children, who want a variety of information and socializing tools from television, are not being served well at all. Even the important needs of entertainment and escape are generally met with second-rate, second-hand programs. Children as children have a low priority. It is children as consumers who are important to the manufacturers of kid entertainment.

Certain things about television are so consistently true they could be carved in stone and left on display for decades. One truth is: The bigger the audience, the bigger the profits. In *Television For Children*, Ralph Garry proposed several questions it might be valuable for kid business broadcasters to ask themselves. The first one is: Are you giving or selling the program to children? "This choice is fundamental," says Garry. "It affects the content of the programs, the production values incorporated in them, the tempo, the attitudes of performers toward their audience. . . . If the decision is to sell, the most profitable approach is to mesmerize the children." Almost everyone in children's television at the moment is selling, not giving.

If the television industry suddenly turned generous, what could it be giving kids? Most important, television could offer many more alternatives. On Saturday mornings, when the kid rating race is most intense, children are offered nothing more than a choice between a *Fantastic Four* and a *Super President*, between a *Spiderman* and a *Frankenstein, Jr.* "The answer to the problem of children's programs is not to do less for children, but much more," writes Harry J. Skornia in *Television And Society*. Professor Skornia believes the balance in children's shows is much too strongly tilted toward simple-minded fantasy programs. "There seem to be no other programs from which to choose at those hours when most children are free to watch television." Those who don't like what is offered, says Skornia, are simply trained to like it. "Scientific discovery, social and international problems, the opening of new nations and cultures . . . heroes who are winning battles over all kinds of natural forces, pressures and ignorance (not merely over gangsters and villains), all suggest new kinds of adventure programs."

With less specifics, Ralph Garry has suggested that television programs could teach children much more of value than they do. "The cleavage between entertainment and education is an artificial result of the particular mold into which American television has been cast," he says. "The broadcaster's aversion to being educational may arise from the fact that he equates being educational with being dull. Talented teachers are as exciting as talented performers. Neither work and play, nor entertainment and education, need be mutually exclusive."

Let's return now to the non-ideal reality and consider what's happening and can happen to children who are watching the present run of television, what's happening in terms of social adjustments and emotional attitudes. For children, particularly younger children, a great deal of their information about the adult world comes from television. Since a child's social adjustments are based on all the information he collects while growing up, the data television feeds in is used in forming these adjustments. The content of most of the shows this chapter has mentioned present a less-than-adequate image of the world, less-than-adequate clues on how to function in it.

The heroes, cowboys and supermen and spies, are usually unprincipled and unrestrained. They define themselves by action, action which includes sadistic vigilante-ism, illegal harassment, and violations of most of the civil and social codes we are supposed to believe in. The biggest difference between hero and villain is that the hero doesn't get arrested for his major crimes or misdemeanors. Plots and patterns have become so ritualized that the motives for actions, and their meanings and consequences, are lost and forgotten. The mass media teach kids, as Dr. Wertham says, that there are three kinds of people in the world. First, heroes, who "are at the top and determine the course of events. Second, the ordinary people, who are merely bystanders and onlookers. That is us. And third, an endless chain of villains, scoundrels, inferiors, enemies, spies, criminals, traitors, dissenters, opponents, bad guys."

The kids who don't want to follow the course of the heroes are stuck with narrow models. The rest of the world, the part that isn't super-righteous heroes or expendable and inferior aliens, is peopled with bumbling conformists, bystanders who don't make waves but who do buy a lot of produce. "Television

extols the spender," observes Harry J. Skornia. "He buys everything. He knows that it is a duty to free enterprise to spend,
rather than to save. . . . If children do not spend on Mother, on
Mother's Day, they obviously do not love her. . . . The saboteur
of our economy is the tightwad father who wants to use the
old car another year, or who objects to the rapidity with which
items are made obsolete."

Television teaches children that it is not good to be different,
that the best thing to be is like everyone else. Much of the
medium is dedicated to the status quo; it has to be, because of
the economics involved. Fads are acceptable, but basic changes
and maverick trends don't fit. Television thus serves as a continuous recruiting drive, aimed at getting children to join, with
enthusiasm and forever, the community of consumers. "Our
job as teachers is to inculcate habits of rational choice and decision," says S. I. Hayakawa. "The advertising profession, however, with all the technical resources of art, expert copy, color
printing, radio, and television at its command, spends most of
its efforts in the encouragement of irrational and impulsive
choice. . . . The teacher's job is to encourage intellectual and
moral self-discipline; the job of the advertiser of consumer
goods is to encourage self-indulgence."

Our concern with the violence so evident throughout children's television comes about not only because there is too
much of it, but because there is too little taught of the real
nature of violence and how to control it. Too many producers
consider violence an ingredient, seeing their responsibility, if
they feel any at all, as determining the percentage of violence
which can safely be added to each kid show. Violence in life,
anger felt, can't be eliminated by not showing it and talking
about it. But continually offering physical aggression and resort
to weapons as the only expression of violent impulses is to be
completely heedless of the consequences and influences of television. "Whether or not he will use violence or avoid it," writes

Bruno Bettelheim, "depends entirely on what alternative solutions are known to a person facing a problem." Children's shows that provide alternate, and convincing, solutions are rare. "Courage is equated with the use of violence," says Harry J. Skornia of the majority of kids' action shows. "Courage which stands *against* violence is rarely shown and virtually never extolled. In all but the most exceptional cases, in order to survive, the heroes of American television finally have recourse to arms and violence."

Violence as an ingredient of shows, physical pain inflicted and murder with a shrug, have a corollary effect. They make killing and torture seem as natural and unavoidable as the sunrise and the fall of rain. So that children are taught not to question the violence that is done by others. Not understanding why, not understanding the real causes of anxiety and its physical expression, children can also be taught to accept the idea, now quite widespread, that the only way to meet violence is with counter-violence. "With the progress of civilization we have learned, slowly and painfully, that violence is not the best way to settle human differences," Dr. Wertham has said, "but we seem to be using the marvelous technical media of movies and television to teach children that it is the only way."

The favorite blanket justification for all mass-media violence is that it helps children get rid of their aggressive feelings in safe and socially acceptable ways, that blood and brutality provide a harmless, make-believe outlet for vicarious violence. In support of this view, psychiatry professor Lauretta Bender once wrote that the violence in comics and television offers "the same type of mental catharsis that Aristotle claimed was an attribute of drama." Though variations of the catharsis theory still appear in mothers' magazines and syndicated advice columns, there is little real evidence that television, or anything else, serves such a function for children, or for anyone else. The most Stanford University's Institute for Communication Research would say, after a three-year study of television in the lives of children, is: "We do know that television is by no means an automatic outlet for aggressive impulses, and it probably builds aggression and frustration as often as it reduces them."

Professor Leonard Berkowitz, also associated with the Stanford institute, doesn't agree with even this modest view. "There simply is not adequate evidence that hostility catharsis occurs through vicarious aggression," he says. "If anything, experimental results suggest that scenes of violence depicted on the screen will have a much greater tendency to incite children to later aggressive acts than to 'drain' them of their aggressive 'energy.' " The UNESCO report on the effects of television on children, issued in 1964, summarized research carried out around the world. With one exception, none of the studies of television violence found any evidence that "a child might rid himself vicariously of pent-up aggression" by watching. In fact, "a series of experiments have now come out with exactly the opposite result." The results of the various studies the UNESCO report found to be "not entirely reassuring, because they leave little doubt that violent programs on television do not serve to reduce aggression vicariously, but if anything increase it and encourage its later expression."

There has been a sort of snobbish class attitude taken by some of those who have commented on the effects of television violence. After the summer riots of 1967, *TV Guide*, in an editorial, remarked: "The underprivileged, the uneducated, the jobless and the frustrated have neither the caution nor the responsibility of the privileged. They are, perhaps, more likely to adopt the violence to which all of us have been exposed, as a means to an end." This bwana attitude, besides its feigned blindness to the more basic causes of urban rioting, assumes that if one is middle-class and well-educated one is virtually immune to television. That children in such fortunate circumstances can select what things on television will affect them and which will not. This is simply not so. Nor does the proposed *TV Guide* solution of reducing "the amount of violence— unnecessary, phony violence—in our mass media" with "a little less shooting in movies, less fighting for the sake of fighting on television" indicate that the real problem has even been thought about. It is not a question of violence or no violence, nor of how much. It's a question of the uses to which physical aggression and weapons are put, and of teaching how to cope with violent impulses and how to create alternatives.

More alternatives to all of what is now presented to children on television are needed. Most of the questions asked in this chapter about what television should be and what it should offer have been answered in the negative. Professional television people like to ward off criticism by calling their critics intellectuals. "There is, and always has been, a broad swatch of professional intellectuals who fear and detest anything new," says CBS employee Eric Severeid in defense of all television, "particularly if it is adaptable to the great mass of ordinary people." There isn't really a conflict between intellectuals and the masses, particularly since two such mutually exclusive groups don't exist. The name-calling, and the just-folks mask put on by network officials and spokesmen, is an avoidance and a cop-out. The history of the last two decades of children's television is a history of carelessness and exploitation.

10. Superman, Inc.

> In drawing style, both in figure and costume, Superman . . .
> set the fashion. Everybody else's super-costumes were copies
> from his shop. Joe Shuster represented the best of the old-style
> comic book drawing. His work was direct, unprettied—crude
> and vigorous; as easy to read as a diagram. . . . When assistants
> began "improving" the appearance of the strip it promptly
> went downhill. It looked like it was being drawn in a bank.
>
> JULES FEIFFER
> *The Great Comicbook Heroes*

> Didja know that more than a dozen college professors thruout
> America now use Marvel mags in their English Litt. courses as
> supplemental material? It's only a start—but we're getting
> there, gang!
>
> STAN LEE
> *The Incredible Hulk,*
> May 1968

In the fall of 1934 a retired cavalry major ran ads in
the *New York Times* saying he was looking for artists to hire.
The major was one Malcolm Wheeler-Nicholson, and he was
about to start a comic book publishing company whose annual
revenue thirty years later would be over 60 million dollars.
Neither Major Nicholson nor Jerry Siegel and Joe Shuster, two
of the young men who responded to his call for new material,
ever saw much of that kind of money. But if the three hadn't
gotten together the entire comic book business wouldn't have
been born, wouldn't have become the 100-million-dollar industry it is today. Comic books are a medium capable of de-

176

lighting children and possibly enlightening them, a medium that can offer a properly rowdy alternative to overly polite and overly art-directed *Jack & Jill* type magazines that are often foisted on kids. How the comic book industry grew and how a medium that has introduced Walt Kelly's *Pogo* and Harvey Kurtzman's *MAD*, and reprinted George Herriman's *Krazy Kat* and Charles Schulz' *Peanuts*, ignored its potential and became preoccupied with murder, torture, sadism and storm-trooper violence is the object of our concern in this chapter.

In a loft on lower Fourth Avenue in New York City, Major Malcolm Wheeler-Nicholson formed, on a very low budget, the Nicholson Publishing Company, and began producing comic books in 1935. Though the major had a terrible business sense, and eventually went bankrupt, he managed to found what would become the 60-million-dollar-a-year National Periodical Company. Major Nicholson, a small balding man in his middle forties, "had a continental air," Creig Flessel, one of the artists who worked for him, told me. "Spats, a cane, a beaver hat, cigarette holder clenched between rotted teeth. He always bowed when he shook your hand."

Born in Tennessee, Major Nicholson had entered the U. S. Army as a commissioned second lieutenant in 1911. Dapper even then, he wore London-made riding boots and Bond Street-tailored uniforms and felt he "invariably roused the hostility of a certain dowdy type of senior officer who ran to quartermaster-issue stuff and resented the wearing of anything else by his juniors." The major served in the Second Cavalry on the Mexican border against Pancho Villa and "other sportive bandits," in the Philippines, in Siberia, and he commanded the American Cavalry Squadron in the Rhineland during the First World War. He was also attached to the embassy in London and later attended the French War College in Paris. He left the service in the 1920's and became a pulp writer.

The pulp magazines were growing increasingly popular in

the '20's, offering a variety of mass literature, from Western and love to science fiction and detective. Printed on cheap untrimmed woodpulp paper, most of the pulps sold for a dime or fifteen cents. Major Nicholson specialized in costume adventure novelets with such titles as *The Song of the Sword* and *Hooves of the Tartar Horde*. The comic books he began publishing in the mid-1930's, *Fun* and *New*, were inspired equally by newspaper comic strips and by pulp magazines. The earliest issues ran to a fat 80 pages and offered one-page humor strips and two- and four-page adventure serial strips dealing with Vikings, aviators, knights, and pirates. The Borgias were always favorites of the major's, and he wrote scripts about them for his new comic books. To keep costs down, the first issues didn't have the coated stock covers which now grace all comic books, and the interiors were short on full color. For all their limitations, what the major had produced were the first regularly issued comics magazines in America to use original art work and not rely on newspaper strip reprints.

The staff the major recruited was eclectic and irregular, a mixture of old-time newspaper cartoonists and teenage art students who dreamed of becoming illustrators: Tom McNamara, who had done a syndicated kid strip for Hearst from 1910 through 1930 and had also helped Hal Roach create the *Our Gang* movie comedies; in the middle 1930's, McNamara was still hoping to get back to syndicate work, and he drew anonymously. And 18-year-old Sheldon Mayer, who would later edit many of the National Periodical magazines. Mayer had been haunting syndicates and newspapers since the age of 14 and was able to place his first cartoons with the major. "No money," he's said, "but a very amusing contract."

Besides putting ads in the *New York Times* which brought in aspiring young illustrators like Creig Flessel, the major sent a representative around to the art schools in Manhattan. Sometimes he got students and sometimes he ended up hiring one of the instructors. Nineteen-year-old Tom Hickey was signed on while teaching night art classes for the WPA. Hickey recalls that Major Nicholson paid him $5 a page. "This included drawing, inking, lettering and, at times, writing."

To edit his shaky magazines, Major Nicholson employed Whitney Ellsworth, who now heads the Superman TV Corporation, and Vincent Sullivan, cartoonist brother of Ed Sullivan. "The major flashed in and out of the place," Creig Flessel remembers, "doing battle with the printers, the banks, and other enemies of the struggling comics. Vin Sullivan and Whit Ellsworth held the editorial reins, bought the art work, created new titles, and in general helped the baby comic magazines learn to walk." Because of the tight money situation at the Nicholson Publishing Company, his editors also used unsolicited artwork sent in through the mail by young artists. Among those who began working for the major this way were two 21-year-old science fiction fans from Cleveland: Jerome Siegel, a writer, and Joe Shuster, a cartoonist. They were able to get monthly spots for their adventure strips *Federal Men*, *Slam Bradley*, and *Radio Squad*. But Major Nicholson and his editors weren't interested in Siegel and Shuster's favorite idea, a science fiction adventure strip called *Superman*.

The major's luck didn't improve, nor did his business ability. "The worst outfit I worked for," cartoonist Matt Curzon told me, "was Major Nicholson's. He kept on promising to pay what he owed us and finally we took him to court. We got a fraction of our money back and Nicholson filed bankruptcy." The last new title the major's company introduced was *Detective Comics*. This was an even closer imitation of a pulp magazine and was crowded with private eyes and sinister Orientals. Of all the hundreds of magazine titles introduced in the comic book field since the '30's, *Detective* is one of the few that still survives. The magazine did much better than the major. One of Nicholson's problems was that, like many pioneers, he was ahead of his time. Not decades ahead, but a couple of years ahead. Distributors were still reluctant to handle comic books, and newsstands even more reluctant to give them rack space. The Fourth Avenue loft was often filled with piles of unsold copies. Had the major been more of a businessman, and perhaps less of a gentleman, he might have been able to hold out until the boom years of 1939 and 1940.

Comic books have been printed in the United States since the nineteenth century. Until the 1930's it had never occurred to anyone to draw original material for them, nor had it occurred to distributors and dealers that comic books could have consistent sales on newsstands. Street & Smith, the dime novel and pulp publishers, seem to have reprinted the early newspaper cartoon *The Yellow Kid* in comic book format in the late 1890's, and as newspaper strips flourished in the new years of the twentieth century many more reprint books and magazines appeared. In the early 1920's, William Randolph Hearst, who seems to have tried almost everything once, experimented with a *Comic Monthly*. It sold for 10¢ and reprinted, in black and white, such then favorite Hearst comic strips as *Barney Google* and *Polly and Her Pals*. The monthly, similar in format to modern magazines, never caught on and was abandoned after a dozen or so issues. Also in the '20's Cupples & Leon, who specialized in hardcover series books about characters like Bomba the Jungle Boy, started reprinting newspaper strips in booklet form. Some of their titles—*Mutt and Jeff, Little Orphan Annie*, etc.—sold as many as 200,000 copies.

The preoccupation with reprinted comic strips continued after the Depression set in. Finally, in the early 1930's, along came Harry I. Wildenberg and invented the comic book as we know it. The reason there's no shock of recognition when you hear Wildenberg's name is because when he thought up the modern-style comic book he was working for somebody else. The Eastern Color Printing Company of Connecticut employed him as sales manager. One of the things Eastern Color did was print the Sunday comic sections of several East Coast newspapers. Having an advertising background, Wildenberg first thought of using the funnies as advertising premiums. He sold Gulf Oil the idea of giving away a tabloid-size book of comics, which proved to be a successful gimmick.

In contemplating extensions of the comics as a premium, Wildenberg and some of his associates noticed that reduced Sunday pages they'd made as a promotion for the *Philadelphia Ledger* would fit two on a page on the standard tabloid-size sheet of paper. Further fiddling and figuring enabled Wildenberg to work out a way to use Eastern's presses to print 64-page color comic books. The next problem was what to do with the resultant magazines. Wildenberg, with the help of a salesman named M. C. Gaines, first interested other advertisers in using comic books as premiums. After an order from Procter & Gamble for a million copies of a reprint called *Comics on Parade*, Wildenberg produced comic books for Canada Dry, Kinney Shoes, Wheatena and other kid-oriented products.

Wildenberg and Gaines then considered sticking a 10¢ price tag on comic books and selling them to children. They approached the Woolworth's chain as a possible outlet but were told 64 pages of old comics wasn't a good enough value. Eventually, in 1934, Wildenberg persuaded the American News Company to distribute a monthly comic book to newsstands. The magazine was named *Famous Funnies*, a title Wildenberg had originally thought up for a soap company premium. The initial issue sold 90 percent of its 200,000 copies. Eastern Color lost over $4,000 on the first issue of *Famous Funnies*, but by issue number 12 they were netting $30,000 a month and the comic book industry had started.

While Eastern was making thousands of dollars, the syndicates weren't doing as well, since the reprint rights to the strips they controlled had been sold for a flat rate of $10 a page.

This and the climbing sales of *Famous Funnies* pushed several large newspaper syndicates into the comic book business. United Features, the syndicate branch of the United Press, introduced *Tip Top Comics* to reprint its *Tarzan, Li'l Abner, Ella Cinders*, etc. King Features entered into a partnership with the David McKay Company to convert all its popular strips (*Flash Gordon, Popeye, Krazy Kat*, etc.) into comic books. The McNaught Syndicate called its magazine *Feature Funnies*, and the Chicago Tribune Syndicate collaborated with Dell and M. C. Gaines, now on his own, to produce *Popular Comics*. All these new magazines were successful, making for a small row of comic books in drug stores and newsstands. And they were profitable, particularly since the syndicates didn't have to pay their artists anything for reprint rights.

It had been Harry Wildenberg's idea that comic books would appeal primarily to kids, and while these early magazines—*Famous, Detective, Tip Top*—were bought somewhat by adults, the real excitement and the majority of sales came from the children who were discovering them. Many kids, like Jules Feiffer who was 8 years old and trapped in Brooklyn, were particularly enthusiastic about the flamboyant pulp action Major Nicholson was championing in his original art magazines. "It was this action-filled rawness, this world of lusty hoodlumism, of Saturday movie serials seven days a week, that made the new comic books, from their first day of publication, the principal reading matter of my life," Feiffer says. In his history of the early comic heroes, Feiffer also remarks that, unlike comic strips in adult newspapers, the artwork in these first comic books didn't have a sleek look. By being "not quite professional . . . they were closer to home, more comfortable to live with, less like grownups." Major Nicholson, because he couldn't pay much, hired many young artists and for the first half dozen years other comic books followed this pattern.

This created a situation in which many of the artists and writers drawing comic books were only a few years older than their readers, circumstances which never happened again in this particular section of the kid business.

For Jerry Siegel and Joe Shuster, 1938 seemed like a good year. After sending their *Superman* strip around to syndicates and publishers for half a decade, they sold it. In the spring of '38, *Superman* appeared in the first issue of *Action Comics.* Siegel and Shuster, now both 23 years old and still mailing their work in from Cleveland, sold not only the comic magazine rights to their character, but all rights forever, in order to see him in print. Siegel and Shuster, both Clark Kent types, had met at high school and became friends through a mutual interest in science fiction and comics. According to Siegel's memory, he thought up Superman one night when he couldn't get to sleep. "I am lying in bed counting sheep when all of a sudden it hits me. I conceive a character like Samson, Hercules, and all the strong men I ever heard tell of rolled into one. Only more so."

Siegel had probably also heard tell of innumerable pulp magazine supermen and also the scientifically created superhero of Philip Wylie's 1930 novel *Gladiator*. From the Wylie character and a patchwork of Old Testament, mythological, and pulp heroes, Siegel put together Superman. Shuster drew it. His style was a grab-bag of pulp illustrators and comic strip artists, but it managed to come alive and be distinctly his own. "Shuster represented the best of old-style comic book drawing," says Jules Feiffer. "His work was direct, unprettied—crude and vigorous; as easy to read as a diagram. No creamy lines, no glossy illustrative effects, no touch of that bloodless prefabrication that passes for professionalism these days. Slickness, thank God, was beyond his means. He could not draw well, but he drew single-mindedly—no one could ghost that style. . . . When assistants began 'improving' the appearance of the strip it promptly went downhill. It looked like it was being drawn in a bank."

The man the partners had sold their Superman to was Harry Donenfeld. When Major Nicholson went bankrupt, Donenfeld, a printer and magazine distributor, had taken over the major's three comic magazines in hopes of retrieving some of the money owed him. Donenfeld's prior magazine experience had been with more adult magazines. One was called *Snappy Stories*, and a writer who worked for Donenfeld in the late '30's recalls "piles of back numbers in the stock room of a magazine with a title like *Silk Stockings*, all showing girls in slips displaying their legs." Whitney Ellsworth and Vincent Sullivan stayed on as editors after the collapse of the major and convinced Donenfeld that the pulp-type format used with *Detective Comics* could be effectively repeated. This resulted in *Action*, a parallel to the adventure pulps.

In gathering features for his first issue, Donenfeld asked the ubiquitous M. C. Gaines, now working for a newspaper syndicate, if he had anything in his slush pile for an action hero magazine. Gaines brought over *Superman*, which Siegel and Shuster had just re-submitted to him. Donenfeld and his editors decided to use the feature, though no one at Detective Comics, Inc. (as Donenfeld was now calling the Nicholson company) was very enthusiastic. There was a deadline to meet, 64 pages to fill, and Siegel and Shuster wouldn't cost much. Donenfeld's general manager offered them $10 a page and sent a release form along to Cleveland. "It is customary for all our contributors to release all rights to us. This is the businesslike way of doing things," the accompanying letter read. The partners signed, and Donenfeld now owned all syndication, movie, radio, and television rights to Superman. Of course in 1938 no comic book character had aroused enough interest to warrant even a comic book all his own. But Detective Comics, Inc., was taking no chances.

The kid response to *Action Comics* was immediate, and it began to outsell Donenfeld's other three titles. A hasty survey showed that the reason was *Superman,* and the Detective Comics Company, which had been following the pulp practice of featuring irrelevant action with Mounties, Arabs, and gangsters on its covers, realized they ought to be showing and mentioning *Superman.* The character quickly became a fad, and to cash in on it Donenfeld and his general manager, Jack Liebowitz, extended the new character every way they could. The comic strip rights were grabbed by M. C. Gaines for his syndicate. A radio show was proposed. A *Superman* monthly was issued and was soon grossing a million dollars a year all by itself. By 1940, with the comic strip in 200 papers, Donenfeld was getting $100,000 from it for himself.

All this success didn't spoil Siegel and Shuster, mainly because it hardly touched them. When they finally came to New York and confronted Detective Comics, Inc., Donenfeld made it clear he owned *Superman* and if they caused trouble he'd simply hire another writer and cartoonist to take over. Siegel and Shuster signed a new contract, increasing their joint income by $1,000 a year, and went back home to Cleveland to keep producing *Superman.*

In the late 1930's publishers didn't have motivational research. Many of the hole-in-the-wall people who jumped into the comic book business after the obvious success of *Superman* couldn't have afforded it anyway. They went by hunches and instinct. What seemed evident was that kids would buy comic books about a guy in tights and a cape. With the single-mindedness that now produces rock groups, publishers put forth supermen. An apparently low budget company calling itself the Fox Feature Syndicate is tied with Donenfeld for the invention of the next superhero after *Superman*. The Fox magazines would later make a major contribution to the collapse of a good part of the comic book industry. In 1939, in the spring, they introduced Wonder Man in *Wonder Comics*. Wonder Man was in reality a mild-mannered reporter, who, when he was in a heroic mood, could leap over tall buildings, race streamlined trains, and catch bullets in his bare hands. Donenfeld felt there was an infringement and sued. At the same time, his own company unveiled Bob Kane's *Batman* in *Detective Comics*. Kane, 19, had until then been sharing office space with a group of young artists who ground out comics for small publishers. His specialties were a strip about Peter Pupp and gag cartoons signed with names like Watt A. Card. *Batman* was a distinct step up for him.

The Fawcett Publishing Company, headed by W. H. "Buzz" Fawcett, Jr., came to prominence with such publications as *Mechanix Illustrated* and *Captain Billy's Whiz Bang*, a primitive girlie joke magazine. Deciding to enter comics in late 1939, Fawcett asked a writer named Bill Parker and an artist named C. C. Beck to create a new superhero and a comic book for him to function in. Parker and Beck came up with a hero who got his powers by saying the magic word "Shazam." When not a full-grown hero, he was a mild-mannered boy reporter for a radio station. The star villain was the mad scientist Sivana, patterned after Beck's neighborhood pharmacist. Parker and Beck called their new hero Captain Thunder, after the thunderbolt which appeared whenever he said "Shazam."

Someone at Fawcett must have been superstitious about Captain Billy's Whiz Bang, and felt the comic book should be close to it in name if not in spirit. At the end of 1939, Fawcett began printing *Whiz Comics* with Captain Marvel, alias Billy Batson. This still left a Bang from the girlie title unaccounted for, and the next year Fawcett used that up on *Slam Bang Comics*. Donenfeld and Liebowitz sued *Captain Marvel*, too, contending a superman in red tights and a white cape was a steal of a superman with blue tights and red cape. The Fox Company had quickly dropped their offending *Wonder Man*. Fawcett was stubborn, and the lawsuit went on for over a decade. For a time in the Second World War period, *Captain Marvel* outsold all the other superheroes.

The proliferation of heroes continued through 1939, 1940, and 1941. Sixty different comic books appeared in 1939, and 160 in 1941. Kids could now enjoy Starman, Doll Man, Sandman, Hydroman, Hyperman, and Strongman, and such colorful supermen as the Blue Bolt, the Blue Beetle, the Red Raven, the Green Lantern, the Black Condor, the Crimson Avenger, the Purple Zombie, the Silver Streak, and Rainbow Man. Not to mention the Owl, the Zebra, the Fox, the Spider, Cat Man, the Ferret, the Shark, and the Flame, the Ray, the Flash, the Clock, the Iron Skull, Tornado Tom, Flash-Lightning, the Blazing Skull, the Human Torch, and Shock Gibson. The publishers behind this assortment included pulp magazine outfits and even the *Saturday Evening Post*'s Curtis Publishing Company, who quietly entered the field and issued *Blue Bolt* and *Target* comics.

Most of the mythology and the psychological symbolism in the early superhero strips was not there deliberately. Siegel and Shuster needed to believe in *Superman* as much as kids did, and there is little calculation in the naive swashbuckling adventures of the early *Batman*. By the '40's many publishers were affluent enough to afford research and deliberation. They could even hire psychologists. Dr. William Moulton Marston had taught and lectured on psychology at Radcliffe, Tufts, Columbia, the University of Southern California, and the New School for Social Research. He had practiced law and was the creator of the lie detector test. In 1941, at the age of 48, he originated *Wonder Woman* for comic books.

"My first sortie into the comics field was in the role of reformer," Dr. Marston revealed in the *American Scholar*. "I was retained as consulting psychologist by comics publishers to analyze the present shortcomings of monthly picture magazines and recommend improvements." The assignment was with Donenfeld's Superman-D.C. chain, where M. C. Gaines who got around a lot, was now producing a series of comic books. Gaines convinced Dr. Marston of the worth of the picture story, the tradition for which "went back to ages past . . . to the early dawn of civilization."

On his own, the psychologist did considerable thinking as to why *Superman* and the others were so popular. "Their emotional appeal is wish fulfillment," Marston concluded. "They satisfy the universal human longing to be stronger than all opposing obstacles and the equally universal desire to see good overcome evil, to see wrongs righted, underdogs nip the pants of their oppressors and, withal, to experience vicariously the supreme gratification of the *deus ex machina* who accomplishes these monthly miracles of right triumphing over not-so-mighty might. Here we find the Homeric tradition rampant—the Achilles with or without a vulnerable heel, the Hector who defends his home from foreign invaders, wronged Agamemnon who pursues his righteous vengeance with relentless fury, and the wily Ulysses who cleverly accomplishes the downfall of attractive if culpable enemies by the exercise of superhuman wisdom." Marston believed he had the superhero psyched out, and he was well qualified, as the quotes from his writings bear out, to script comic book continuities.

Dr. Marston was equally certain about the effects the best comic book heroes should, and did, have on children. "What life-desires do you wish to stimulate in your child? Do you want him (or her) to cultivate weakling's aims? . . . The wish to be super-strong is a healthy wish, a vital, compelling, power-producing desire. The more the *Superman-Wonder Woman* picture stories build up this inner compulsion by stimulating the child's natural longing to battle and overcome obstacles, particularly evil ones, the better chance your child has for self-advancement in the world."

The specific thinking that led to Wonder Woman herself grew out of Dr. Marston's insights into the myth qualities of comic book heroes and his belief that children could be positively, in his terms, affected and influenced by the heroes. The early episodes of *Wonder Woman*, which appeared in a magazine with the self-advancing title of *Sensation Comics*, were rich with badly assimilated Greek and Roman mythology and snappy pleas for virtue. Dr. Marston's theories on the mechanical creation of a character seemed to work. *Wonder Woman* sold well, graduated to her own magazine and comic strip, remaining a valuable property even today.

What exactly were some of the lessons Dr. Marston hoped to teach children is not quite clear. Discussing the reasons for his super-Amazon, Dr. Marston said, "It seemed to me, from a psychological angle, that the comics' worst offense was their blood-curdling masculinity. A male hero, at best, lacks the qualities of maternal love and tenderness which are essential to a normal child as the breath of life. . . . It's sissified, according to exclusively masculine rules, to be tender, loving, affectionate, and alluring. . . . Not even girls want to be girls so long as our feminine archetype lacks force, strength, power. . . . Women's strong qualities have become despised because of their weak ones. The obvious remedy is to create a feminine character with all the strength of a superman plus all the allure of a good and beautiful woman." So Dr. William Moulton Marston took the pen name "Charles Moulton," hired veteran cartoonist H. G. Peter, and produced *Wonder Woman*.

To doubts on M. C. Gaines' part that boys would buy a strong woman, Marston replied, "Give them an alluring woman stronger than themselves to submit to and they'll be *proud* to become her willing slaves!" The success of his character, Mars-

ton believed, was due to his formula of "super-strength, altru-
ism, and feminine love allure, combined in a single character."
Although Dr. Marston was saying things like this throughout
the early 1940's, no other psychologist or psychiatrist thought
to critically examine *Wonder Woman* until nearly ten years
after her debut.

In addition to psychologists, the new comic book industry
gave employment to a complex assortment of people, particularly in the year or two just prior to Pearl Harbor. "When the
comics boom began," says Alfred Bester, "there was a mad
scramble for editors, artists, and writers. Most of the editors
were hired away from Standard Magazines and they brought
some of their writers along with them, myself included." Bester
was just out of Columbia and breaking into science fiction in
the Standard pulps. He was still years away from his remarkable science fiction novel *The Demolished Man*, and even
further from his current position as writer and senior editor
for *Holiday*.

Bester signed on at Superman-D.C. to write scripts. "We all
had to learn the new business together, and they were exciting
days for a writer," Bester told me. "There was a constant demand for stories. You could always experiment and try things."
He wrote continuity for Batman and created his own character, a parody superhero Genius Jones. "Comics were simon-
pure in those days; no sex, no sadism. Our biggest fight with the
editors was over the issue of The Trap. Inevitably, every hero
had to be placed in a fiendish trap by the villain, and as the
conventional ones were exhausted, the writers had to reach
farther and farther out. Then the question would arise: Is this
trap good clean fiendish, or is it sadistic?"

Other writers in the comics field then included science fiction
men like H. L. Gold and Henry Kuttner, future novelists like
George Mandel, and future critics such as Stanley Kaufman.
The most affluent alumnus of comic writing is Mickey Spillane.

He ran a writers' workshop which produced scripts for the Human Torch and similar heroes.

The artists who drew the strips included C. A. Voight and Frank Godwin, men who had in better days illustrated in the major slick magazines and done syndicated comic strips. Neither of them thought enough of the new field to ever sign their work in it. Ed Wheelan felt differently. His comic strip *Minute Movies* had been a widely read one in the 1920's, and he happily revived it for one of the Gaines magazines. Wheelan not only prominently signed the feature, he included a letter column in it and gave tips to young cartoonists. Emerging young artists who were trying out in the comic books included William A. Smith, later a *Saturday Evening Post* illustrator and gallery painter, and Louis Glanzman, whose illustrations now appear in most of the surviving slick fiction magazines.

Just prior to the war, a young Colorado-born cartoonist named Bert Christman left his job drawing for the Associated Press and began doing two features for Superman-D.C. One was *The Sandman*, a cloak-and-mask character who followed the pattern of crime fighting set down on radio by *The Green Hornet*. Christman, an aviation buff, also drew *The Three Aces*. This strip dealt with "three winged soldiers-of-fortune, sick of war and tragedy, who pledge themselves to a new kind of adventure. They came to roam the globe, working for peace and sanity." Christman believed in a world where a soldier-of-fortune was still a possibility, and he quit magazines and went to Pensacola to take flight training. He then joined Chennault's American Volunteer Group, the Flying Tigers. In January of 1942 Christman's P-40 was shot down when the Flying Tigers went up against a 72-plane Japanese attack on Rangoon. Christman bailed out, and a Japanese plane went after him and machine-gunned him as he dropped. Christman was dead before he hit the ground. It was a new world now, and nobody would believe in the Three Aces again.

In the first year after Pearl Harbor, the comic book publishers took in 15 million dollars. Their audience was increasing, and changing. Servicemen took up the comic book, an accessible and easy-to-read kind of escape fiction, quickly disposable. More adult civilians had discovered comic books now as well. The rising age of readership and the war fever spreading through the country brought about changes in magazine content. Violence and sadism broke out completely now that there was an acceptable target.

"World War II was greeted by comic books with a display of public patriotism and a sigh of private relief," Jules Feiffer has said. "With the advent of the war it was no longer necessary to draw villains from the swarthy ethnic minorities: there were the butch-haircutted Nazis to contend with—looking too much like distorted mirror images of the heroes, perhaps—but no less bold an innovation for the conceit that Anglo-Saxons could be villains. . . . But the unwritten success story of the war was the smash comeback of the Oriental villain. He had faded badly for a few years, losing face to mad scientists—but now he was at the height of his glory. Until the war we had always assumed he was Chinese. But now we knew what he was! A Jap; a Yellow-belly Jap; a Jap-A-Nazi rat." All three of these designations were widely in use in war-time comic books, and the Japanese got much more attention from the avenging super-patriots than the Germans did. Buck-toothed drooling Japanese soldiers were burned alive by the Human Torch, drowned by the Sub Mariner, machine-gunned by Blackhawk, and fair game for any hero. Even the Japanese-Americans interned in California detention camps were used as villains in a number of comic stories.

World War II brought a rise in decorative sex, and there were many more raised skirts and torn blouses. At Superman-D.C., despite Donenfeld's background in girlie magazines, there was hardly any of this. In *Wonder Woman*, in fact, the company had given kids the most unsexual girl ever seen. In many other magazines women as victims became more evident. The sadism, on the villain's side, was often directed against a chained or tied-up girl. Sex and violence in a home-front setting were being provided by an emerging publishing company headed by Lev Gleason. Gleason had worked for Wildenberg and then edited the mild-mannered *Tip Top Comics*. Early in World War II he concocted, borrowing not from the pulps but from the true crime magazines, a new comic book entitled *Crime Does Not Pay*. Working with cartoonists Charles Biro and Bob Wood as editors, Gleason turned the true stories of Dillinger, Legs Diamond, Lepke, and numerous other crooks and killers into comic book form.

For an earlier magazine of his, Gleason had thought up the slogan "The comic book that dared to be different," but the line seems better suited to *Crime Does Not Pay*. Gleason's magazine was one of the first comic books to show people being strangled, shot in the face, burned by acid, hanged, beaten, tortured, and dissected. All in complete detail. Gleason's magazine approached murder and crime with the same deftness of *The Police Gazette* and depicted them with all the subtlety of a tabloid photo. The pages of *Crime Does Not Pay* were heavy with pools of blood and dead girls stretched out in the foreground of scenes. The covers of the magazine, usually drawn by Biro or one of his ghosts, specialized in anticipation rather than the depiction of violence. Biro showed the moment just before the pool hustler has his throat cut, the moment just before the two gas station attendants are buried alive, the moment just before the bootlegger is dropped into a lime pit. *Crime Does Not Pay* was the first example of what would become a dominant comic book genre. When the comics industry, ten years later, decided to set up a code authority to control the excesses of crime comics, Lev Gleason was the first president.

The war years also brought the partial integration of the comic books. Negroes had rarely appeared in the comic magazines of the 1930's, except as background. Porters, janitors, maids, cannibals, perhaps comedy relief. In 1942, though, to cite a few examples, Captain Marvel acquired a Negro sidekick, a group of fighting kids called the Young Allies recruited a Negro, and The Spirit was fighting crime with the help of a young Negro. Captain Marvel's black friend was named Steamboat, the Young Allies' Negro member was called Whitewash, and the Spirit's pal was known as Ebony. Steamboat spoke like this: "Heah dat, Mistah Billy? He don't believe Captain Mahvel's really heah!" And Whitewash: "Mah mammy always say dat 'ceptin' fo me, you is de dumbest boy she knows!"

These black characters, along with several others, also shared giant lips, flashing teeth, and oval heads either glistening bald or tightly covered with kinky hair. Many of them dressed in zoot suits. Exactly what the comic book industry was up to is hard now to determine. Maybe they were trying to reach a Negro audience and didn't know how. The Superman-D.C. chain avoided the problem, though they did run a scattering of public service strips presenting realistic Negroes and speaking against prejudice. In the main, those Negroes evident in comics were caricatures.

Criticism directed at comic books had started appearing at the same time as all the Superman impersonators, in the late 1930's. It ranged from the usual viewing-with-alarm which follows any new children's entertainment to specific complaints about brutality and the too-heavy reliance on a vigilante concept of justice. The bigger publishers, Superman-D.C. and Fawcett for example, hired or otherwise acquired advisory boards "to help us maintain high standards of wholesome entertainment in our comics publications." The respected educators and public figures assembled to advise and put off critics included the above mentioned Dr. William Moulton Marston, Dr. C. Bowie Millican of NYU, Dr. Robert Thorndike of Columbia, Rear Admiral Richard E. Byrd, Pearl S. Buck, Dr. Norman Vincent Peale, Gene Tunney, and Eleanor Roosevelt. An editor I asked said he doesn't recall ever seeing Mrs. Roosevelt around the office, but that some of the consultants did have more than simply honorary titles. In spite of the counsel and defensive prestige of celebrities and scholars, there was increasing criticism of comic books as the 1940's progressed. For one thing, many of the more obvious excesses were committed by magazines operating without benefit of either consultants or scruples.

An increasing number of writers—journalists, educators, psychiatrists—were expressing concern over what was happening to kids' magazines. The then-prominent radio program *Town Meeting of the Air* concerned itself with what was wrong with comics, and the then-prominent weekly *Collier's* printed Judith Crist's attack, *Horror in the Nursery*. A less widely circulated critique of crime and violence in comic books appeared in a book called *Love and Death* by Gershon Legman, published at the end of the 1940's.

Legman, expatriate expert on erotic literature and ribald limericks, was overzealous and not completely fair in his assault. Nonetheless, many of his points were relevant to the situation in the postwar period. "The price of comic books being only ten cents apiece, and the distribution national, every American child can and does read ten to a dozen of these pamphlets monthly. . . . If there is only one violent picture per page—and there are usually more—this represents a minimum supply, to every child old enough to look at pictures, of 300 scenes of beating, shooting, strangling, torture, and blood per month." Legman felt that, because the child will identify "with the hero who is handing out beatings and gun shots," the comics were "being used to teach him—and in no quiet professional tone, but rather in flaming color and superhero dialogue —that violence is heroic."

To Gershon Legman the abundance of violence in the popular arts was there because of the forced repression of sexuality, and he scorned critics who saw the partly dressed girls in the comic books as the major problem. "The really surprising thing," he wrote, "is the hypocrisy that can examine all these thousands of pictures in comic books showing half-naked women being tortured to death and complain only that they're half-naked. If they were being tortured to death with all their clothes on, would that be all right for children?"

When advisory boards proved unsuccessful at either forestalling complaints or controlling the conduct of the entire industry, the publishers formed an association with a code authority. The Association of Comics Magazine Publishers was born in the late 1940's and included the major companies as members. The criticism in the mass magazines and the concern of parents had helped produce bills to curb the sales of comics, local censorship boards, and assorted boycotts. The first code, therefore, was as much an attempt to protect an investment as it was a sincere effort to protect children. The 14-point code of the Association included cautions against nudity and unduly accentuated busts. Further, "no woman or girl should be shown being tortured," though no similar provision was made for men and boys. Ridiculing minorities, using overly frightening monsters, the glorification of criminals and glamorizing of divorce were also out. It's optimistic to expect much immediate improvement in a medium where you have to warn its artists and writers specifically to avoid showing the torture of women, and this early code had little effect.

Other things had happened to the comic books in the war years. From the point of view of Jules Feiffer, who was breaking into the field as World War II ended, his idea that comics could be a creative, exhilarating art form faded. Part of it was because of his own growing up, but part was because the war changed the comics, too. "The best men went into the service. Hacks sprouted everywhere—and, with sales to the armed forces booming, hack houses also sprouted. . . . The business stopped being thought of as a life's work and became a stepping-stone," Feiffer has said. "If you weren't in it for the buck, there wasn't a single other reason. Talk was no longer about work . . . it was about wives, baseball, kids, broads . . . the same as in any office anywhere."

I've talked to other cartoonists who suffered similar lost illusions during this same time. Publishers, with fewer illusions to lose, worried about sales when VE and VJ days arrived. Profits had risen because the magazines had had a chance to reach a wider, less exclusively kid, audience—a captive PX audience often. While children might accept a return to less violent, jumping-over-tall-buildings kind of stuff, the adult and adolescent audience probably wouldn't. Some of the schlock houses folded, but many publishers retooled and adjusted to the postwar world by abandoning superheroes and taking up gangsters, detectives, and other acceptable killers. In the five years following the end of the war, most comic books became harsher, strident with violence and death. There was the new medium of television to compete with now. It was already killing off the pulp magazines, and comic books had to fight hard against being the next to go under.

The first new genre could be called the Lev Gleason school. Gleason's *Crime Does Not Pay* and its later companion *Crime And Punishment* were claiming a circulation in the millions. They were joined by *Real Clue Comics, The Killers, Crime Can't Win, Crime Exposed, Law Against Crime, Murder, Inc., War Against Crime, Lawbreakers, Penalty, Crimes By Women,* and *March Of Crime*. Even the now relatively sedate and enor-

mously successful Superman-D.C. chain dabbled in crime with
Mr. District Attorney and *Gangbusters*. While these Donenfeld
titles kept the more violent crimes off stage and allowed only
an occasional machine-gunning on a cover, their competitors
dealt in the direct depiction of slaughter and destruction. Besides a flourishing of murder in an urban setting, there was an
increase in open-spaces murder. *Two-Gun Kid, Western Out-
laws, Western Killers, All-American Western,* and *Blazing
West* now appeared, joining the crime comics on the news
racks.

That *All-American Western*, by the way, was started in the
1930's as *All-American* by M. C. Gaines. Its superheroes and
comedy fillers were dropped and replaced by cowboys and gun-
slingers. Gaines himself had started still another company,
Educational Comics, Inc., which experimented with *Picture
Stories from the Bible* and *Picture Stories from American History*. When he died his son, William, took this company over
and began printing true crime comic books.

Some accounts of this postwar period, particularly that of
Stephen Becker in *Comic Art In America*, give the impression
that there was only an "occasional comic book which specialized in gore and grue" and that "only a handful of such comic
books" were published, all by small shabby publishers. None of
this is true. The small shabby publisher pulled out more stops,
but the major publishers of comic books issued hundreds of
thousands of copies of crime and murder comics. Superman-
D.C., Martin Goodman's Marvel Group, Fawcett, E.C., all
had crime titles. Only Dell, with its strong bunny-rabbit orien-
tation, refrained.

After crime came war and then horror comics, and some
curious blends of all three. The Fox Feature comics, long dedicated to superheroes and science fiction, now shifted completely into sado-masochist funnies. This would have seemed
an improbable genre ten years before, but Fox didn't look

startlingly out of place now. The late 1940's Fox comics featured whips and boots, girls being tortured, lesbians wrestling, and numerous other diversions formerly only mailed out in plain wrappers. The single precedent, in the kid world, for these Fox comics was a line of undressed girl comics begun in the early '40's by the pulp publisher Fiction House. In *Jungle Comics* and *Jumbo Comics*, which starred Sheena, Queen of the Jungle, a more cautious form of what Fox was now attempting had prevailed. Since Fox and Fiction House shared many of the same artists and writers, the later magazines could be called the logical development of the earlier ones. The postwar years apparently provided a healthier climate for sadism.

The Association of Comics Magazine Publishers continued to function into the 1950's, with members displaying the Comics Code Seal on their publications. The code was "to assure good taste and high editorial standards," and parents and children were further promised that "the Association is constantly working to give you better entertainment and more information about the world we live in." The head of the ACMP now was *Crime Does Not Pay* publisher Lev Gleason, and among the other officials was William Gaines, whose Educational Comics Company was issuing *Tales from the Crypt*, *The Vault of Horror*, and *Crime Suspenstories*.

While the ACMP had been establishing codes and making promises, Dr. Fredric Wertham had been starting his crusade against the crime and horror comic books. Wertham, then senior psychiatrist at Bellevue, was writing articles and making speeches against the comic books and what he believed to be their effects on children. Also a consultant to the LaFargue Clinic, a free psychiatric clinic he'd helped found in Harlem, he had done considerable work with disturbed children. In 1953 Dr. Wertham's *The Seduction of the Innocent* was published. In this book Wertham contended that "the bad effects of crime comic books exist potentially for all children," and among these bad effects he listed the atmosphere of cruelty and deceit that crime comic books create, the suggesting of criminal and sexually abnormal ideas, and providing the rationalizations for them. These magazines also suggested the forms a delinquent impulse might take, supplied details of technique, and might even tip the scales toward maladjustment or delinquency. Wertham did not say that these magazines were a direct cause of juvenile delinquency, but that they could be a contributing factor.

To the frequently made suggestion that there has always been a certain amount of violence in children's books and entertainments, Dr. Wertham said, "The atmosphere of crime comic books is unparalleled in the history of children's literature of any time or any nation. It is a distillation of viciousness. The world of the comic book is the world of the strong, the ruthless, the bluffer, the shrewd deceiver, the torturer, and the thief. All the emphasis is on exploits where somebody takes advantage of somebody else, violently, sexually, or threateningly."

Wertham's book included a portfolio of scenes from comic books, scenes showing murder and torture in numerous forms. One of the samples most widely commented on pictured, to use Robert Warshow's description in *Commentary*, "a baseball game in which the ball is a man's head with one eye dangling from its socket, the bat is a severed leg, the catcher wears a dismembered torso as chest protector, the baselines are marked with stretched-out intestines, the bases are marked with the lungs, liver, and heart, the rosin-bag is the dead man's stomach, and the umpire dusts off home plate with the scalp." Warshow said, in his piece on Dr. Wertham and the crime comics, "I don't suppose I shall easily forget that baseball game." But he assumed it had come from "the underworld of publishing." This would give substance to the claims that only schlock houses went in for this sort of thing. Actually the panels showing the grisly ball game were from a story in one of William Gaines' E.C. publications, drawn by the reputable Jack Davis.

Dr. Wertham was also distressed by the advertising in most comic books, particularly ads offering guns, knives, and whips for sale. "Comic book stories teach violence," he said; "the advertisements provide the weapons." He was concerned as well with the open race hatred shown in comic books. Heroes were always tall and regular-featured. Those they opposed, challenged, and frequently destroyed were "natives, primitives, savages, 'ape men,' Negroes, Jews, Indians, Slavs, Chinese, and Japanese, immigrants of every description, people with irregular features, swarthy skins, physical deformities."

To halt the excesses of kids' magazines, Dr. Wertham proposed laws that would restrict what could appear in children's comics and also would forbid the sale of crime comic books to young people. Unfortunately, this seemed too close to censorship. The *New York Times* said: "We think the comic books have on the whole had an injurious effect on children . . . , [but] public opinion will succeed in making the reforms needed. To wait for that to happen is far less dangerous than to abridge freedom of the right to publish."

Speaking for the National Cartoonist Society, Walt Kelly and Milton Caniff issued a statement reading: "The National Cartoonist Society views as unwarranted any additional legislative action that is intended to censor printed material. . . . We believe the offensive material can be weeded from the mass of worthwhile publications by the exercise of existing city, state, and federal laws. . . . We believe good material outsells bad. We believe people, even juveniles, are fundamentally decent. We believe, as parents and as one-time children ourselves, that most young people are instinctively attracted to that which is wholesome. Our belief in this sound commercial theory is only in our addition to our belief in the free expressions and the noble traditions of our profession."

The comic book publishers did not seemingly share the NCS' belief in the fundamental decency of people, at least not of people in the funny book business, and they now regrouped as the Comics Magazine Association of America and drafted a more thorough code, one with over three dozen provisions. This code was tougher about the depiction of crime and horror and also prohibited the advertising of knives, concealable weapons, and realistic gun facsimiles. By this time local restrictions and boycotts by newsdealers, distributors, and parents were causing serious trouble. An editor who was with E.C. then told me that hundreds of thousands of copies of their magazines were being returned, whole bundles not even untied.

This automatic rejection of any magazine devoted to crime and horror prompted the code authority to suggest "restraint in the use of the word 'crime' in titles and subtitles," and that "no comic magazine shall use the word 'horror' or 'terror' in its title." Most of the major companies abided by the code, and self-regulation forestalled outside policing. The idea of a code diminished parental anxiety, though again it is less than comforting to think that children's entertainment is being created by editors, artists, and writers who have to be reminded that "all scenes of horror, excessive bloodshed, gory or gruesome crimes, depravity, lust, sadism, masochism shall not be permitted." The publishers who wouldn't, or couldn't, abide by the code dropped out, and the crime and horror fad faded. The present effectiveness of the code will be examined shortly.

Long before the fall of the comic book gangsters and graverobbers, the superheroes had declined. Now in the mid-1950's, as the surviving publishers dug out after the attacks of parents and critics, the masked men and caped avengers vanished almost completely. Captain Marvel, plagued by bad sales and the persistant Superman lawsuit, closed up shop. The field was left to Superman himself and the various Donenfeld spinoffs. The Superman character had been entirely a product of the publisher since 1948, when Siegel and Shuster had sued for a bigger share of royalties. After the settlement that followed, Siegel and Shuster lost all control of their character, their names were dropped from the feature, and the staff of assistants they'd helped organize took over. Both Jerry Siegel and Joe Shuster have spent their time since then trying alternately to create a new character as successful as Superman and to get back some part of the Superman empire. They haven't had much luck. Though they both live on Long Island, the partners have not seen each other for years. Siegel, tired of trying to repeat the Superman formula and of long periods of unemployment, is said to be back writing Superman scripts anonymously. Shuster lives with his mother in Forest Hills. He has never married because, he says, "I never met a girl who matched up to Lois Lane."

After superheroes the comic books tried toned-down crime and Western magazines, plus true love. The Marvel Comics Group did, too, but its chief editor, a script writer named Stan Lee, occasionally tried to revive the old Marvel hero properties—Captain America, the Human Torch, Sub Mariner—that had done so well during World War II. "I like Shakespeare more than anything. Everything there is on such a grand scale —so heroic," Lee has said in explaining his preoccupation with larger-than-life heroes. "I guess I'm corny at heart." Lee, who got his first writer credit with a Nazi-killing hero known as the Destroyer, persisted in his reincarnation efforts and eventually had a batch of superheroes on the stands at the exact moment a new fad was waiting to be born. The '60's brought in a nostalgia for the '30's, a fascination with camp and pop art, and a new generation of kids who were curious about what was being called the Golden Age of Comics. Lee's hyped-up heroes, art-directed by Captain America's creator, Jack Kirby, fit perfectly. *The Fantastic Four, The Incredible Hulk, The Amazing Spiderman, The Mighty Thor*, and, yet again, *Captain Amer-*

ica, The Human Torch, and *The Sub Mariner* attracted a continually growing audience.

While the Comics Magazine Association believes in the
comic book as an implement for inspiring and teaching children and an art form "vastly entertaining and instructive," its
individual members are not above abandoning teaching and
enlightening for a quick ride on the bandwagon. Sales of the
Stan Lee Marvel comics and the best-seller popularity of *Batman* on television led to a renaissance. National Periodical
Publications, the present title of the Superman-D.C. outfit, re-
activated dozens out of its mothball fleet of superheroes. New
muscle men mingled with old on the magazine stands: the
Black Hood, the Blue Beetle, Thunderbolt, Captain Atom, the
Spirit, T.H.U.N.D.E.R. Agents, Fat Man, and the Peacemaker
("a man who loves peace so much that he is willing to fight
for it!"). A new golden age seemed to have arrived.

The acceleration of trends, the quick peaking characteristic
of the toy business, have spread to the comics magazine field.
The superhero fad of the middle 1960's expanded and con-
tracted more rapidly than any previous fad in comics, with the
exception of 3-D comic books, and publishers suddenly found
there wasn't room for one more. For many, the good times
lasted a year or two at best, leaving them over-extended and
over-spent. The union-suit hero craze died so soon several companies had their magazines refused shelf space. A few second-
string publishers dropped their hero line at a loss. For the
American Comic Group, a firm established in the 1940's, speculation in superheroes led to its extinction.

"We've managed to make ourselves the undisputed leaders
of the comics industry," Marvel Comic Group editor Stan Lee
told his readers in 1968. "We doubt that any group of magazines has ever before been so imitated, so universally acclaimed,
so zealously supported by its fans!—No, strike that word!
You're more than fans! Much more! We've always thought

of you as friends—and we always will!" For these friends Lee produces over a dozen comic book titles, including *The Fantastic Four, Spiderman, X-Men, Sgt. Fury and His Howling Commandos, Captain America,* and *Nick Fury, Agent of S.H.I.E.L.D.* He also sells Marvel Super-Hero T-Shirts ("only $1.60 each"), Marvel sweat shirts ($3.15), and memberships in the Merry Marvel Marching Society fan club ("for the paltry sum of $1.00"). *Esquire* has reported, "Should anybody still suspect that children are the only Marvel readers, it might be pointed out that the company has sold 50,000 printed T-shirts and 30,000 sweat shirts, and it has run out of adult sizes of both."

Much of the enthusiasm for the Stan Lee product has been on campuses, where students, apparently sharing Lee's style of expression and gift for put-on, have told him things like, "We think of Marvel Comics as the Twentieth Century mythology and you as this generation's Homer." Lee shares this view, how seriously it's hard to tell, and a recent British interviewer says, "He sees the superhero fantasies as fulfilling the same function that myths, legends, and tales of romance and fairy stories did for earlier generations." The appeal to college-age people is attributed to this myth quality and the tragic flaws Stan Lee has built into his heroes. "Spiderman, in real life a college student named Peter Parker, is guilt-ridden, money-conscious, socially insecure, and gets blamed for things he didn't do," explains *Esquire.* "The Fantastic Four are always quarreling among themselves. Thor's father won't let him marry the girl he loves, and the Hulk is totally alienated. This, plus a tongue-in-cheek approach, which takes more than a third-grade education to appreciate, is Marvel's appeal."

After blurbs like this it's disappointing to look into the Marvel magazines themselves. The heroes there are not only flawed, they are, in many cases, flaming psychopaths. The tongue-in-cheek humor often comes while the hero is getting, or giving, a kick in the face. In one recent issue of *The Mighty* *Thor*, for example, the hero himself is dead on the opening page. This seems to be the result of an attack by a musclebound villain known as the Wrecker. (Lee's continuities, by the way, ramble on from issue to issue and are laced with references to the past. Besides being Homer, he's also the Proust of the funnies.) Hela, goddess of death, shows up now, decked out like a psychedelic drag queen, and tries to take Thor's astral self. Meanwhile, in the cavern kingdom of the Norns, a knight named Balder is impaled against a tree by a giant barbaric warrior. Balder survives, has a two-page battle with the warrior, and ends up smashing the barbarian's head. The Wrecker all this while is smashing streets and buildings with a giant crowbar, while half a dozen policemen shoot at him. Balder, meanwhile, is shot with a blowgun and trussed up on a rolling catapult device and delivered to the enchanted chamber of the Queen of the Trolls. The queen then sends an indestructible robot to the world of humans, and he has a two-page fight with the Wrecker.

After the Wrecker breaks his crowbar over the robot's head, the robot, whose name is the Destroyer, gives him a judo chop in the head and a shot of electricity in the stomach. The Wrecker cries "Arrgghh!" and falls over. Thor, who seems to be alive now, cries out, "The Destroyer hath returned!" He challenges the Destroyer to a battle to the death, not realizing the Queen of the Trolls has placed the living ego of Thor's girlfriend inside the robot. The episode ends at this point, followed by a full page ad for the latest Verve record by Frank Zappa and the Mothers of Invention.

Most of the drawing in the Marvel magazines, no matter who the artist, is heavy with forced perspectives and exaggerated figure work. Heroes and villains loom gigantic and seem to be all torso and ropey muscles. In the issue of Lee's *Daredevil* on sale alongside the Thor we've just skimmed, the

20-page adventure is almost exclusively a loud and vicious fight between two of these distorted giants. One of Stan Lee's current preoccupations is the transmigration of souls, and here the hero and the villain have had their mental essences exchanged. The bad guy is a cloaked robot named Dr. Doom (Lee is strong on myths, weak on names), and he has a gang of musclebound hoods in his employ.

The plot notion, perhaps one of Lee's humorous touches, is that while Dr. Doom is walking around with his essence in Daredevil's body, his own men jump him and beat him up. This battle takes two-and-a-half pages, with the Daredevil figure being slammed into the pavement and then having fists smash into him. He kicks one of the heavies in the face and is able to convince the men he's not what he seems, but actually Dr. Doom. Younger readers, who haven't yet achieved a third-grade education and don't know much about mental essence transference, might assume it's the hero who has been kicking people in the face. When the thugs realize their mistake, they rush and find the Dr. Doom figure, who is really Daredevil inside, and beat him up for three pages. They drop-kick him in the head, pummel him (in close-ups and long shots), and are finally stopped by the police. The episode ends with a four-page confrontation between hero and villain, themselves again, that ends with Daredevil smashing the mind-transfer machine with an axe. This yarn is followed by an ad for a mansize karate dummy.

The high point in the Marvel line, at this writing, is the magazine featuring Nick Fury, Agent of S.H.I.E.L.D. Fury is a tough talking operative for the Supreme Headquarters International Espionage Law-enforcement Division, whose members have little resemblance to any of the other initial groups like U.N.C.L.E. The S.H.I.E.L.D. staff has gotten as far from being plainclothes operatives as you can under current postal regulations.

Dr. Wertham was chided for finding homosexual elements in the superheroes of the 1950's, and possibly it would be safer to avoid such comparisons now. Still, Nick Fury's costume resembles nothing quite as much as those tight leather outfits worn by the characters on the homosexual and fetish magazines they keep under glass in cigar stores. On the cover of a recent issue of his half-a-million-circulation monthly, Nick Fury is presented in a skintight leather suit. He wears black leather boots and white leather gloves, has a knife strapped to his calf, another piece of gear strapped to his thigh, a holster strapped to his shoulder, two unspecified belts across his chest, a bracelet around his right bicep, and a pistol two feet long squeezed in his fist. He also wears a black eye patch on his left eye. His male companions are similarly decked out, and the one girl in the group is shown charging at the reader in a cutdown version of the basic uniform, more skin and fewer belts. In the background is a large American flag.

The Fury adventure inside this particular issue, a story titled *Armageddon!*, begins with a full-page drawing of a barechested Chinese FBI agent holding the dead body of his girlfriend, a victim of the Oriental villain Yellow Claw, who can be seen in the distance. The Yellow Claw is an updated sinister Oriental, looking as Fu Manchu would if he joined the Hell's Angels.

The death of the girl inspires Nick Fury to go wild, and the next four pages are given over to one gigantic fight scene. The Claw's minions are as fond of tight clothes and straps as the Shield bunch, and are given to attacking with claw-covered maces. To keep the Claw from making a getaway "into the space-time continuum beyond human reach," Fury breaks into the Claw's secret den and faces him. Several of the panels are buttocks views of one or the other of the protagonists, one scene uses Fury's widespread muscular legs to frame the action. Fury now rips off his eye patch and gives the Claw a psychedelic evil eye, which causes the Asian to explode and spill his insides all over the floor. To Fury's surprise the Claw turns out to be a robot.

There's nothing in the comics code that forbids freaking out, and apparently the code administrators don't think whips and boots and the other fetishes of the underground should be ruled out as sadistic and masochistic. Since smashing in the head of a robot doesn't cause bloodshed, and a boot kicked in the face of a human being is standard practice in all the entertainment media, there's probably nothing officially wrong with the Merry Marvel group. But I don't believe that if Homer or the Brothers Grimm transferred minds with Stan Lee they'd produce this kind of junky storm-trooper entertainment.

Though National Periodicals had kept Superman dull, talky, and middle-aged for years, they have lately shaken up their staff and in the late 1960's many of their comics are close to the Stan Lee style. The cover of the Christmas 1967 issue of *Batman*, for instance, shows the hero flat on his back while two formidable women in boots, masks, and skin-tight uniforms argue over who will get him. "You'll take Batman to your catacombs over my dead body, Cat Woman," says the girl on the left. "Have it your own way, Batgirl," the Cat Woman replies. In her hand she is holding a long whip, the coils of which are wrapped around the prone Batman's leg.

National has revived old superheroes such as The Spectre. The latest version of this feature is full of mind swaps, judo chops, fists in the face, and enormous male torsos. The issue I'm looking at has "Die, Spectre! Again—and again—and again!" written bold across the cover. Going the Spectre one better is National's newer hero, Deadman. Deadman comes by his name because he is dead. He was a circus aerialist and someone murdered him. "It started with the crack of a rifle and a burning fire in his chest!" the comic book tells us. "Arrgh! I've been shot," says aerialist Boston Brand. Artist Neal Adams spares his kid readers from actual bloodshed by drawing Brand from behind and showing his body spread-eagled and quivering on the moment of bullet impact.

The continuing theme of Deadman is the search of Brand's ghost for his murderer. He, too, can send his mental essence into the bodies of others. Whoever Deadman takes over then becomes involved in ferocious battles with the current suspect. The clashes between hunter and quarry involve kicks in the face, attempted stranglings, giant close-ups of fists hitting agonized faces, victims being thrown off buildings. This knock-down, brutish violence can be found in most of the National adventure titles now. The fetish element has been strongest with the Green Lantern, who with his skin-tight two-tone vinyl costume, white gloves, green boots, and green finger ring is the most fetching of the surviving supermen.

All these current superheroes and muscle men, unlike many of the simpleminded do-gooders of the 1940's comic books, are arrogant in their power. Often as corrupt as their enemies, their pride and their exaggerated strength is of the kind used by empty and doubt-ridden people. "The person who feels weak becomes a bully," says psychologist Rollo May, "the inferior person the braggart; a flexing of muscles, much talk, cockiness, an endeavour to brazen it out, are symptoms of covert anxiety in a person or a group. Tremendous pride was exhibited in fascism, as everyone knows who has seen the pictures of the strutting Mussolini and the psychopathic Hitler." Anyone who has looked through one drugstore rack of current comics will see the same kind of flexing and strutting heroes.

The comic books of the 1960's have muted and disguised some of the impulses of the 1950's and there is less open blood-letting, but Dr. Fredric Wertham is still concerned. In 1966 he wrote: "The mass media Superman is a symbol of power, force, and violence. The rationalization is that he imposes pun-ishment. . . . Superman, like Oswald, can choose all by himself who the proper adversary is. He is above all democratic law.

In the child's mind a hostile world is created." Since the comic book is a product, we can expect that if the newer kind of heroes remain successful there will be more of them coming off the assembly line.

The majority of the comic books surviving today are of the muscle hero and war hero types. They may be much admired by college students and collected as fad objects by middle-aged readers, but they are not for kids at all. Younger children can buy all the Furys and Avengers they want, but they are really peeking in at somebody else's entertainment. While the comic book can never be a substitute for literature, it could certainly be an entertaining kind of trash for kids. In many of the large countries of the world—France, Italy, England, for example—comic format magazines specifically for kids are produced. They are usually well done, excellently drawn and beautifully printed. In our country, with the exception of a few funny animals hanging on from the past, it is all monsters and superheroes. The Comics Magazine Association talks often about the educational values inherent in comic books, about how they can be a stimulus to learning to read and learning about the world. They never mention the lessons really being taught, the kind given by Stan Lee and the artists and writers in the Marvel bullpen.

11. Delicious and Nutritious

> If a man has all his life been fed a combination of marzipan and ethyl alcohol—if eating, to him, is a matter of being knocked unconscious by an ice cream soda—can he, by taking thought, come to prefer a diet of bread and wine, apples and well-water?
>
> RANDALL JARRELL
> *A Sad Heart At The Supermarket*

Strange things blossom in the artificial air of the supermarket. Not foods, but food products. Items. Over seven thousand new food items have been born in the Sixties. To the food industry, food is merely a means, a raw material. Metal, wood, vinyl, food. The basic purposes of food are not as important as what it can be made into, what can be said about the result. "The American public each year not only wants a constantly wider range of product, size, and brand, but is more able to buy and try the new and different," says a grocery industry spokesman, adding that young, under-30 people are the most frequent buyers of new food products. This is natural, since 20 years of intense television advertising has endeavored to persuade children that food can be bought as casually as toys or any other mass product.

Good processed food exists in quantity and balanced eating is still possible. But there has been too much romancing of negligible foods. Too many dubious and outright false statements about nutrition have been taught and implied. There are too many openly slipshod and dangerous processing prac-

212

tices. In spite of all the care and quality in some areas, these negative gifts of the food industry and the supermarket have been the ones most often heaped upon children. They have helped to bring about in this country a situation in which the older a child gets, the poorer his diet becomes; where the middle-class middle-income child is usually overfed and undernourished; where one of the major problems of children when they reach their teens is obesity and overweight. Food habits are set early. A child who escapes the out-and-out poisons and hazards of mass food will still, because of the early eating patterns the food advertisers have drummed into him, run a risk of heart disease and other physical complications. The odds against a child are large, the chance of escaping all the traps and dangers is small.

Because of the commercial exaggerations, dubious proclamations, and not infrequent untruths surrounding mass-produced food, such simple concepts as good nutrition and proper diet get lost. "Good nutrition is not complicated," says Dr. Frederick J. Stare, who heads Harvard's nutrition department. "Everything that is required is in everyday foods . . . in splendid and varied profusion: minerals and vitamins, proteins and carbohydrates, foods with low fat and foods with high fat, foods for all ages and for all needs." Even though the Department of Agriculture's chart of basic and essential foods has been seen by practically everyone in America, there is still a strong notion, certainly encouraged by many of the manufacturers of food aimed at children, that the chart was made up chiefly to decorate schoolroom walls and has no other value. But these foods really are essential and there is, as yet, no way to get an adequate diet without relying on all of them.

Before we consider the abundant pile of false nutrition knowledge that's been built up by the processed food makers, let's take another look at the basic foods and what they are supposed to provide kids with.

The Department of Agriculture breaks food down into the meat group, milk group, vegetable and fruit group, and bread and cereal group. It is the recommendation of the Department, as well as of most dieticians and nutritionists, that a child needs two or more servings a day of meat, fish, poultry, or eggs; four or more servings of vegetables and fruits; four or more servings of bread and cereal; and three to four glasses of milk. Simply in terms of calories, a child of 3 needs, according to the National Academy of Science's recommended daily allowances, 1300 calories a day. A 7-year-old needs 2100 calories. By the first teen year, a girl requires 2600 and a boy 3100 calories.

Children must also have proteins, vitamins, and minerals, usually in amounts that are larger in proportion to their body weight than those needed by adults. A child of 3 should have 40 grams of protein daily, a child of 10 needs 70 grams. Protein is essential to the building and repairing of all body tissues. The best sources of complete protein are milk, meat, eggs, fish, and poultry. Miriam E. Lowenberg, head of the Pennsylvania State nutrition department at the time she contributed a chapter to the Agriculture Department's explicitly titled *Food*, says: "The child needs one good serving of meat, poultry, or fish at least one meal each day. The amount may vary from a 2-ounce portion for children 1 to 4 years old to a man-size serving of at least one-fourth pound for the hungry child of 6 to 13 years."

From fruits and vegetables a child gets vitamins and minerals, that he needs; from the cereals and bread he gets carbohydrates, needed for energy and to allow the body to utilize nutrients from other foods for their basic purposes. The dairy foods give calcium, Vitamin D, and other valuable nutrients.

Considerably opposed to the recommendations of the nutrition and diet experts is the philosophy of much of the kid food business. The philosophy of eating espoused in far too many commercials is false nutrition, often used to sell false products,

products that have low food value, or products that can be dangerous in the long run—and sometimes dangerous at once. While a balanced diet is economically possible for at least two-thirds or more of our children, many of them aren't getting it. Instead they are being filled with false information and empty calories. In recent years, for example, the overall consumption of fats and sugars has risen until these foods furnish a third of all the calories available for consumption in the average diet in America.

One of the consequences of the false notions promoted by kid food makers is the increasing prevalence of what can be called affluent malnutrition. "We Americans are the *most*-fed people in the world, but not necessarily the *best*-fed or the healthiest," says nutrition expert Dr. Robert S. Goodhart. "Malnutrition is not confined to cases of under-nutrition or outright starvation. It means 'bad nutrition'—this can apply to the overfed as well as the underfed." This overstuffed and underfed condition is a particularly American problem. In the developing countries, up to half of the children die before their fifth birthday and 7 out of 10 of all these children suffer from some form of basic malnutrition. In Latin America, Libya, Vietnam, the children simply do not have enough to eat. In the midst of all this, in a world of starvation, most American children eat plentifully. Though even in America there are several million children quietly starving to death. But for the children who eat plentifully, it is usually the wrong kind of plenty.

Studies of the diet of children and teenagers, reported by the U.S. Department of Agriculture, show that 6 out of every 10 girls and 4 out of every 10 boys have poor diets—diets which provide only two-thirds or less of the nutrients recommended for their age. The biggest reason for the undernourishment of most American children is the growing consumption of foods which provide empty calories. "Empty calories—foods made up chiefly of fat, sugar, and starches," explains the Agriculture Department, "have small amounts of vitamins, minerals, and protein in proportion to the calories."

As children in the United States mature, their diet grows worse, reaching a low point with the average teenage girl. The teenage girl is the poorest fed member of the family, undernourished and frequently obese. "More older girls are overweight than younger girls," according to the Agriculture Department, with studies showing that "19 percent of Iowa girls aged 9 were overweight. This increased to 44 percent of the 16-year-olds. In Oregon about 39 percent, and in Washington and Maine 25 percent of the 16-year-old girls were overweight. Sometimes this corrects itself as the adolescent body readjusts, but the amount of overweight is far too high."

The *Consumer Bulletin* has stated that sugar and starches today commonly provide as much as 50 percent of the calories in the average American diet, with fats making up another 40 percent. "Sugar, common starchy foods, and commercial fats are all highly unnatural foods," in the opinion of the *Bulletin*. "Though constituting 90 percent of the intake, they provide less than one-twentieth of the essential nutrients." The popularity of empty calories is on the rise, as Peter Wyden reported in his *The Overweight Society*. The use of sugar, starches, all fats is climbing, while consumption tables show that "foods that are highly recommended for low-fat, anticholesterol diets performed indifferently or worse. Fish consumption dropped . . . veal eating plunged precipitously. . . . Most remarkable is what happened to fruits and vegetables. . . . Total consumption of fresh, canned and frozen vegetables fell," and the eating of fresh fruit dropped from the late 1940's to the early 1960's by over 50 pounds per person.

Obesity in children is rarely caused by a glandular disorder (in one study of obese children, only 2 cases out of 400 were found to have a glandular cause), but by overeating, usually of the empty calorie kind. A strong push toward this eating pattern, aside from the personal emotional causes, comes from the vast and incessant advertising of the sweet and empty foods. Our affluent malnutrition is encouraged by the same ads and commercials.

The Mars Candy Company, as one of many examples, advertises its Milky Way bar on kid shows as "the good food candy bar," although the candy bar's most prominent ingredients, as shown on the wrapper, are milk chocolate, corn syrup, and sugar. Coca-Cola promotes its Hi-C as being high in Vitamin C and implies it's as good for children as orange and other fruit juices. According to Sidney Margolius, Hi-C has 60 percent less Vitamin C than canned orange juice. Most drinks of this type are water and sugar with fruit flavoring, and many times the fruit flavoring is artificial. It is possible to buy, and perfectly legal to manufacture, a fruit drink containing no natural fruit at all. A big tie-in advertising promotion in 1968 was one teaming Hi-C and Kellogg's Pop-Tarts, which we'll meet again in the next chapter. This Pop 'N' Pour promotion suggested Pop-Tarts and a glass of Hi-C as an enjoyable snack, stressing the fact that both products have real fruit flavor. Pop-Tarts are mostly flour and shortening, Hi-C is mostly water. The emphasizing of their minimal connection with real fruit is one of many examples of the flimsy nutrition championed in the food advertising directed at children.

A diet heavy in sugars and starches is not only bad for the child when he is in the process of growing up, it can determine what his adult life will be like. "Heart disease is highest in countries where fatty and starchy and sugary foods are cheap and plentiful," says *Consumer Bulletin*. The commercials for snacks, sweets, and starchy foods aimed at children exaggerate and heighten what is already a less than satisfactory national eating pattern. Furthermore, a great deal of the advertising aimed at mothers strives to equate love with rich foods and pastry. "Someone wonderful just baked Toll House cookies," reads a Nestle's headline in one recent ad in women's magazines. The picture shows two grateful children munching the cookies. General Foods runs numerous Baker's Chocolate ads which show giant rich cakes juxtaposed with photos of pleased kids. One of their typical child-pleasing frosting recipes calls for 6 squares of chocolate, 5 tablespoons of butter, and 6½ cups of sugar. The Pillsbury people have of course spent millions of advertising dollars preaching the doctrine that love is something you bake in the oven.

The food makers' love of sugars, starches, and grains has a less than spiritual basis. Carbohydrates are among the cheapest ingredients for food products, capable of being stretched and advertised into massive profits.

Promoted as incessantly as love is protein. "Kids think it's treat food, but it's protein food," Chef Boy-Ar-Dee tells mothers in slick magazine ads. "Just one serving of Chef Boy-Ar-Dee Spaghetti and Meat Balls has more protein than most lunchtime soups or sandwiches." In advertising statements such as this, the good grey Chef is managing the facts, counting on working sales magic with the word "protein." What a can of spaghetti and meat balls gives kids most of is carbohydrates. The protein present is mostly vegetable protein which, while valuable and usable in diet, is not the same as meat protein. The standard 15-ounce can of the chef's supposed protein food contains only four small meatballs—padded with crackermeal—from which a kid could get any meat protein. Most food charts list an 8-ounce serving of canned spaghetti and meatballs as providing a total of only 10.7 grams of protein of all kinds.

The average cheeseburger, a fairly common lunchtime sandwich, provides a child with between 30 and 35 grams of protein, over 20 of those grams coming from the meat. A plain tuna sandwich using only one ounce of fish will give over 12 grams of protein with much less fat than either the canned spaghetti and meatballs or the hamburger. And while a bowl of most canned soups does give only half the protein of the canned spaghetti and meatballs, there is usually much less carbohydrate present. By not giving any actual weights or measures, by not specifying what sandwiches and soups the product is being compared with, and by not differentiating between kinds of protein, advertisements for a processed food like this can usually give the impression that it is much more valuable and healthful than it really is.

Protein source foods containing all the essential amino acids are classified as offering complete protein. "For the body to build a protein, all the required amino acids for it must be available at the same time. If even one acid is missing, the body will not build that protein, and will allow the other amino acids to be converted into energy and fat, rather than storing them for future tissue synthesis," writes Dr. Harold Aaron in *The Medicine Show*. "Many amino acids can be manufactured within the body, but there are at least ten which can't be made in the body and therefore must be present in the diet. They are generally called the essential amino acids." The best sources of these essential amino acids are animal-derived foods such as meat, fish, milk, and eggs. Peas, beans and peanuts can be useful substitutes. Cereal grains and most vegetables, because they are usually lacking some of the amino acids, must be supplemented by meat and dairy sources of protein. Cereal foods, of which spaghetti is one, are mainly sources of carbohydrates. If they are eaten to the exclusion of other protein sources, their protein cannot be efficiently put to use by kids' bodies. This applies to high-protein breakfast cereals and breads as well.

Miracles from a single food, though they may come with the close of our century, do not exist. Still, they are constantly being promised or intimated. Wonder Bread has been engaged in polite miracle huckstering for years. "Every delicious slice of Wonder Bread is carefully enriched with foods for growing bodies and minds," Wonder tells prospective customers in full-page magazine ads. All enriched white bread is essentially the same, and most supermarket bread is enriched. A slice of enriched white bread gives your child 60 calories, 2 grams of cereal protein, and 6 times that much starch and sugar, a trace of Vitamin A and ascorbic acid, plus some iron, thiamine, niacin, and riboflavin. Wonder Bread can not contribute any more to growth than any other enriched bread, especially since it's mostly fuel food. No food now known to science can do anything for your kids' minds, and that part of the Wonder Bread claim is, at best, meaningless. Perhaps they feel the polka dots on their wrapper provide an artistic experience.

Spreading false nutrition and selling hollow foods can be harmful, often in slow quiet ways, but there are much worse things happening. One of the most dangerous assaults on childhood has come from the meat industry, and the Wholesome Meat Act of 1967 provides only a partial defense. The deceptive and harmful practices of meat packers and processors have always been particularly easy to get away with in the making of the meat products most favored by children—hot dogs, hamburger, and lunch meat. "Contaminated meat, horsemeat, and meat from sick animals originally intended for dog and cat food has ended up in hamburger and processed meat," Ralph Nader reported in 1967. "Eyeballs, lungs, hog blood and chopped hides and other indelicate carcass portions are blended skillfully into baloney and hot dogs." A Department of Agriculture study of non-federally inspected meat plants done five years earlier found, as summed up by Washington newspaper man Nick Kotz, "unbelievably foul sanitary conditions, the use of diseased animals, adulteration of meat products, and labeling practices which mislead consumers as to the contents of luncheon meats, wieners, and sausage." And the international vice president of the Amalgamated Meat Cutters said last year that "it is impossible for the consumer to be able to tell what meat is in ground hamburger and processed salami."

Current technology has not led to improvements in meat products, but, in many cases, only to more and better ways to cover up shoddy practices. "Modern chemicals and drugs completely nullify the usual tests of sight and smell with respect to meat," said Senator Joseph Montoya, author of the meat inspection bill finally put through Congress. Ralph Nader elaborates: "Meat is doped with aureomycin as a substitute for sanitation, and detergents are applied to freshen up unfit meat. . . . It takes specialists to detect the deception. What is more, these chemicals themselves introduce new and complicated hazards." The artificial smoking and coloring agents used in processed meats and the numerous additives are, in the words of the Deputy Assistant Secretary of Agriculture, "potentially deceptive and dangerous to one's health when their use is not regulated."

The excesses and suspected excesses leading to the stronger meat inspection laws were not limited to small-time meat packers. "Brand names and labels provide no protection. The largest meat packing companies in the nation have established plants doing business only within a state and therefore escape the stringent requirements of federal meat inspection which products from their other operations must undergo," Senator Montoya said late in 1967. "For example, the meat industry's big three—Swift & Co., Wilson & Co., and Armour & Co.— have admitted operating more than 100 intrastate meat plants which slaughter, process, and prepare millions of pounds of meat each year without federal inspection." Operating an uninspected plant within a state allowed for the use of lower quality meat and gave a competitive advantage. An official of one big meat company admitted, off the record to Nick Kotz, that "his company could not compete effectively in the sales of luncheon meats in several important markets if the company's branch plants had to meet federal requirements for sausage and wiener ingredients."

The unsanitary conditions, adulterations, and high chance of contamination that have long existed in many meat-packing plants came about because most state regulations and requirements have never been as strict as those of the United States Department of Agriculture. "At present, few if any state inspection systems match the federal one," *Consumer Reports* said in 1968, "especially in its insistence on continuous inspection of all slaughter and processing; 22 states do not yet require meat inspection of any kind." Before the Wholesome Meat Act was passed, a national packer could open a plant in a state and as long as he sold his product only within the state he would not have to meet any federal standards or, in some cases, any standards at all. The only consistent thing about a brand of hot dogs advertised nationally might be the label and trademark.

The bill passed in 1967, against tremendous pressure from almost the entire meat industry, gives the Secretary of Agriculture the right to put his inspectors into any meat plant, whether its products are intended for interstate or intrastate use. However, those meat plants which manufacture only for sale within a state can be inspected by the USDA only if the state fails to bring its own standards up to those of the Agriculture Department. And the states and meat plants have two or three years to do this. "Two or three more years of putting chopped eyeballs, hides, and all kinds of other things in the meat," commented Senator Neal Smith, also active in the fight against bad meat. The contamination and lack of sanitation will probably continue for awhile—while the incidence of diseases like salmonellosis, with symptoms similar to those of intestinal flu, continue to increase. "The rapid growth of new frozen food products and 'ready to serve' dishes that are eaten following short cooking periods," Nadar has said, "are increasing the danger of trichinosis and other bacterial diseases."

There are many other less than comforting things that can happen to meat as it becomes a product, most of them still legal. For one thing, meat can be stretched. The federal regulations allow a processor to add varying percentages of extenders to the product. Hot dogs, for instance, can be up to 3.5 percent cereal, starch, or nonfat dry milk, so long as the package label says so. Franks and lunch meat can also be as much as 10 percent water and pass government inspection. A 1964 sampling of hot dogs, conducted by *Consumer Reports* in New York state, found up to 9.5 percent extender in some products. There was cereal and nonfat dry milk in franks sold as "all beef." Ham, thanks to pressure and court action taken by the big packers, can now be as much as 16 percent water. This doesn't mean just the natural moisture in the meat. Packers often inject water into the ham, thereby increasing its weight.

Nowhere is meat more disguised and extended than in the TV dinner, another product with a large kid following. Here the USDA permits all sorts of stretching. Salisbury steak can be part cereal, fish sticks can be as little as 51 percent fish, meatballs can have water as their second most important ingredient. In some frozen turkey dinners there is less than 25 percent turkey. "A famous TV dinner of 'meat loaf with potatoes and peas' lists ingredients in order of importance as potatoes, tomatoes, beef, peas, skim milk, and water," says Sidney Margolius in *The Innocent Consumer Vs. the Exploiters.* "The real cost of this 11-ounce package is almost $1 a pound, for a meat-loaf dinner that is more loaf than meat."

In a large sampling of TV dinners carried on by *Consumer Reports* in 1967 the conclusion was that most of the dinners didn't even provide the minimum amount of meat suggested by nutritionists. "Home economists generally accept a portion of cooked lean meat weighing 2.5 to 3.5 ounces as a standard serving," said the consumer magazine. Sometimes even more is recommended for growing kids. Testing of the meat portions in 75 different dinners showed that hardly any of them, except the frozen chicken dinners, came near to furnishing 3.5 ounces of meat. The average for sliced beef was below 3 ounces, for turkey below 2 ounces. Some Salisbury steaks weighed in at 3 ounces, but an unknown portion of that is cereal filler. The amount of actual meat included in all TV dinners has dropped steadily in the past decade. Not only don't TV dinners provide enough protein and nutrients, they don't provide even enough calories. According to calorie charts prepared by the Smith Kline & French laboratories, a complete meat loaf TV dinner gives only 370 calories, a complete Swiss steak only 250.

TV dinners present problems beyond their relatively low food value. There is considerable mishandling of these frozen products as they travel from packager to supermarket. "They may be shipped or delivered to stores in un-refrigerated trucks," states *Consumer Reports*. "Left standing for hours on a ware-house loading platform, or at a back door of the food store, or in the supermarket aisles waiting to be loaded into display cabinets. And they may be kept in those cabinets for long periods at well above 0°F." Any, or all, of such practices can result in mold, rot, and increased bacteria content. A frozen meat handling code may develop yet as a result of the 1967 meat act. But this is not, at the moment, certain.

There are numerous other foods beside meat which can be stretched, extended, and added to. As an illustration, take peanut butter. As of now the FDA hasn't ruled on what exactly peanut butter is. A few years ago Procter & Gamble's Jif peanut butter was found to be 75 percent peanuts and almost 25 percent Crisco. The Food and Drug Administration tried to make a 95 percent peanut content necessary before a product can be legally called peanut butter. This suggestion was met with much opposition in the peanut butter field, and the percentage is now hovering around 90 percent. The quantity of peanuts in this product will effect the amount of protein available in each jar, and vegetable fat is not much of a nutrient.

Water is another frequent ingredient in food products. Cheese and cheese spread in jars have been known to contain as much as 60 percent water, and obviously much less food value than you'd expect in real cheese. Corn syrup and cornstarch are regular additions to kid foods such as jam and pies. The U.S. Food and Drug Administration requires that jams and preserves be only 45 percent fruit or fruit juice, the rest is usually sugar or corn syrup. Mass-product pies, especially frozen, have been continually cutting down on fruit and boosting the amount of fill, often cornstarch.

Water and corn syrup are the least dangerous of the additives now present in most of the supermarket foods children are eating. There are several thousand chemicals allowed for use in processed foods: thickeners, bleaches, dyes, stabilizers, artificial flavors, emulsifiers, preservatives, and anti-mold agents. "Any distinctly new type of food is fairly certain to be unsafe in some respect," believes the *Consumer Bulletin*. "There have been numerous cases in which a one-time 'safe' material has later turned out to be toxic or carcinogenic."

Among the most controversial of the newer additives are the artificial sweeteners. "All synthetic sweeteners (saccharin, cyclamates) are drugs; they have no food value and their safety has not been established," reported *Consumer Bulletin* in 1967. "No synthetic sugar substitute should be used regularly, except under the direction of a physician. The Food and Drug Administration does *not* permit the use of artificial sweeteners in cereals and candy (except as a dietetic food). . . . It is not yet clear whether the cyclamates have a direct toxic effect or cause some kind of interference with the absorption of nutrients in the gastro-intestinal tract. So-called low-calorie beverages are not suitable for children."

But the cyclamates are much cheaper than sugar, and they are used in sweet drinks quite openly intended for children. Pillsbury's Funny Face imitation drink mix has cartoon characters on the front of its packets, one for each flavor. Their artificial lemonade, for instance, says "Lefty Lemon" in large red letters on the front side of the package and features a goofy lemon-headed character in a baseball cap. Most anyone, particularly a child, would figure Pillsbury's Funny Face is a kid product. Yet on the back of the package, in the body of small-type descriptive copy, Pillsbury tells customers the sweeteners used in their product, calcium cyclamate and saccharin cyclamate, "should be used only by persons who must restrict their intake of ordinary sweets." General Foods is even more obvious about appealing to kids with their artificially sweetened version of Kool-Aid. They put Bugs Bunny on the front of the packet. The dutiful cautionary statement on the reverse side of the Kool-Aid package apparently satisfies the FDA. And funny faces and Bugs Bunnys on the front make sure the kids buy the stuff anyway.

Potentially harmful non-food products are plentiful in the supermarket, too. The cosmetic and toiletries industries are paying increasing attention to going after young children, and their products are virtually uncontrolled by any government agency. The FDA can not inspect or regulate. The 1960 federal Hazardous Substances Labeling Act exempts cosmetics, so that no warning is required on a cosmetic which may contain a known and possibly fatal poison. The poison need not be identified on the label, no emergency directions need be given. As Toni Stabile indicates in her book *Cosmetics: Trick Or Treat*, not only adult products that can also be used by children (toothpaste, talcum, suntan lotion, shampoo, etc.), but products specifically aimed at little girls (bubble bath, home permanents, and cosmetic play kits), can be marketed without any preliminary testing or inspection. And this even though ingredients

in shampoos, home permanents, soaps, and other such prepara-
tions have resulted in countless cases of poisoning, blindness,
and permanent disfigurement.

Dr. Bernard E. Conley, former Secretary of the AMA Committee on Toxicology, has said: "The most potentially hazardous ingredients in such products are the strongly alkaline
substances, metallic salts, and a multitude of organic chemicals.
. . . The toxic effects of these ingredients, especially on the very
young person, have been demonstrated clinically as well as
experimentally." As of now nothing is being done to effectively
control what goes into cosmetics and soaps, not even those that
are sold specifically for children. One of the larger manufacturers makes 4.5 million dollars a year from the sale of children's cosmetics alone. These industries will not, as I. F. Stone
has said of slumlords, volunteer to profit less.

Sharing shelf space with cosmetics are a number of supermarket kid drugs, medicines, and nostrums—some worthless,
some potentially lethal. The drug most frequently involved in
accidental poisoning of young children is aspirin. Each year
about 25 percent of all poison accidents involving children
under 5 are due to aspirin. One reason for this is the prevalence
of flavored aspirin for children. "The number of aspirin poison-
ings among children has mounted with the availability of such
products," says the Consumer Reports book *The Medicine
Show*. "Children apparently mistake it for candy."

Colds and sore throats have been a great source of inspiration to advertisers, with much of the cold-preventing claims
directed toward families with young children. Mouthwashes
like Listerine are fond of implying that if children gargle with
their product they will have fewer colds and sore throats. Listerine and similar product commercials can slip this nonsense
past the National Association of Broadcasters by having it
mouthed by matronly young actresses who preface their quack-
ery with lines like, "Now, Hazel, I'm no scientist, but I really

think Bobby and Nancy have had less colds since we started gargling with this stuff." Dexter Masters, formerly with *Consumer Reports*, points out that "proof of the effectiveness for products of this sort is hard to come by. Bacteria normally exist by the millions in the mouth and throat and are held in check by the natural defenses of the body tissues and fluids. Moreover, viruses belonging to the group known as adenoviruses probably cause upper respiratory infection more frequently than bacteria, and neither Micrin nor any other oral antiseptic destroys or inhibits them. Moreover again, if a sore throat is truly minor, no mouthwash is needed for that, and if a sore throat is major, no mouthwash will help, although it might delay treatment long enough for a strep throat to lead to rheumatic fever."

The makers of kid-aimed vitamins also like to insinuate that vitamin pills and capsules are effective against colds. Again, there is no evidence for implying this. Worse, the vitamin people continue to promote the notion that vitamins are a substitute for food. Miles Laboratories tells parents in magazine ads for their fruit-flavored Chocks vitamin tablets: "You may convince your children that all vegetables are good for them. But they still might not like them. And if they don't like them, they won't eat them. So to make up for the things they don't like, give them something they will like." True enough, Miles Labs admits in the small type that vitamins are not a replacement for food. But their ad is 80 percent illustration, and the illustration clearly implies that if children don't like vegetables, the perfect substitute is Chocks.

Advertising and promotion is particularly important to all supermarket drugs and sundries. "It is advertising that makes one branded goods company successful; another less so," explains *Forbes*. "Soap and aspirin may be 'low-cost' to the consumer, but they still sell for many times what they cost to produce. There is thus a big profit in them, but only for those companies that can build enough volume to justify a strong ad campaign." Not satisfied with reaching children and young people through television, many drug and cosmetic manufacturers rely heavily on giving away samples. Several firms are in the business of distributing these samples. One of the largest is Gift-Pax, Inc., which distributes millions of gift packages to students each year. Gift-Pax concentrates on college and high school, promising its clients that two million young men and women in high school "will receive your brand in hygiene classes and homerooms across the country and throughout the school year." A typical pack, for high school girls in this case, contains Bufferin, Hidden Magic hair spray, Head & Shoulders shampoo, and Tampax.

While children are important to every company with products on sale in the supermarket, to the food industry they are essential. The food processing industry is the largest in the nation, with Americans spending more than 100 billion dollars a year for food. Leading the lists of fastest-growing and most profitable companies are giants like Standard Brands, General Foods, Corn Products, Borden, and Campbell Soup. Kids as consumers are vital to all of them: to Standard Brands with its Royal puddings and gelatins and its Shake-A-Pudd'n; to General Foods with everything from Jell-o to Kool-Aid; to Corn Products who, besides controlling all of Best Foods, make Karo syrup, Skippy peanut butter, and Bosco. And if it weren't for kids, Campbell Soup wouldn't take in the over 700 million dollars it does each year. Not only does Campbell have 90 percent of the canned soup market, it owns Swanson and Franco-American and is thereby responsible for the TV dinner and Spaghetti-Os. "It's the first spaghetti children can eat neatly," Campbell's president says of this bland hybrid.

The breakfast food industry was the advance guard into the children's world. Most of the rest of the exploiters and false nutritionists of the food business came after them. The snap-crackle-pop tycoons will be covered in a separate chapter of their own. The mechanisms and ideals of the rest of the kid food and drink makers can be illustrated by examining a couple of other specimens.

Almost completely dependent on youth is the soft drink industry, a major portion of whose 3.5 billion dollars a year in sales are accounted for by the younger end of the population. "The essential nature of the business is quite simple," said *Wall Street Reports*. "Just add a sweetening agent and flavoring to water and market it either in bulk, cans, or bottles. The success of the operation lies in vigorous advertising and selling." The most vigorous and successful mammoth in the soft drink business is Coca-Cola, unquestioned leader in the field with annual gross sales of 900 million dollars. Next in line is PepsiCo, a soft drink complex with sales of over 500 million dollars coming from Pepsi-Cola, Diet Pepsi, Mountain Dew, and Fritos corn chips. When the Frito-Lay company was taken over, PepsiCo president Donald Kendall had a simple, logical explanation for diversifying into corn and potato chips. "Salted snacks," he said, "make people thirsty."

There are numerous soft drink makers in the United States, and more than 3,800 bottling plants, but Coca-Cola and Pepsi do 60 percent of the business, trailed by Canada Dry, Dr. Pepper, Royal Crown, and the New York American Beverage Co., which controls Hires Root Beer and the Dr. Brown delicatessen soft drinks. Since the end of the Korean War, with the increase in the number of Americans under 30 an important contributing factor, sales of soft drinks have more than doubled.

Several new trends have contributed to the great rise. The most important is, once again, diversification. New fruit flavors, some real, most artificial, have increased until soft drink sections now display some 40 different flavors. Chocolate-flavored soft drinks have been gaining momentum, with a 25 percent gain in sales in 1967 alone. Diet soft drinks have been the most impressively salable: 10 million cases of artificially sweetened soft drinks were consumed in 1960, ten times that many in 1963, and 200 million cases by 1964, and sales are still galloping upward. Low-calorie brands account for over 50 percent of the gains in total soft drink sales in the 1960's. The target for almost all soft drink advertising is the under-30 age group, with particular attention being paid to what *Television Age* magazine designates the 10-to-29-year-old age group. This is the major market for all soft drinks, regular and low calorie. Television is the major advertising medium used. In 1964 major bottlers spent 55 million dollars on TV advertising. Coke and Pepsi usually lead the list of the top hundred of all users of television spot commercials.

"The soft drink is not a serious thing. Nobody needs it," says PepsiCo's William C. Munro, vice president in charge of marketing. "But above all, this generation wants happiness. And the soft drink is a fun thing. It's connected with fun and happiness." Besides fun and happiness, what does the soft drink give to kids? At best, empty calories. A glass of regular Pepsi or Coke contains about a hundred sugar-derived calories. "This is the same number of calories provided by eight ounces of orange juice, which is an excellent source of ascorbic acid and other essential nutrients not present in the soft drink," points out nutrition professor E. W. McHenry. "It should be noted that eight ounces of skim milk, containing calcium, riboflavin, and high-quality protein, has a calorie value of 87," Dr. McHenry adds, hoping to reach all those teenage girls who think milk is too fattening to bother with.

Dr. Hazel E. Field, of Occidental College, says about soft drinks: "They are just an expensive way of getting sweetened water. If they do relieve fatigue more than any other form of sugar, the suspicion arises that they contain small amounts of caffeine or a similar drug. Some of the colas are said to be slightly habit-forming." The *Consumer Bulletin* goes further in its criticism. "Sugar soft drinks—along with alcohol and liquor—are now shown to be an important cause of liver damage. Cirrhosis, a dangerous inflammatory disease of the liver, is turning up even in teenagers who drink a good deal of soda pop," says the 1967 *Consumer Bulletin* annual. "For children, whose parents all too often think bottled sodas and even cola drinks, with their content of caffeine and teeth-eroding acids, must be harmless and refreshing as advertised, consumption of any soft drink is definitely undesirable."

The effects of caffeine on adults and children are still under investigation, with a link between coronary disease and caffeine consumption suspected. At a late 1967 symposium on human genetics held at the University of Chicago, Dr. Wolfram Ostertag, a German geneticist, said: "The possibility exists that caffeine is one of the most dangerous mutation-causing agents in man." He warned against the use of coffee and caffeine by pregnant women, "since it is known," said Dr. Ostertag, "that caffeine penetrates to the human germinal tissue and through the placental barrier to the human fetus."

The possible damaging effects of caffeine, and the fact that it is a mild poison, are well known in the soft drink industry. This has not led anyone to stop making cola, but it has given the competitors of Coke and Pepsi a clout to use against them. The faltering Canada Dry Company, with a tough new president borrowed away from the soap trade, went after Coke in the spring of 1968 with Sport Cola, said to be 99 percent caffeine-free. Canada Dry's president, David J. Mahoney, denies he's trying to hurt the big two cola makers. "We are simply trying to carve out our own niche in the cola market with a fun product," says Mahoney, whose company also produces Johnny Walker Scotch and Pedro Domecq brandy.

It is obvious from the market breakdown figures available that children are drinking a good percentage of the artificially sweetened low calorie drinks. The most-used sweetening agents used for the low calorie soft drinks are, again, the cyclamates—sodium cyclamate and calcium cyclamate. The earliest cyclamate on the market was the sugar substitute Succaryl, introduced in 1950. It was followed by many others, among them Sweet-10 which is now owned by Pillsbury. As we've seen, the cyclamates are much less expensive than sugar—about ten times cheaper. As with the use of cyclamates in the drink mixes and edible toys, the FDA insists all soft-drink use of them should be only by persons who must restrict their intake of ordinary sweets.

In 1966 *Consumer Reports* concluded, "More research is urgently needed before cyclamate can be pronounced safe for people of all ages and in all conditions of health." A decade earlier the National Academy of Science said of cyclamate, "There has not yet been extensive controlled study of its use by people in various physiological states. . . . There is a lack of data on the relation of body weight to response to specific dosage of cyclamate. . . . The possibility of deleterious effects in the case of lower bowel disease should be considered." Unfortunately, most of the research in recent years has been undertaken either by those, such as Abbott Laboratories, who manufacture cyclamates, or by the sugar industry. The Food and Drug Administration is said to be carrying out new studies of the artificial sweeteners, but, at this writing, no results have been made public. Studies done by the Wisconsin Alumni Research Foundation, and financed by the Sugar Research Foundation, showed that cyclamate affected the rate of growth and the general health and appetite of the experimental animals.

Mars, Inc., has the only president who has definitely been observed going down on his knees at board meetings and praying for candy bar sales, but the entire candy industry is anxious and zealous in one way or another. The big companies are competing for an annual sales intake of a billion and a half dollars. Sales of candy have risen steadily for over a decade. Each

American—and particularly the young ones—is now consuming an average of between 18 and 20 pounds of candy a year. Candy bars account for 500 million dollars' worth of all candy sold, candy bars, with 10¢-bar sales jumping and 5¢-bar sales dropping. *Candy Industry*, a trade magazine that has long championed the cause of getting as much as you can for a bar, says of developments such as this: "There is no limit to what creative production and marketing can do for candy."

The leading direct outlets for candy bars are supermarkets and grocery stores. The growing sales of candy bars, and the growing importance of the supermarket as the place for these sales, is due to a much more aggressive use of advertising by many of the large candy makers. Mars is a heavy user of television, as are Nestle and Peter Paul. The Connecticut-based Peter Paul, Inc., recently doubled its advertising budget to 5 million dollars. Hershey, with the name "Hershey bar" long a generic for chocolate bar, has never done much advertising. Mars, Inc., already has 10 percent of all domestic candy sales and is still expanding (the company also makes M&M Candies and Uncle Ben's Rice), and Peter Paul's Mounds have begun to outsell the Hershey bar. This worries Hershey, some, and the company has already begun advertising campaigns in its Canadian markets.

The TV candy bar, like the TV toy before it, is becoming important, and company survival will now depend on the ability to compete with national television advertising. "The candy industry, made up of small, struggling companies," reported *Time* in the fall of 1967, "is astir with mergers and sellouts." The Pet Milk Company has absorbed the Whitman Candy organization, P. Lorillard Tobacco bought out Reed Candy, and the mergers are not yet over.

The candy industry's favorite crusade involves tooth decay. When implications that eating candy can result in cavities appear anywhere in the mass media, they are followed by charges that the candy makers are being used as "a whipping boy." Not even fellow television advertisers are safe from reprisal. When Bristol-Myers, for instance, aired a commercial which "makes the comment that if a person resists candy, soft drinks, and ice cream, and uses Fact Toothpaste regularly, then tooth decay will be reduced," the trade papers of the candy industry attacked Bristol-Myers in a front-page way. The major candy manufacturers protested and sent messages to Bristol-Myers and its advertising agency expressing shock and demanding that the offensive commercial be withdrawn.

Candy, soft drinks, and ice cream do contribute to tooth decay. This is an undisputed truth, even in this era of fluoridation. The candy industry's continued tilting at those who even mention the link between their products and cavities seems stubborn and heedless. Like the cigarette manufacturers, they can't afford to admit their product can be harmful at all. So they overlook the realities completely and go on touting the joys of giving in to the impulse to consume candy in conspicuous quantities. They even call it good food. While the inconsistencies in what the candy makers try to tell us and our kids are more obvious, the triumph of the profit motive over common sense and concern is not restricted to their branch of the kid food business. The waiter who drops the steak on the kitchen floor usually picks it up and puts it back on the serving dish. Many of those in the children's food business have similar ethics.

12. Autocrats of
the Breakfast Table

"Our marketing management saw an opportunity for a cereal that was crunchy, did not get soggy in milk and was sweet enough for children," says Quaker Product Manager Larry Baker. "We asked our agency to develop the concept." Quaker's agency, Compton Advertising, got right on it and came up with the cartoon character Cap'n Crunch, a sea captain around whom animated commercials could be devised. "It was not long after that that the product was developed," says Baker.

Forbes,
October 15, 1966

What the majority of children in the United States eat for breakfast and what they think and feel about it is dictated by less than half a dozen giant companies. These are the cereal manufacturers who dominate the breakfast table and sell over half a billion pounds of breakfast food to children each year. The companies in control are Kellogg, General Mills, General Foods, Quaker Oats, Nabisco, and Ralston. And they were among the first to advertise food directly to children. They spend 100 million dollars a year convincing us we should spend 650 million dollars for wheat, corn, and rice, with and without sugar. By calling these inexpensive grains Trix, Quake, Sugar Jets, Sugar Pops, Lucky Charms, Cheerios, etc., the cereal makers realize an incredible profit.

In promoting these cereals, many of which also contain a

236

considerable amount of air as an ingredient, the six cereal giants promote inadequate eating habits and a fair share of false ideas about nutrition. Many of the tricks of exploiting children used throughout the food industry were developed by the cereal makers, who still excel in conning kids. They did it on radio and in Sunday comic sections. Now they do it on television. "With television, we began to sell children our product before they could talk. They know who the TV characters are before they can say full sentences," explains one official in the cereal trade. "Now they tell their mothers what to buy. Their mothers don't tell them." What many people in the kid business are still striving for, the cereal business has long had: the ability to make children demand their products.

There's no possibility that cereal can, despite all the sunshine and health implied in breakfast food advertising, provide an adequate breakfast for anyone. A child who has only a bowl of pre-sweetened cereal with milk and a glass of orange juice for breakfast is getting between 300 to 350 calories, with an average serving of sweetened dry cereal contributing 110 of them. Even if calories were the only consideration, a breakfast like this would still be recommended only for a dieting adult. A child of 6 needs between 1700 and 2100 calories a day, and a 12-year-old as many as 3000. Breakfasts suggested by nutritionists average 500 to 600 calories.

This is not to say cereal can't be part of a good breakfast. But it can't contribute everything needed, even in terms of calories. All the careful box-side notations about vitamins and essential nutrients to the contrary, breakfast cereals are mostly starch—between 65 and 75 percent by weight. What carbohydrates, such as starch and sugar, provide is energy, and therefore they are important—as part of a balanced diet. To buy carbohydrates in the form of Cap'n Crunch and Lucky Charms is, as we'll see, to pay a remarkably high price for some of the cheapest of food elements.

Most dry cereals, along with bread, macaroni, and cooked cereal, are a source of iron and several B vitamins. An average serving of dry cereal, though, may provide as little as 5 percent of the minimum daily requirement of iron and as little as 8 percent of the B1 requirement. Fortified cereals offering the full daily minimum requirements of all vitamins are still mostly starch. And even though commercials imply a mother can relax as long as her meal-skipping family gets all its vitamins, this is nonsense. A number of television commercials, usually full of artificial rain and kids splashing in mud puddles, try to persuade us that vitamins, including those pumped into some cereals, will prevent or relieve infectious diseases, especially colds. This is nonsense, too, since there is absolutely no reliable evidence to prove that taking in greater amounts of vitamins will build up a resistance to disease or germs. Proper diet depends on a mixture of various food elements, and a child could get all the vitamins he needs and still be a victim of malnutrition.

Years of breakfast cereal advertising has had a backlash effect which is harmful to the cereal industry, and to many older children. In going after the prime cereal target, the young child, the cereal giants have committed themselves to convincing kids that breakfast food is made especially for them. This effort has been so successful that when a child reaches an age when bunny rabbits and superheroes no longer attract him, he drops out of the cereal habit. No cereal propaganda has yet been able to convince the public that breakfast food isn't kid stuff, with the result that growing up in America now involves giving up cereals. Unfortunately, an increasing number of teenagers give up on breakfast altogether. Skipping breakfast is one of the biggest diet problems listed by nutritionists who work with young people. There are several reasons for the teen aversion to breakfast, but the millions of dollars spent on equating breakfast with children is certainly one of them.

The American dry cereal business was created by a Seventh-Day Adventist sanitarium proprietor, his young brother, and one of their former patients. Dr. John Harvey Kellogg, who had acquired his medical training at Bellevue, assumed the superintendentship of the Seventh-Day Adventist health institute at Battle Creek, Michigan, in 1876. By 1878 he was marketing a dry oatmeal and cornmeal health food he called Granola. The Battle Creek sanitarium, known as the Western Health Reform Institute, was built the year after the Civil War ended and was dedicated to Adventism, abstinence, women's rights, vegetarianism, and general physical well-being. One of the institute's founders had received a divine revelation indicating it was God's will that everyone keep healthy.

Dr. Kellogg's contributions to Battle Creek and the cause of good health were enormous. "Kellogg made of Battle Creek a veritable fountainhead of faddism," writes Ronald M. Deutsch in his history of food fads. "It became the nation's chief clearinghouse for an astonishing array of nostrums, messianic food promoters, and international quacks. It became the source of a torrent of misinformation about food, a good deal of which still engulfs us. . . . It would be hard to find a man or woman in this country who does not hold some erroneous belief about health propounded by Dr. Kellogg."

Helping out around Battle Creek was Will Keith Kellogg, eight years the doctor's junior. W. K. served as clerk, keeping records and shipping out the tracts and books his scholarly brother wrote. He also assisted in the various therapies practiced at the institute, which changed its name to the Battle Creek Sanitarium in 1878. Dr. Kellogg placed great faith in proper diet and in purging the body of poisons. Patients treated at his sanitarium found careful attention paid to both. The doctor was against meat-eating, on the grounds that it not only poisoned the system but encouraged savagery and lust, and so the Kellogg diets favored fruit and vegetables. One therapeutic menu required the patient to eat nothing but grapes, up to 14 pounds of them a day, for two weeks. The Kellogg brothers believed in the enema, and the Battle Creek spa made frequent use of an enema machine capable of flushing gallons of water through a patient's system.

The doctor's enthusiasm for dry cereals grew out of his religious and vegetarian beliefs, plus his theory that individuals needed large amounts of roughage to keep the bowels in order. After he invented Granola, Dr. Kellogg in the spring of 1895, came up with the first wheat flake cereal. This he named Granose. Three years later, doing business as the Sanitas Nut Food Company, the Kellogg brothers started producing the first corn flakes known to man. Early in the twentieth century, W. K. split away from his brother and promoted his own Kellogg Toasted Corn Flake Company into national prominence and success.

The third Battle Creek pioneer was a Texas-born real estate and blanket salesman named Charles W. Post. He came to Kellogg's sanitarium in the early 1890's, suffering from a series of unspecified complaints. Post, who favored white Stetson hats, spent nearly a year at the sanitarium riding in a wheelchair. He assimilated the eclectic Kellogg philosophy, and when he left them he opened his own health establishment in Battle Creek. He professed to believe not only in the powers of diet and faith but in his own personal powers as a healer. He wrote a book about the efficacy of Natural Suggestion. He also invented Postum, a cereal coffee, no doubt inspired by the Kellogg brothers' earlier brand of pseudo-coffee.

Post, by advertising in newspapers, achieved sales of over a quarter of a million dollars in his first year with Postum. Real coffee could cause neuralgia, heart disease, and even blindness, Post told prospective customers. Postum didn't, and, more important, it made red blood. What C. W. Post helped do with his Postum campaign was bring the approaches and claims already long in use in the selling of patent medicines into the food business. When he followed Postum with Grape Nuts cereal and Post Toasties corn flakes, he adapted similar patent medicine techniques. "The deceits and tricks of cereal advertising," says former Consumers Union director Dexter Masters, weren't "too much different from the deceits and tricks of advertising that had made fortunes for the patent medicine entrepreneurs. Indeed, the old patent medicine health claims promising vitality, health, and regularity—and as groundless as ever—were used for Shredded Wheat, Postum, Grape-Nuts, and other new products of the sort." White-hatted Post even attempted to tie religion in with his cereals, originally giving Post Toasties the biblical name of Elijah's Manna. This was overzealous, and public and pulpit pressure caused him to rechristen his corn flakes.

The Kellogg boys, Post, and the other manufacturers joining the rush into cereal production were trying to reach a health-minded, possibly vegetarian public. They had little or no thought of their products being used as breakfast food. In fact, Dr. Kellogg believed adding milk and sugar to his dry cereals would adulterate them, rob them of any value. Even the inventor of shredded wheat, a dyspeptic lawyer named Henry Perky, had thought of his discovery as a digestion aid to be eaten dry or perhaps with soup. Gradually, as the new century began and sales of dry cereal increased, manufacturers and promoters learned that people were using the flakes and shreds as a convenient breakfast food. Battle Creek flourished because of the cereal makers who were able to exploit and vastly disseminate this idea. Packaged cereal benefited from the twentieth-century shift to packaging and canning foods, the industrializing of food which would eventually replace the general store with the supermarket and shopping center.

Most of the major cereal makers of the 1960's can trace their beginnings to the last century, to the sanitarium and vegetarianism era. Kellogg and Post, of course—and Ralston Purina, a venerable grain processor, more heavily involved in animal food than in human breakfast food, took the Ralston portion of its brand name from Dr. Ralston's Health Club. Quaker Oats has been in the breakfast business since the 1870's, concentrating on hot cooked cereal. Despite the name, there is no religion in the background of the company. The trademark and the name came about when an executive saw a picture of a Quaker. General Mills is a composite of millers from the last century, put together in the 1920's.

By 1966 there were almost a hundred different brands of breakfast food. The industry was selling over 650 million dollars' worth of dry cereal a year, but had reached an uncomfortable plateau. Sales, which had been leaping forward by 10 percent a year, began to level off concurrently with the leveling-off and slight decline in the national birth rate. Kids who had eaten enough ready-to-eat cereal in the early '60's to jump sales 43 percent were turning into teenagers. "The group between 14 and 44 years of age," explained *Fortune*, "the group that is most indifferent to cereal (in fact, most likely to skip breakfast altogether), now constitute 42 percent of the population, and the proportion is growing."

This slight shrinkage in the kid market obliged the cereal manufacturers to continue, and if possible intensify, their advertising attack on youngsters, in the hope of increasing their percentage of customers in the diminishing ranks of pre-teens. The situation also prompted diversification, doing different things with the same old raw materials of wheat, corn, and rice. Breakfast cereals aimed more at grownups, often implying Geritol-type powers, started appearing on the shelves, bearing names such as Special K, Total, Product 19, and Life. "The breakfast food companies have begun applying dry-cereal technology to new kinds of products," wrote *Fortune* in 1967, "and have also begun promoting products for consumption at new times of the day." All this reapplied technology has brought forth cereals disguised as snack foods and called by such names as Whistles, Corn Skis, Dippy Canoes, Bugles, Daisies, Salty Surfers, Buttons and Bows. Kellogg, Post, and Nabisco have also become preoccupied with the family toaster. Cereal-based jelly-filled tarts are the result. These tarts, variously named Pop-Tarts, Toast-'Em, Pop-Ups, and Toastettes, aren't the kind that would have tempted the Jack of Hearts. Nevertheless they chalk up sales of 45 million dollars a year. After the initial success of plain Pop-Tarts, Kellogg's smeared a thin sugary paste on top and thereby had a new product. This one they dubbed Frosted Pop-Tarts.

General Mills, which was diversified to begin with, has been spreading out into new areas beyond even snacks and adult-aimed cereals. Former Air Force General Edwin W. Rawlings has been largely responsible. Rawlings, who became president in 1961, first pulled General Mills out of the animal food business and then closed nine of the company's flour mills. Rawlings must have felt you could still make more money with less children being born, if you simply sold them more things. He was behind General Mills' taking over of Playskool toys, Kenner toys, and Parker Brothers games. Post's efforts at diversification led them to freeze-dried fruit. The fruit, freeze-dried strawberries, blueberries, and peaches, was mixed with corn flakes. When you mixed milk you were supposed to get the equivalent of cornflakes and fresh fruit. You didn't. By the end of 1967 the Post division of General Foods had lost an estimated 12 million dollars on this particular new direction.

The biggest share of the dry cereal market still belongs to Kellogg's, who sell over 40 percent of all breakfast food and manufacture four of the five best-selling brands. The Kellogg company concentrates almost exclusively on cereal; 90 percent of its U.S. business is in the nearly two dozen cereals it manufactures. Defending their as yet relatively modest diversification, the Kellogg president and chairman, Lyle Roll, says, "We're just a li'l ol' country company doing the best we can. We'd rather do what we do right than do lots of other things and not do them right." In 1966 Roll's li'l ol' company had gross sales of 427 million dollars, a net profit of 38.3 million dollars, and spent 46 million dollars on advertising.

When Carnation's Instant Breakfast appeared in 1965 and Carnation was able to force enough of this essentially dairy product onto the breakfast food shelves, it unsettled the cereal kings. General Foods retaliated with Post Instant Breakfast, which didn't catch on. Kellogg's tested a similar product, though only in Canada. It did not do well. "It isn't the right way to eat," Chairman Roll says. "It's fundamentally not the right way for a family to live." Significantly, the head of Kellogg's said this publicly only after their instant breakfast had proved a failure in sample markets. "Occasionally, your men talk you into something and you have to let them get it out of their system," Roll said after the fact. "That's the way they learn."

After Kellogg, General Mills, Quaker Oats, and General Foods' Post cereals, nobody, except Nabisco with 5 percent of the market and Ralston Purina with 3 percent, makes the list of cereal big-timers. "Some 50 other companies have mere trace elements in the field," reports *Fortune*. "Collectively they share about 2 percent of the market." The reasons the control of the cereal business remains in the hands of a few are many. "A very high order of energy, brains, cold cash, and marketing sophistication is required to secure a position at the breakfast table," says *Fortune's* Sheldon Zalaznick. "There are other problems for anyone thinking of getting into the market. Capital equipment is expensive—a fifty-foot dryer used to process those beguiling shapes costs $100,000; a packaging line to seal them in boxes might run to $150,000 or so. Moreover, the cost of advertising and sales promotion is so high that several million can disappear in a few months without even leaving a ripple."

Experts, such as Cornell University food economist Dr. David Call, have pointed out that in the entire food industry today food itself is merely a means, something to make products out of. "There are no really new foods on the market," says Dr. Call. "You have different services added to the same raw materials. Companies are putting a new bundle of services around the same old food." The food industry refers to this new-way-of-doing-the-same-old-thing philosophy as selling convenience and variety.

Hardly any other segment of the food industry has been more successful than the cereal business in coming up with new ways to process the same old basic ingredients. The gross profits are enormous, as *Forbes* has reported. "The ingredients that go into a box of cereal selling for 37¢ cost only a few cents," the financial magazine reported in its survey of the cereal field. "A top-selling brand can net as much as 20 percent after *all* the expenses of making and marketing it, including the TV commercials." The raw materials' cost makes up an incredibly low percentage of the cost of packaged breakfast cereal. Though the retail price of corn flakes has gone up well over 50 percent since the early 1950's, the wholesale price of corn has dropped. Today the farmer averages only 2¢ for the corn in a 29¢ box of corn flakes. In other words, as Sidney Margolius points out, "if he gave the corn to the manufacturer free, you would still pay 27¢ (provided they passed on the saving)."

The more the cereal giants fuss with the basic grains, the bigger their profits. The cheapest ingredient yet utilized is air. Cereal makers have been inflating grain for years, puffing and krisping it, even shooting it from guns. Another way to cut down on grain used and to push up the price is sugar-frosting the cereal. This was first tried in the late 1930's, didn't catch on. Post attempted it again, in the more affluent years just after the Second World War, with Sugar Crisp, and began what is now the pre-sweetened boom. All new cereals appearing today are pre-sweetened. Cereals with a coating of sugar added account for 25 percent of the sales of all cereal sold.

The addition of air and sugar to grains causes consumers to pay ten times what the basic ingredients are worth. Projecting the box prices shows we pay about 45¢ a pound for a simple brand-name box of corn flakes. If we buy our kids corn in a puffed-up and sugar-enhanced form, such as it appears in Post's Honey Combs, it costs us nearly $1 a pound. Puffed rice and puffed wheat also go for $1 a pound or more. The sugar in a box of frosted flakes is costing you about 7¢ an ounce. That is, you're paying well over $1 a pound for the sugar conveniently added. Even a supposedly convenient shape can double the price. Spoon-size shredded wheat, for example, is sold for twice the price of regular shredded wheat.

Hot cereal, the market for which has been declining steadily, is much less costly. A pound of oatmeal costs around 40¢, which is one reason why even hot cereal is now being given the convenience treatment. Eventually it will not be relatively cheap, either. All the inflating and shaping costs aren't noticed because all boxes of cereal appear to be on sale for about the same price, around 39¢ for the usually-purchased size. However, the weight of the cereal inside fluctuates considerably from brand to brand. The same money that buys you 16 ounces or more of corn flakes will buy only 12 ounces of Rice Krispies, 14 ounces of Raisin Bran, 10 ounces of Sugar Smacks, and merely 8 ounces of Cap'n Crunch, Alpha Bits, and Quake/ Quisp. This practice of setting the price for the box size and regulating the margin of profit by cutting the weight of the contents is known as packaging to price.

An executive with one large cereal manufacturer explains: "Most food products sell at 19¢, 29¢, 39¢, and so forth. This is what is called a psychological price, and people will buy items at 29¢ or 39¢ when they won't buy at 28¢, 38¢, etc., even if the price is cheaper. . . . If we are going to try to price in a way that the retailer can finally come out to 29¢ or whatever, we can only put so much product into the package. In short, as a manufacturer, we begin by figuring what kind of retail price we can get, and we work back from that point to determine what weight of product we can fit in the package." Playing with the contents also allows cereal makers to raise the price of an individual breakfast food without the customer's being aware of it. The price on the box stays 39¢, but the weight of the cereal inside drops from 9 to 8 ounces.

The package itself, particularly in kid cereals, is the ultimate salesman. Children are not concerned with how many ounces they get for 39¢, and all cereal boxes are designed to grab kids in the most obvious of ways. In instructing advertisers on how to reach consumers and potential consumers in the younger generation, a design authority said, in the pages of *Advertising Age*, that you have to "leave personal taste out of package plan." Good taste and bad taste doesn't mean as much as an effective package. The only good package is the one which gets carried from the shelf to the checkout stand. Since many of the prime potential customers for dry cereal can't read, the cereal box must hit hard with a big picture. The picture is most often that of the cartoon character who's being used in the television commercials—Cap'n Crunch, the Honeycomb Kid, Bullwinkle, the Smackin' Brothers, Linus. Next in importance is the premium, and there is usually a picture of a plastic sub, a Batman printing set, a Woody Woodpecker whistle, or a pioneer fort on the package front as well.

A child who can't read has no way of knowing that while the eight plastic cowboys and Indians shown on the Honey Comb box are really inside there, the stamp printing set on another brand is not and has to be sent for with 25¢ and a boxtop.

More sophisticated older kids can be conned with a variation of this gimmick. An 8-year-old knows the bicycle shown on the box can't be inside obviously. He still may think he can get one with cash and some boxtops, and not realize the only chance he has of getting the bike is by entering the blind sweepstakes explained in fine print on the box's backside.

Another frequent dodge is to put a premium in the box for awhile, then withhold it. New cereals almost always use the premium/no premium gambit. When Quisp and Quake came into some new markets, the packages contained free comic books, nicely drawn by Al Kilgore, about the characters Quisp and Quake. The boxes of the cereals put on the supermarket shelves a couple of months later were without comic books or other premiums. Although there was no attempt to imply that the newer boxes contained a free comic book, a younger child will assume that if he got a free comic book once he'll get it again. This is the child's fault. He is too naive. And the cereal people are counting on it. The whole kid business is built up on that fact.

13. Overthrowing the Kid Business

> Whatever the one generation may learn from the other, that which is genuinely human no generation may learn from the foregoing. In this respect every generation begins primitively, has no different task from that of every previous generation, nor does it get further, except insofar as the preceding generation shirked its task and deluded itself.
>
> S. KIERKEGAARD
> *Fear And Trembling*

There are alternatives to being Superkid, to being the eternal consumer. The best alternative for a child is to become himself. This is not easy, and being processed and programmed into an identity can seem simpler, less strain and more fun. "The attainment of an individuality is a long and painful process," writes British child psychologist Frances G. Wickes, "one which is not actually achieved by many so-called adults. It is certainly not the possession of the child. He is, as we have said before, a mass of potentials." The potentials of each child are assaulted and worked over by the masters of the kid business we've become acquainted with in this book. It is our task as parents to serve as a counterbalance to the tremendous pull of the mass media and the mass society. We are involved in our children's passages toward autonomy.

Autonomy can be defined in several ways. Psychiatrist Eric Berne explains it as "manifested by the release of three ca-

249

pacities: awareness, spontaneity and intimacy. . . . Awareness means the capacity to see a coffee-pot and hear the birds singing in one's own way, and not the way one was taught; . . . [it] requires living in the here and now, and not in the elsewhere, the past or the future. . . . Spontaneity means option, the freedom to choose and express one's feelings from the assortment available. . . . Intimacy means the spontaneous . . . candidness of an aware person."

Such qualities as spontaneity and awareness cannot be imposed from outside, and so we can't counterbalance the assault of the kid business with an assault of our own. Our obligation is to be aware but not to interfere, to offer help but not force it on the child. The parent who can relax, who can be helpful, will not have his kids manipulated away from themselves by the mass men. This entails not stepping in, not ordering and forbidding, but understanding. It means, too, not letting the juggernaut of the kid business run you over.

As we've seen by now, the propaganda of the toy tycoons and the cereal merchants is aimed at parents, too. Though love and affection can have an infinity of vocabularies, mass-produced objects are not automatically on the list. Though admen will spend a million dollars to promote such notions as the one that nothing says lovin' like something from the oven, such nonsense is still not true. Anybody who has to have a cinnamon roll, or a plastic commando, before he feels loved is a nitwit. People are the ones who express affection: Barbie dolls, Sugar Smacks, Mickey Mouse, and Davy Crockett, don't. Many of the products of the kid business are clutter and trivia, and the only real messages they speak are the messages of the kid business. We, parents, are the ones who can provide affection, stability, and security. Eventually kids grow up, if they haven't been made into Superkids, and can move away from us.

The world at times, to kids especially, seems to be full of people who are trying to stop something—to suppress, stamp out, and get rid of. Many of them seem to kids to be dry, humorless people, and their obvious dedication doesn't erase the image. Pioneer vice suppressor Anthony Comstock once even went after the Rover Boys-type books which flourished in the early 1900's. They were, he declared stiffly, "devices to capture our youth and secure the ruin of immortal souls." So let's avoid being latter-day Comstocks. Anger at the kid business can be helpful, as can indignation and laughter. One weapon against mass media which is often advocated is censorship. Like many weapons, censorship can easily fall into the wrong hands. The history of the use of censorship in America indicates that unpopular opinions and dissent are suppressed more than any real evils. Censorship, particularly that imposed by the government, is always worse than the problem it is supposed to be controlling.

Being an individual insurgent against the mass media requires patience and endurance, an awareness that many of the victories will be partial. "There are only three great instruments which society may use to encourage or prod the mass media to responsible performance," says Professor Wilbur Schramm in dismissing the use of censorship. "These are government and its various regulatory bodies, national, state, and local; the media themselves, their individual personnel, and their formal and informal associations and administrative organizations; and the general public, with its formal and informal organizations and associations."

One of the things the general public can do is complain. Protests can oust kings and presidents and change foreign policy. Sufficient complaining can affect television networks and producers. A letter of protest is not as impressive to a consensus-ridden television executive as a drop in the rating. The first response to outside complaints is to minimize them. Early in 1968, *TV Guide* reported that while the magazine had received a flood of protests about the Saturday morning wave

of monsters and superheroes, the networks claimed they themselves hadn't received many. At the same time, the day time
program chief of NBC complained about criticisms by saying,
"When we were kids, our parents had no idea what we were
seeing in the movies on Saturdays. But because we go into the
living room, parents are suddenly critical." By the fall of '68,
however, the networks had, after several hundred thousand
more letters of complaint, decided to prune their crop of killer
heroes. Unfortunately, however, television violence had gotten
irrationally linked with the assassinations of Martin Luther
King, Jr., and Robert F. Kennedy in the press and certain segments of the public mind. The networks were probably giving
in as much to mass superstition as to reason.

Obviously a parent can't be a child again and look at children's entertainments and diversions as a child does, but neither
can a parent be a very good mentor or guide through territory
and experiences he knows nothing about. Concern does not
mean intervention. I would suggest watching and sampling
rather than forbidding. Watching and sampling a large variety
of kid entertainments and trying to find out what it is the child
likes in each and what the individual implications of the di-
version are. For example, it's useless to try to eliminate violence
or to ask a network to do so. The specific uses of violence are
what must be criticized. Commenting on his private detective
character, Philip Marlowe, author Raymond Chandler said,
"Marlowe has as much social conscience as a horse. He has
a personal conscience, which is an entirely different thing." The
personal conscience of the hero of a kid show, the ethical frame-
work stated or implied, can be more important than the amount
of violence. Children must know not only that violence exists
but how to handle it within themselves and how to meet violence
when it is exhibited by others. Viewing kids' television shows
and comics with some discernment can enable parents to sort
out the good trash from the bad trash and may even lead them

to finding real value where they did not expect it. After exploring, then protest, then attempt to understand and possibly restrict the child's involvement with a particularly bad cultural product.

Some of the more open intrusions of the mass media people—running product tests in class rooms, giving away free samples at school, and administering motivational research quizzes to students—have to be met on a local level. It is my feeling no advertising agency or private research firm should be allowed inside a public school to try out new products and ask questions of children. A kid's feelings are his own business. In various localities ad men get through the school boards in different ways, and no single technique of stopping them will apply everywhere. Industry propaganda in the schools has to be cut down, but much of public education would collapse should free films and documentaries be kept out of schools. A real and useful education should be as free of propaganda and lies as possible. But unless we are willing to put considerably more money into the public schools, they'll remain dependent on the handouts of the giant corporations and advertising agencies.

Those who make a strong effort to cope with and counteract the excesses of the food industry get the label "consumer" stuck on them by food and advertising publications. In this instance, a consumer is an advocate of consumerism. "Consumerism," which sounds and looks in print like another unpopular ideology, is frequently written up in the trades, its progress and setbacks charted. "Consumerism losing White House foothold," headlined *Advertising Age* when Mrs. Esther Peterson was eased out of her job as chairman of the Committee on Consumer Interests and advisor to President Johnson. Though the White House gave no reasons for replacing the dedicated Mrs. Peterson with Betty Furness, *Ad Age* believed she had been scrapped because she "became a lightning rod who drew directly to the President the indignant reactions of business men who didn't like what was going on."

Mrs. Peterson attracted wrath to herself and the White House with rather modest proposals and plans. She advocated conferences between representatives of consumers and representatives of business, and the giving out of consumer information and buying advice to lower-income families. *Printer's Ink*, the advertising trade journal, called Mrs. Peterson "the most pernicious threat to advertising today." Her attempts to support the establishment of consumer education courses in high schools were met with intense opposition. Sample products and industry propaganda can be given out in schools with greater ease and less contention than can unbiased information about these products and industries. Business and food industry agitation over Mrs. Peterson was also forceful enough to cause very tentative plans to establish a Consumer Department to be shelved in Washington.

To the food and ad people, the crusade of Senator Philip Hart, the persistent sponsor of what became the truth-in-packaging bill, was further evidence that Washington was a hotbed of consumerism. Hart's long struggle was to establish uniform package standards which regulate size and weight, how they are described on packages and cans, and the type size in which the information is given. He also, finally, got restrictions placed on the use of exaggerating adjectives like "jumbo" and "giant" and promises of servings that don't exist.

The Grocery Manufacturers of America, basically a food lobby set up to fight food and packaging legislation and hand out anti-consumerism information, fought long and hard against Senator Hart. The lobby raised, early in 1964, nearly half a million dollars to carry on its work. When more money was needed, the Grocery Manufacturers, according to the *New Republic*, "put the touch on TV networks, women's magazines, and member's advertising agencies—all of them dependent on food advertising—for about $225,000." Hart's opposition was not limited to the makers of adult food items, and some of his most aggressive attackers were the kid food people, the cereal men and the canned food crowd.

Though Senator Hart had a partial triumph, there is still strong resentment over "the heavy hand of government" coming to the aid of Mrs. Joe Public, as a long article in *Advertising Age* calls her. Speaking for the anti-consumerism forces, University of Chicago business administration professor James Lorie said: "Consumers may be competent to select presidents, wives and husbands, and schools for their children, but not to pick breakfast foods." Professor Lories is defending in his late 1967 piece the fundamental American right to be exploited. Professor Lorie, like many another professional champion of the food industry, also attempts to make even a concern with food values seem foolish. Progress, he feels, has meant "foods are frozen, dried, canned, and packaged in enormous variety, with very marked reduction in gross margins at the retail level and in the amount of work necessary for the housewife to get dinner on the table." He adds, "I'm not going to comment on the quality of the dinners . . . in terms of calories—amino acids, vitamins, and minerals."

Vigilance is essential in coping with the food industry. The more open and obvious tricks and dangers are usually caught by the United States Department of Agriculture, which now has more power, under the new clean meat bill; by the Food and Drug Administration, which got broader authority from the truth-in-packaging bill; and by the Federal Trade Commission, whose job it is to halt unfair competition and deceptive sales and advertising practices in all business areas. Paul Rand Dixon, FTC chairman, addressed himself to one of the central problems in a recent speech to advertising men. "It takes no great clairvoyance to predict why false advertising cases will continue to flood the Commission," he said. "It will be because too many advertisers, with or without the connivance of their advertising agencies, and with or without the advice of their lawyers, will take a chance on trading truth for sales." Despite national and state and local authorities, personal vigilance is still a necessity. Lies and exaggerations are still going to be plentiful.

Developing a habit of label-reading is one way to police the food industry. On most labels the manufacturer must tell you what is in his container. And the most prevalent ingredient has to head the list. A can of spaghetti that has promised much protein in its commercials, and yet lists tomatoes and water as its chief components, has been bending reality some. A TV dinner promising to provide your children with a well-balanced meal can't do so if it's actually made mostly of potatoes and cracker meal. A frankfurter that calls itself all-beef and has dextrose as its second ingredient is operating under an assumed name. The USDA seal, in some form, has to appear on all meat inspected and passed by the Department of Agriculture. Meat products without any seal or stamp can be made of anything your state at the moment allows.

It isn't really safe to depend on what food ads and commercials tell you about vitamins and nutrition, either. Having encountered many food copywriters, I'd say the majority of them can't tell a calorie from a vitamin and often just repeat in their advertisements whatever information their food client has handed them. Since all too many food merchandisers have the style and objectives of quacks, information on food and diet really should come from sources outside the food business. Children won't always automatically eat what is good from a nutritional standpoint, and probably a certain amount of junk food can't be avoided. But it should be kept at a minimum, used in addition to essential and valuable foods.

Even though nothing can persuade a kid to eat broccoli and drink orange juice, or whatever the passing prejudice is against, a Pop-Tart and a glass of Hi-C are not substitutes. The foods with suspect ingredients should be approached with caution and usually avoided until reliable research has been done and made public. An Abbott Laboratory chemist told a 1968 Chemical Society meeting that critics of the cyclamate sweeteners have no other motive save holding back the advance of science. "We can expect lobbying by established interests to retard progress here," said the Abbott man, whose company is the chief producer of cyclamate, "as it has throughout history." He also predicted that by 1972 a billion dollars' worth of artificially sweetened foods will be sold each year, twice as much as presently.

Much of the grownup world still fails to fully acknowledge that children are going anywhere, that they are in process and not locked into childhood, that their existence has significance. The mass men, because of where they place their emphasis, reinforce the idea that childhood is pointless, a time only for indulgence and chaos. Childhood has to be much more, however, unless a child is to remain forever ungrown inside. "Man does not grow automatically like a tree," observes Rollo May, "but fulfills his potentialities only as he in his own conscious plans and chooses. Fortunately the long protracted period of infancy and childhood in human life . . . prepares the child for his difficult task. He is able to acquire some knowledge and inner strength so that, as he must begin to choose and decide, he has some capability for it." This is the real business of kids, and the toy tycoons and the cereal makers and the electronic uncles and the camped-out supermen do not contribute in any positive way.

The most applicable means of overthrowing the entire kid

business, of minimizing its effects, involves getting our own notions about being parents sorted out. If we're not sure, if we're impressed by the propaganda of the kid business, then we can't really function as mentors, as guides and teachers. We become either casualties or implements of the assault on childhood.

Bibliography

These lists contain only the titles of the books and articles which can, in various ways, expand on the topics *The Assault On Childhood* has dealt with. They're not meant to serve only as a place to check quotation sources, but to have some more useful purpose.

CHILDREN

Aries, Philippe, *Centuries of Childhood*, Alfred A. Knopf, 1963.

Coles, Robert, *Children of Crisis*, Little, Brown, 1967.

Erikson, Erik H., *Childhood and Society*, Norton, 1963.

————, ed., *The Challenge of Youth*, Anchor, 1965.

Friedenberg, Edgar Z., *Coming of Age in America*, Random House, 1965.

————, *The Dignity of Youth*, Beacon, 1965.

————, *The Vanishing Adolescent*, Beacon, 1959.

Goodman, Paul, *Growing Up Absurd*, Vintage, 1962.

Hechinger, Grace and Fred M., *Teen-Age Tyranny*, William Morrow, 1963.

Ilg, Frances L., and Ames, Louise Bates, *Child Behavior*, Dell, 1956.

Jersild, Arthur T., *Child Psychology*, Prentice-Hall, 1947.

Lear, Martha Weinman, *The Child Worshipers*, Crown, 1963.

Mann, Erika, *School for Barbarians*, Modern Age, 1938.

Miel, Alice, *The Shortchanged Children of Suburbia* (pamphlet), American Jewish Committee, 1967.

Mok, Paul P., *Pushbutton Parents and the Schools*, Delta, 1965.
Spock, Benjamin, *Baby and Child Care*, Pocket Books, 1957.
————, *Problems of Parents*, Houghton Mifflin, 1962.
Wyden, Peter, *Suburbia's Coddled Kids*, Doubleday, 1962.

FOOD AND DRINK
Carson, Gerald, *Cornflake Crusade*, Rinehart, 1957.
————, *The Old Country Store*, E. P. Dutton, 1965.
Consumer Reports, *The Medicine Show*, Consumers Union, 1963.
————, *Report on Smoking and the Public Interest*, Consumers Union, 1963.
Deutsch, Ronald M., *The Nuts Among the Berries*, Ballantine, 1967.
Field, Hazel E., *Foods in Health and Disease*, Macmillan, 1964.
Goodhart, Robert S., *The Teen-Ager's Guide to Diet and Health*, Prentice-Hall, 1964.
Kahn, E. J., *The Big Drink*, Reinhardt, 1960.
McHenry, E. W., *Foods Without Fads*, J. B. Lippincott, 1960.
Margolius, Sidney, *The Innocent Consumer Vs. the Exploiters*, Trident, 1967.
Masters, Dexter, *The Intelligent Buyer and the Telltale Seller*, Alfred A. Knopf, 1966.
Mooney, Booth, *The Hidden Assassins*, Follett, 1966.
Mowbray, A. Q., *The Thumb on the Scale*, J. B. Lippincott, 1967.
Packard, Vance, *The Waste Makers*, David McKay, 1960.
Stabile, Toni, *Cosmetics: Trick or Treat*, Hawthorn, 1967.
Wyden, Peter, *The Overweight Society*, William Morrow, 1965.

MASS MEDIA
Beaumont, Charles, *Remember? Remember?* Macmillan, 1963.
Becker, Stephan, *Comic Art in America*, Simon & Schuster, 1959.
Bernays, Edward L., ed., *The Engineering of Consent*, Univ. of Oklahoma, 1955.
Carnegie Commission, *Public Television*, Bantam, 1967.
Craven, Thomas, *Cartoon Cavalcade*, Simon & Schuster, 1943.
Denney, Reuel, *The Astonished Muse*, Grosset & Dunlap, 1964.
Feild, Robert D., *The Art of Walt Disney*, Collins, 1947.

Garry, Ralph, et al., *For the Young Viewer*, McGraw-Hill, 1962.

————, *Television for Children*, Foundation For Character Education, 1966.

Gilbert, Eugene, *Advertising and Marketing To Young People*.

Goodman, Ezra, *The Fifty-Year Decline And Fall Of Hollywood*, Simon & Schuster, 1961.

Hall, Stuart and Whannel, Paddy, *The Popular Arts*, Pantheon, 1964.

Harmon, Jim, *The Great Radio Heroes*, Doubleday, 1967.

Jacobs, Lewis, *The Rise Of The American Film*, Harcourt Brace, 1939.

Jarrell, Randall, *A Sad Heart At The Supermarket*, Atheneum, 1962.

Meerloo, Joost A. M., *The Rape Of The Mind*, World, 1956.

Packard, Vance, *The Hidden Persuaders*, David McKay, 1957.

Postman, Neil, *Television and the Teaching of English*, Appelton, 1961.

Schickel, Richard, *The Disney Version*, Simon & Schuster, 1968.

Schramm, Wilbur, *Responsibility in Mass Communication*, Harper & Row, 1957.

————, *Television in the Lives of Our Children*, Stanford, 1961.

Shulman, Arthur, and Youman, Roger, *How Sweet It Was*, Crown, 1966.

Skornia, Harry J., *Television and Society*, McGraw-Hill, 1965.

Stephenson, Ralph, *Animation in the Cinema*, A. S. Barnes, 1967.

Thomas, Bob, *The Art of Animation*, Simon & Schuster, 1958.

Turner, E. S., *Boys Will Be Boys*, Michael Joseph, 1957.

————, *The Shocking History of Advertising*, E. P. Dutton, 1953.

TV Guide, *The Eye and I: Television and Its Effects on Our Society*, (pamphlet), 1966.

Unesco, *The Effects of Television on Children and Adolescents*, 1964.

Warshow, Robert, *The Immediate Experience*, Doubleday, 1962.

Waugh, Coulton, *The Comics*, Macmillan, 1947.

Weinberg, Meyer, *TV in America*, Ballantine, 1962.

Wertham, Fredric, *Seduction of the Innocent*, Rinehart, 1954.

TOYS AND PLAY

Fraser, Antonia, *A History of Toys*, Delacorte, 1966.
Hartley, Ruth E., et al., *Understanding Children's Play*, Columbia, 1952.
Huizinga, Johan, *Homo Ludens*, Beacon, 1955.
Lowenfeld, Margaret, *Play in Childhood*, John Wiley, 1967.
McClintock, Inez and Marshall, *Toys in America*, Public Affairs Press, 1961.
Russell, David H., *Children's Thinking*, Blaisdell, 1956.

GENERAL

Allen, Frederick Lewis, *Since Yesterday*, Harper, 1940.
Bettelheim, Bruno, *The Informed Heart*, Free Press, 1960.
Boorstin, Daniel J., *The Americans: The National Experience*, Random House, 1965.
————, *The Image*, Harper Colophon, 1965.
Ellul, Jacques, *The Technological Society*, Alfred A. Knopf, 1964.
Galbraith, John Kenneth, *The Liberal Hour*, Houghton Mifflin, 1960.
Henry, Jules, *Culture Against Man*, Random House, 1963.
Laing, R. D., *The Divided Self*, Pelican, 1965.
Riesman, David, et al., *The Lonely Crowd*, Yale, 1950.
Swados, Harvey, ed., *Years of Conscience: The Muckrakers*, Meridian, 1962.

MAGAZINE ARTICLES

"Barbie Is a Million-Dollar Doll," William K. Zinsser, *Saturday Evening Post*, Dec. 12, 1964.
"Captain Kangaroo," Edith Efron, *TV Guide*, March 19, 1966.
"Children Should Learn About Violence," Bruno Bettelheim, *Saturday Evening Post*, March 11, 1967.
"The Dolittle Explosion," *Newsweek*, Jan. 1, 1968.
"Don't Underestimate the Power of a Kid" (on breakfast food), *Forbes*, Oct. 1, 1966.
"The Fight for a Place at the Breakfast Table," Sheldon Zalaznick, *Fortune*, December 1967.

"Food Processing," George C. Lodge, *Harvard Business Review*, October 1966.

"Has TV (gasp!) Gone Batty?," John Skow, *Saturday Evening Post*, May 7, 1966.

"Horror in the Nursery" (on comic books), Judith Crist, *Colliers*, March 27, 1948.

"How the Comic Book Started," John R. Vosburgh, *The Commonweal*, May 20, 1949.

"Let's Keep Christmas Commercial," April Oursler Armstrong, *Saturday Evening Post*, Dec. 18, 1965.

"The Magic World of Walt Disney," Robert De Roos, *National Geographic*, August 1963.

"Mickey Mouse," Alva Johnston, *Woman's Home Companion*, July 1934.

"Mickey Mouse, Financier," *Literary Digest*, Oct. 21, 1933.

"The Most Popular Doll in Town" (on Barbie), *Life*, Aug. 23, 1963.

"Movies for Young Children," Pauline Kael, *McCall's*, June 1966.

"Not So Educational TV," James Ridgeway, *New Republic*, Aug. 21, 1965.

"Old Invincibles Return," (Superman), Alexander Ross, *Maclean's*, March 19, 1966.

"Preliminary Report on Superman," Gilbert Seldes, *Esquire*, November 1942.

"Ralston Ties on a Bigger Feed Bag," *Business Week*, Dec. 3, 1966.

"The Sweet, Secret World of Forrest Mars," Harold B. Meyers, *Fortune*, May 1967.

"Teaching Children to Think," Joseph Featherstone, *New Republic*, Sept. 9, 1967.

"Tear Off a Box Top," Ron Goulart, *P.S.*, June 1966.

"Toy Makers at Work," *Financial World*, Nov. 9, 1966.

"Up, Up and Awa-a-y!," John Kobler, *Saturday Evening Post*, June 21, 1941.

"Watch That Hamburger," Ralph Nader, *New Republic*, Aug. 19, 1967.

"Welcome to the Consumption Community," Daniel J. Boorston, *Fortune*, Sept. 1, 1967.

"We're Still in the Jungle," Ralph Nader, *New Republic*, July 15, 1967.

"What TV Is Really Doing to Your Children," Marshall McLuhan, *Family Circle*, March 1967.

"What's Not So Funny About the Funnies," Ponchitta Pierce, *Ebony*, November 1966.

"Why 100,000,000 Americans Read Comics," William Moulton Marston, *American Scholar*, Winter 1943–44.

"The World of Walt Disney," *Newsweek*, Dec. 31, 1962.

ADDITIONAL BIBLIOGRAPHICAL SUGGESTION

Anyone who wishes to remain up-to-date with the planners of the assault on children can check the latest issues of the trade magazines below to see what the kid business is saying about our children and what it has in mind for all of us. Most of these publications can be found in the larger public libraries.

Advertising Age, Billboard, Media/Scope, Playthings, Printer's Ink, Sales Management, Sponsor, Television Age, Toys & Novelties.

Index

INDEX